Music Comes
in
Springtime

Psalm 23

To Frank and Ann,
Blessings to you! Thank you for being a light and a godly example. I pray this book is an inspiration to you!
— Jared Kuykendall

JARED KUYKENDALL

ISBN 979-8-88943-086-5 (paperback)
ISBN 979-8-88943-087-2 (digital)

Copyright © 2023 by Jared Kuykendall

All rights reserved. No part of this publication may be reproduced, distributed, or transmitted in any form or by any means, including photocopying, recording, or other electronic or mechanical methods without the prior written permission of the publisher. For permission requests, solicit the publisher via the address below.

Christian Faith Publishing
832 Park Avenue
Meadville, PA 16335
www.christianfaithpublishing.com

Printed in the United States of America

To my parents, BJ and Elaine Kuykendall, who have faithfully taught me the ways of the Lord. Thank you for your loving example!

To my grandma, Sally Kuykendall, who has inspired me in writing to give my best. Thank you for your unwavering encouragement.

To Matt Young, my English professor in college. Thank you for instilling in me a love of writing and for your thoughtful instruction.

CONTENTS

Introduction: An Exercise in Romanticism vii
Chapter 1:   It's What You Make of Life 1
Chapter 2:   Destined to Be a Man 10
Chapter 3:   Across the Sea 16
Chapter 4:   Rugged Travels to Oregon Country 28
Chapter 5:   Raised Rural 33
Chapter 6:   Better Together 53
Chapter 7:   Yet Another Story 69
Chapter 8:   The Kansas Clan 91
Chapter 9:   Changing Horizons 118
Chapter 10: The Innocence of Youth 145
Chapter 11: Love and War Together, Part I 165
Chapter 12: Love and War Together, Part II 183
Chapter 13: Love and War Together, Part III 193
Chapter 14: The Years That Followed 217
Epilogue 241
Bibliography 243

INTRODUCTION

An Exercise in Romanticism

Dear reader,

I love history! Everything about it intrigues me: the struggles, the valor, the hardships, and the victories. Through the course of human history, we in our "modern" age can observe how our ancestors lived and ponder the effects their consequences created. Some of these we should strive to emulate, while others we need to leave behind. But regardless, collectively, they portray a contiguous story of humanity.

Can we, or should we, romanticize everything from the past? This question has burned in the hearts of many and should be considered carefully. I contend that things that are against God's law should not be celebrated. Much evil has occurred under the sun since the fall of Adam and Eve and continues until this day. Yet we must remember what good has happened.

I understand not everyone wants to be a historian, yet we all need to know things about the past. Understanding the values, beliefs, and goals of past generations allows us to more deeply understand *why* they did what they did. Without understanding the historical context of this world, we remain lost and confused trying to forge new paths alone.

We need to understand our own lives and choices in light of a historical context. We need to have the ability to identify where we

INTRODUCTION

align with and don't align with values and ways of life from the past. In so doing, our lives will feel more grounded. People today talk about how they feel a disconnect between themselves in the twenty-first century and the untouchable past. But, dear reader, the past really holds a lot of the key to the future. The right, proven ways from the past are ours for the taking if we would but take the time to learn about them.

And that is what this book is all about. Yes, it will take time to complete. But I don't want it to seem like a homework assignment. Enjoy! Think about it as a steppingstone to your own historical discoveries! Let me explain my own journey.

The story of my own family has intrigued me ever since I was a little boy. For years, I have sat and listened to my parents, grandparents, and great-grandparents, besides many aunts, uncles, and other relatives, to hear bits and pieces of our story. Life is made up of stories. It is how we understand the world around us. And learning about my family—where they came from and how they lived, for example—has greatly enhanced my ability to live in the modern age. Why? Because I feel rooted and grounded. I know where I'm from, where my family's been, and how we made it through.

My great-great-grandmother put together a memoir of her family in 1976. Between 2008 and 2011, my great-grandmother put together four books of family history. One book contained her mothers' memoirs, and the other three she wrote. My grandma and great-aunts helped with the project, and the four books collectively—containing hundreds of stories and photos—are a treasured family jewel.

I grew up hearing about these stories and later read them myself as a teenager. Around 2019, I had the notion to take these four family-history books and turn them into a novel. I wanted them to be based entirely on what happened (factual), or what might have happened, as I needed to take liberties to fill in the details. The project began in 2020 as I used the books as a guide to create a narrative of our family's history.

At times, trying to write a cohesive story felt overwhelming, yet I thoroughly enjoyed the process. I realized how I had the ability to control the narrative of my family's history, and that was a huge responsibility. Should I paint a family member in my story in a positive or negative light, for some situations? Throughout the book, I strove to remain fair and include a realistic, balanced picture. I wanted to portray real life, which at times is sunshine and roses but also can be thorns and storms.

But for me, it was an exercise in romanticism, as I strove to look for, understand, and highlight the positives throughout my family's life. Adopting a romanticist mindset has allowed me to deeply appreciate and celebrate the wonderful things in life and the good that has happened in human history. There is so much we can learn from the past!

Now, dear reader, I have never really enjoyed long introductions to books, have you? So I want to keep this brief. Besides, we have a long journey ahead of us. Think of it! There are stories to be told, adventures to be had, places to be, and experiences to ponder, with all the added blood, sweat, tears, and adrenaline throughout. Let's get started!

Jared Kuykendall
Soli Deo Gloria
October 2022

CHAPTER 1

It's What You Make of Life

Today is December 22, 1899, in Marne, Germany. At the Dressler residence, Christmas excitement is in the air. All the children, many there were, rushed into the back bedroom—the father's orders. Only the father is allowed in the living room right now. The children are rambunctious, pacing about the room with excitement. My own father is one of those children—Herman Robert Fritz Dressler, age seven. He meanders over to his older sister, Alma, and asks with childish ignorance what father is up to in the other room. He hears noises—fun noises, such as bells and even the whistle of a train.

Outside the closed door, the father is decorating the living room—tree, decorations, and all. It is another German Christmas in the city of Marne, and only the father is allowed to decorate. The father, whose name is also Herman, is just putting the finishing touches on the tree. He hangs tinsel and brightly colored glass ornaments upon the seven-foot-tall tree. Little animated toys, clowns, and trains adorn the tree and its branches. In the lights, including the firelight, the room is a masterpiece—an ode to the creativity and nostalgia of German Christmas tradition.

Two days later, the whole family gathers in the living room for a celebration. Young Herman is finally allowed in the room. His eyes gleam with awe. He takes his place beside his younger sister, Louise, on the couch to hear their father talk about the meaning of Christmas. They then sing carols, such as "Silent Night," only in German which becomes "*Stille Nacht.*" The family sings and sings more—"Joy to the World," "Hark! The Herald Angels Sing," and then one of the younger children's favorites. Everyone gathers around the tree, holds hands, and sings, "O Tannenbaum." Just then, Louise exclaims, "O listen, the church bells are ringing." She goes to the window and peers out. Snow blankets the road and is even on top of the lampposts—spaced evenly every few yards. She strains her eyes and can make out a few sleighs and happy people in them, going their merry way.

At the end of the bells, the family sits around the table for the big Christmas dinner, which includes roast and apple sausage. The older girls have spent hours preparing the beloved meal. After the father gives thanks, they serve up in an orderly way. Herman loves the food—especially the sausage—but his mind right now is more on Saint Nicholas coming to bring presents later in the night. For dessert, there is a sort of fruitcake, called Stollen, with nuts and fruits. The father sighs as he takes his first bite. This has been a special Christmas—even though it has been three years since the mother died. However, the father presses on and tries to make each Christmas special for the kids. They don't know it yet, but tomorrow, he plans on telling them the news. He has decided to marry Katherine Heeschen.

Now, the Dressler family at this time already included seven children. Marrying Katherine would add her eight children to the family. Things might become a little chaotic! But the father hopes for the best—he knows he needs another woman around the house although he is grateful for all the work the older girls have done keeping the house together since Emma died.

Saint Nicholas finally arrives, and gifts are distributed to everyone. After another joyful Christmas Eve, it is time to say goodnight or *guten nacht.*

*****

MUSIC COMES IN SPRINGTIME

On Christmas Day, the children learn the news that their father plans on marrying Katherine Heeschen. The father thanked Alma and Carolla, the older girls, for all the work they had done in the last three years in keeping the family together. However, he explains how it gets sort of lonely without a partner in life, and he feels this is the best decision for the family. Young Herman is slightly excited but more disappointed. *This means a few new kids to play with, but what if Father doesn't give me all the attention that I am used to? Will these new kids "steal" my father—and all the love that goes along with it—away from me?*

This scene reminds me of the movie *The Sound of Music*, for in it, the captain is enthusiastic about remarrying the rich lady from Vienna, but the children are not amused.

Anyhow, whether or not Herman or the rest of the kids fully agreed with their father's decision, they respected it. They were soon going to have a new mother.

After the wedding and honeymoon, the day finally arrived, and the Heeschen family moved in with the Dresslers. Herman could not believe how much new stuff was being brought into his home. Why would anyone want this many clothes anyways? And where to put them all? At least there were some new toys and kids' books for him to enjoy.

The Heeschen child closest to his age was Lisbeth. She came walking right into the Dressler home as if she owned the place. And her hair! Herman thought Lisbeth to be an outright little prig tramping into his place like that!

The first dinner together—all together—was sort of awkward, to say the least. Here is the father sitting next to his new wife, and all their fifteen kids about them—at two tables. Poor Alma and Carolla! They had to prepare quite a big meal for everyone. However, the night went pretty well—all the new kids in the family found where they were to sleep and keep their things and the like.

At times, Alma felt she had to just go outside and take a walk down the street—she could not stand her new siblings taking so much space. *Oh well, Father needs the peace to be kept at such a crucial time anyway*, she thinks. *I will let it go.* Alma had always tried hard to be a peacemaker in the family. Although her younger brothers and sisters thought it was great fun to scare her with spiders—Oh, goodness!—but their father doesn't have the energy to try and break up another war. Her patience would prove invaluable to the family in the coming months and years.

*****

The coming weeks and months came quickly, and the Heeschens became a part of the family. However, not all relationships between the new "family members" were wonderful. Katherine seemed to have an uncanny ability to prove her daughter, Lisbeth, was innocent in every fight between her and young Herman.

Let me explain. There was a certain seat at the table which was Herman's very own—before his new brothers and sisters arrived, however. On many occasions, Lisbeth would sit at this particular seat during dinner or supper simply to irritate Herman. Once, Herman became irate at this and threatened to pull her right out of the chair if she would not leave. Lisbeth refused by smiling and sticking her tongue out. Herman kept his promise, and out of that seat came Lisbeth faster than you can say "Jackie Robinson." Lisbeth responded by pinching him so hard it left a welt on his skin for a week.

Of course, by this time, both kids were bawling. Katherine came rushing over and hugged Lisbeth as she listened to her daughter explain how it was unfair how Herman didn't share anything with her. Katherine's mood changed. She slowly and slyly looked up at Herman from under Lisbeth's shoulders and screamed at him to go to his room immediately, and don't he even think about getting supper that night. Herman was so scared he did not even try to explain anything and ran as fast as his little legs could.

Such events occurred quite frequently—at least once a week—and on each occasion, the father would try to make peace between both parties. This sometimes irritated Alma and Carolla, but their father knew best. One day, after a long argument with Katherine about how she treated him, he came and sat beside Herman on his bed.

MUSIC COMES IN SPRINGTIME

Herman lay there under the quilt that his grandma had made for him and was trying to hide the tears. The father sat there and looked down at the rug. He didn't know what to say exactly but wanted to show Herman that he would be willing to stand up for him.

"I know things are not easy for you right now, but they will get better, Herman. Please try to be a peacemaker and get along with Lisbeth. She is your sister now and maybe just needs your love and attention."

"I'm trying as hard as I can, but she doesn't seem to even care," cried Herman. "She gets away with everything. 'Mother' ignores the bad she does but always punishes me."

"You are right. Lisbeth does need discipline. It is hard to correct her, though, when your mother thinks she is the perfect child. Sometimes I overhear you two arguing and can tell she is the one in the wrong—just by the tone in her voice."

"I admit I do tease her sometimes and am sorry for that. But is she sorry for all the mean stuff she does to me?"

"That is something I will have to ask her. As a lawman and working in the courthouse all day, I know I am not here for you most of the day. Sometimes I feel I have hardly the strength to try to appease everyone. But don't worry about that. For now, I want you to get some sleep."

Herman lay there in the dark after his father left the room feeling just a little bit better. "Mother" had sent him to bed without a meal again; however, Alma sneaked in a plate of sausage and bread to him. She did this whenever Herman was sent to bed without supper. But as he lay there, inwardly, he knew anger was not the answer. He did not know exactly what that answer was yet but was determined to try to be as good a boy as possible.

*****

Months passed, and life began to change. Katherine gave birth to a girl—they named her Hanna. Louise, Herman's young sister, was in love with the new baby. Who needs toys when there is a real baby to play with? Often, Louise would play dress-up with Hanna and pretend to be a good, loving mother to her. Some of the older children took care, though, that Louise did not go too far and be too rough with her. Anyway, Louise admired the new baby—such soft skin and bright beautiful blue eyes. Oh! And her fingers and toes were the tiniest things she had ever seen. Louise offered to help change the diapers, but Katherine wasn't quite ready for the help yet.

First Alma and then Carolla married fine young men. Alma's husband was a butcher; they remained in Marne. Carolla married an architect. Her husband often would travel around Germany for his job, so that meant Carolla had a lot of alone time at the house. She would visit Alma or go over to the "ol' house," as she called it, to see the kids and her father and mother. Their father missed their help but was glad to have them married. He was fond of his new sons-in-law, thinking highly of them.

Back at the house, Herman began getting along better with his stepbrother, Emil. Emil was the closest Heeschen boy in age to him. They often got rowdy, so Katherine would send them outside to play. They loved especially playing in the pine forests, where they would be there for hours. The gently rolling hills always provided a splendid place for races. Whoever won made the other carry him up the next hill! This was the country, however. In the city, they enjoyed being with other boys—talking and laughing and joking—on the streets and near the canals.

As much as the story should go—that Herman and Katherine's relationships improved—sadly, the situation became even worse. Alma and Carolla—who had stood up for Herman—were now gone. No one would stand up for him now—not even Emil.

Little things angered Katherine too easily. The father thought that perhaps she was just tired and had weak nerves. But the truth is, ever since the night those two kids got in a fight over the chair, she disliked him. Then came a situation that happened all too often, but it finally led to a drastic change.

Herman came down the stairs and headed straight for the breakfast table. Food is usually one of the first things on a boy's mind in the morning. Eggs and bacon—what a tasty meal. He sat down at the table with the rest of his family; they always ate breakfast altogether. After the father's prayer, everyone began. "Please pass the salt and pepper, Louise," the father said. With hearty appetites, everyone around the table ate fairly quietly. The morning was quite typical, and after breakfast, the father said goodbye to everyone and went to the courthouse.

Both Herman and Lisbeth had not quite finished breakfast when their father left. She did not intend on making him too mad but "just" wanted to see his reaction to it: Lisbeth took her fingers and squished the eggs on Herman's plate. Herman gasped and looked at her in anger. "How dare you mess with my food!" He grabbed her hair and started pulling it. "I am so sick of you! You are a nasty sister."

Upon hearing Lisbeth's screaming, Katherine rushed into the scene. She jolted over to them, grabbed Herman by the arm, and flung him out the door, and she locked it.

"Oh, my baby…my baby girl." She panted as she hugged her sobbing daughter. This had gone too far. Her husband's son would pay for this.

When the father returned that evening, all seemed too quiet at the house. He passed through the kitchen and saw Katherine wiping her hands with a towel. "Dinner will be ready soon, but I wish to have a word with you. Upstairs please." Louise, who was playing with Hanna in the next room, was scared. She ran to tell Herman he had better hide. So he went and got Emil, and the two boys went outdoors and headed to one of their favorite out-of-the-house places—the canals.

Katherine ushered father into the room, and then she slowly shut the door behind them. He knew something must be wrong, again. "What is it now, Katherine? Who did what and why?"

"Your son is irresponsible and a challenge for me. I am trying to keep the peace between all the siblings, but he seems to have an uncanny ability to undermine everything I am trying to accomplish," shouted Katherine.

"And who are you referring to?"

"Herman, of course."

"Of course, it is Herman. You two have never been able to get along. Katherine, have you ever thought about spending quality time with him? He is really a good boy and has a sweet heart."

"I have done all I can. But he is disobedient and mean to his sister, Lisbeth. Today, I caught him pulling her hair. That is unacceptable! Herman, I want you to whip him. He has many lessons to learn."

The argument went back and forth. Herman knew she was being unfair and did not know exactly what to do. In the end, he half-promised to talk with Herman, but he also said he was going to have a talk with Lisbeth as well—to get both sides of the story.

After playing in and around the canals for a few hours, the tired boys decided it was probably time to return home. They came back racing—everything was always a race to them. The streets of Marne were beautiful at night back in those days. Street lamps ran down each lane, and the windows of homes were decorated with pretty curtains and glowed by candlelight. Emil almost accidentally ran into an elderly lady while trying to peek into someone's window while running! "What are you doing? Spying, prying, and peeking, are you?" teased Herman.

After supper, the father went and first talked to Lisbeth in his bedroom. She did tell the truth more than Katherine but then felt that her poking Herman's eggs that morning was "just a test to see what would happen." The father then talked to Herman, again.

"Son, the situation between you and your mother is growing more dire day by day. She wants me to whip you. I want you to hide out when I am home, so she cannot find you for a whipping. I love you, but we have a large family, and I need to keep the peace. Do you understand?"

Herman nodded, slightly perplexed, but in a loving way.

Whenever the father was home, then, outside of meal times, Herman kept to being out of the house, mostly by the canals and oftentimes with Emil. Water seemed fascinating. There was so much he could do with and in it, especially in the summertime! Swimming was great, as was boating and skipping rocks. Emil had tried his hand at making a makeshift boat once, but it lasted only about ten minutes! So instead, he and Herman saved up summer earnings so they could buy a used, beat-up boat; this, they bought with pride. It needed a little work, so they washed, repaired, and repainted the boat. After their little renovation, they carried it from their house to the canal, one boy on each end.

"I hope this thing works. We worked the greater part of summer for it!"

After putting it in the water, hobbling in, and getting the paddles out, they were ready to try out their favorite new toy. Herman sat in the front, and Emil in the rear. *Whir, whir, whir* went the water as they paddled along. How fun, this is the best thing ever—after swimming! They loved the smooth ride although the coordination of their paddles needed some practice.

They spent many sunny afternoons the rest of that summer in their boat. It was their own little world—a world different from the pace of early twentieth-century Germany. No brawling or tittle-tattling allowed on those few square feet. They could be anything their imagination thought of—pirates, sailors, explorers, warriors, or travelers lost at sea. From reading so many children's history books, their minds were filled with scenes of ancient battles, explorations, and discoveries. They even loved the story from 1620 of how a group of people from Western Europe, such as they were, set sail aboard the *Mayflower* to seek a new life for themselves in the Americas.

Herman could only dream of such stories. Before becoming a lawyer and working in a heated courthouse all day, Herman's father had served in the German Navy for over twenty years. His father had many stories to tell about faraway places, towns, and people. As fun as their little imagination boat could be, every night, they returned home—a place they genuinely loved but maybe not as much as the boat. It became a place for Herman to forget the worries, the arguments, and the fights at home and just be a kid—something which everyone needs.

CHAPTER 2

Destined to Be a Man

As all boys do, Herman soon grew up faster than he thought. When he was only ten years old, in 1902, his father thought it best for him to attend military school in Annaberg, Germany. Serving in the military and fighting for one's country were something that the older Herman took to heart. He had been a sailor for more than twenty years, and because of this, he was able to send Herman to school for free.

The day finally arrived for young Herman to leave his home, family, friends, and city of Marne to embark on his military journey in Annaberg. He hugged his mother, father, and all his siblings before boarding the train. Emil was one person he especially did not want to leave. They had had much fun together. But all his fond memories passed through his head quickly. The train whistle blew, and off he went.

Sitting third class on the train meant a rough ride, but maybe even the hopes and fears and dreams were more worrisome for a ten-year-old boy. What did the future hold? Would he fit in at this new school—a military one? Were the boys as nice there as they had been in Marne? Oh, how he missed his father and mother and Louise and everyone already! *Oh well, it is what it is, and I am on my way to military school*, he thought. He peeked through the curtains of the windows to watch the countryside flash past him. It was actually a beautiful day outside; he thought he saw one of his favorite birds.

But the train moved so fast that the trees sort of blended together to make a streak or blur of green.

The military school—what a sight to behold! What interesting buildings and precise formalities. The leaders here were much stronger than anyone he had seen back home. A burst of excitement and pride leaped in his heart as he saw a way of life that intrigued a ten-year-old boy. The older boys at this school, those who had been in the program for a few years, looked and acted older than their real age. This was a place of strict discipline. Life meant order. It was not hard to find one's place in the school—everyone ranked in some way. Only the strong, only the passionate, and only the fiery had the chance to progress through and make it to higher ranks and the glory that came with being in a higher rank! The shining of medals and decorations on the higher officers was enough to intrigue new attendees, such as Herman.

As he lay in bed that night, in a less-comfortable bed, far away from his parents and home, and in a room with many other boys he did not know, he thought about how long he would be at this school. Certainly, to progress and make it to high levels, he would have to fully commit himself—his life—to the military. Yet at his age, he did not know really what he wanted to do. At any rate, this was what his father thought he should do. If his father made it, so could he.

The school proved to be difficult. Herman knew he could do it, but it took about every ounce of strength to get up so early in the morning, perform exercises, learn about military machinery, and study military science. The food did not taste as good as he thought it would, but at least he got a good helping! His new clothes were worn with pride; he liked the color.

The most important thing to him was that he was learning how to be a man. He so greatly wanted to grow up as fast as he could and admired the older boys who had been there for longer than he. He learned to acquire discipline, say no to his body, and obey authority. Although he would never make the military his career, the skills and disciplines he learned during this time would prove invaluable during his later life.

Herman would study at this school until the age of fourteen in 1906. The only time he came home was during summer vacation.

*****

The day eventually came when Herman, age fourteen, left the military academy for good and came home in the summer of 1906. He had mixed emotions about leaving—especially because of the friends he had to leave behind.

One boy he had become acquainted with in the last two years was Ralph. Ralph came from a wealthy family in Berlin and had been sent to military school to fulfill his duty to his country. Herman used to confide in Ralph. The future seemed vast and scary, and the two boys, when not busy, would talk as much as they could about what to do with their lives. Ralph had a hunch he might be interested in becoming a butcher although he would have to overcome any and all fear of blood. Herman thought about that profession but also considered becoming a lawman like his father. On his mind, however, was if he could stand being in such a heated debating place all day. Though the two boys talked about future work, life, and even possibly marriage, they kept to themselves about it and only hoped for a good future.

Now Herman thought back to these times as he rode the train once more to Marne. Sorry to leave Ralph, he was excited though to see how big Hanna had grown since he last saw her.

The train pulled into the station, and as the smoke cleared, he could see Louise, his father, Emil, and even his mother waving to him on the wooden platform. Herman felt surprised to see how excited his mother seemed at having him home. *I really am happy to be home*, he thought.

The first meal back at home was always a favorite for Herman. After an entire school year at the military academy, a home-cooked meal tasted better than anything else. He sat in his old chair, exhausted from the day's travel, but thankful for his family. His father said something then that caught him slightly off guard.

"Well, Herman, what are your next plans? What are your interests, son?"

In Germany, it was expected of every boy Herman's age to learn a trade. Herman seemed shocked his father would ask about his future plans so soon after he had returned. But the question did need to be asked, he knew. In an instant, his mind went back to his discussions with Ralph. Only then the future seemed so distant. Now he was being asked to make a decision about the near future! It seemed exciting but a lot more nerve-racking than he had imagined.

"Father," he stammered, "could we talk after dinner about this? I have several dreams but am not sure if I should pursue them."

"Go on, Herman," his mother budded in. "I am interested in hearing what you have to say."

Herman did not have a concrete answer. He said something about possibly going into the meat business. Or perhaps he could pursue a career like his father. It was evident to his mother that he did not have his future planned out after all.

"I might have a suggestion," his father mentioned. "I know of a bookbinder in Hamburg who is looking for someone to come and help him in his shop. The trade could prove to be in line with your skills, Herman. I think you ought to at least consider the proposition."

The father gave Herman a few days to consider the idea. He went out on his beloved boat again in the canals to think it over. Would he really enjoy bookbinding? It seemed interesting, but what if the fascination with it only lasted a few days? Could he see himself doing this for the rest of his life?

One day while out in the boat, he realized this was the only viable option for him right now and that he must do it. *Who knows, maybe I will end up owning my own bookbinding shop one day,* he thought.

After what seemed like only a very short time at home, again, he ventured out to a new place. This time, he was going to the town of Hamburg, located on the Elbe River, close to the North Sea. *What a beautiful city*, he thought! There were many more canals and immaculate bridges in this town. The striking cathedrals, ringing bells, and busy people mesmerized Herman. And from near the docks, he could see the turquoise sea stretching without end and smell the salty aroma about.

Soon, he was situated in his boarding house, only a block from where he would work at the local bookbinder's shop. On his first night, he took a warm bath, for it had rained heavily for part of the day. Afterward, he came downstairs to enjoy a warm meal the cook, named Frau Maria, had prepared for him. Maria took an instant liking to the boy and made sure he got a big helping of food.

The next morning, bright and early, Herman arose and dressed in some of his best clothes. After a quick breakfast, he walked one block over to where the bookbinder shop was located.

"I have been expecting you, Herman," a burly man with a deep voice said. "Welcome to the bookbinding business. As your father has told you, my name is Herr Wilhelm. Please, come inside and let us begin. We are already burning daylight."

Herman was mesmerized by the stacks of papers awaiting to be completed. On an old, wooden table lay a pile of completed books, ready to now be sold. In another pile, which was much larger, lay papers in bunches that still needed to be bound.

"Today, I need you to run a few errands for me," he told Herman. "Please go and deliver this note to Herr Struber. His office is located just over on Wasser Street. Then I need you to take this cart over there in the corner and deliver this stack of books to Herr Schmidt's bookstore across from this building."

It did not take Herman long to realize that Herr Wilhelm was not very interested in training him how to become a bookbinder. Rather, he seemed to want Herman to simply take care of the day-to-day menial tasks. Of course, this was not learning—anyone could do the types of things he was being asked to do.

After one week of being Herr Wilhelm's "errand runner," Herman had had enough. He wrote home to his mother explaining the situation. Katherine was irate. She wrote back telling Herman to return home so they could look for a better opportunity for him.

Although Herman was sad to leave the exquisite city of Hamburg, he could not leave the bookbinder's shop fast enough.

The only decent person he felt he had met on this quick trip was Maria!

As he rode the train home, again back to Marne, he could not help but appreciate his mother wanting the best for him. They had clashed over the years, and there were many hurts on both sides. Yet, for once, he thought to himself, she was doing something nice for him. It felt good that he was returning home in peace.

Now after arriving home, the question again, was, What is next? The answer to this question is one Herman could never have imagined.

CHAPTER 3

Across the Sea

Herman sat alone on his bed wondering where he would go next. Hopefully, his next endeavor would turn out better than the last. He mused about the future while his mother, in the other room, just received some amazing news.

Katherine's older son, Gerhard Heeschen, as well as her brother, Emil Martin, lived across the ocean in Island City, Oregon, United States of America. They had graciously sent enough money so Emil could go to America. *What an opportunity for him*, she thought. With Gerhard and Emil there, he would not be lonely.

She announced this arrangement at dinner that night. Both Herman and Emil looked at each other in shock. Emil had never even considered going to the United States, and Herman was sad about the proposition. They had grown close over the last several years.

It was to Katherine's great disappointment, however, when her husband informed her that this proposition couldn't happen. The government would not let Emil out of the country.

"For heaven's sake, why on earth?" she fumed.

"Because," father explained dryly, "Emil is military age. I am sorry, Katherine, but there is no way of his being able to go to America. Either the money will have to be returned, or someone else will take his place."

Everyone went into uproar mode that night as they went to bed. The money was a considerable sum. What would happen? Who would go instead of Emil? Certainly, Herman thought, his mother would never allow him to take Emil's place.

Imagine his surprise when at breakfast the next morning, the father announced that Herman would be the one to leave for the United States! Herman could hardly breathe! Going to Hamburg was one thing; going across the Atlantic to another continent felt entirely different. Herman wondered why they chose him, but to his father, he was the most logical person to go.

Herman, a boy of fifteen and a half, would soon be sailing for New York City.

*****

That last morning at home arrived as Herman and his family rode the train back to Hamburg to see him off. While riding, Herman lovingly held his toddler sister Hanna close to him. This was the last time he would see her for what would seem an eternity. He gazed over at his beautiful sister Louise. She had grown up so much while he had been away at military school. Now she was practically a lady. He longed that they all might be able to come with him, but he knew they would not be able to afford all of the travel expenses. Besides, their lives were rooted in Germany. That was home.

As the train rolled along into the Hamburg station, his father and Katherine did a head count to make sure everyone was accounted for. After departing, they all headed for the docks. The day had become quite sunny, and the waters beamed in the sunlight.

There was not much time before Herman would be leaving his homeland. For how long, he cannot say—perhaps he may never return. However, at present, even though saying goodbye would be painful, he wanted to be a man. At fifteen, he was ready to face the world and step out into its vastness on his own two feet.

He gave a gentle hug to Lisbeth and then almost cried in Louise's arms, but he refrained himself from doing so. Next, he gave a man hug to Emil and a hug to his mother. His father hugged him too.

Herman's heart raced. He was excited; he was scared. After bidding them and his beloved homeland farewell, he turned to board the ship.

He would be riding on the *Pennsylvania*, a ship 579 feet long and 62 feet wide. On this particular voyage, there were 162 first-class, 180 second-class, and 2,382 third-class passengers, Herman being in the last category.

The ship was larger than he ever could have imagined! He had seen ocean-going vessels from his last stay in Hamburg but never before had he ever been on one. How enthralling to watch the crowd of cheering people slowly vanish out of sight as they crept farther and farther into the vast ocean. As exciting as it was, though, he also felt a wave of deep solemnity and sadness at the sight of seeing his family, friends, and homeland vanish.

How interesting life on deck could be! All around him lay a vast ocean beaming and dancing in the sunlight. On board, people were busy everywhere talking, playing games, gawking at the sight, and for some trying not to puke. For the first two days, he felt mildly seasick; but after a while, he got used to the feeling.

The food for third-class passengers was not particularly special, but he ate it for daily strength. For some meals, he would eat a little bread, cheese, meat, or fruit. He could not believe how elegant the first passengers ate! They had more than enough food—and the finest. Their accommodations were extravagant, clean, and large. Servants waited upon them. During the day, the women would stroll along the ship with their white gloves and parasols, with men in suits and big hats at their sides.

Herman, however, did not really care about dainties. He was a boy of fifteen. The goal of his passage was not a vacation but just a way to get him to America. America! Wow, he could hardly believe he was going to the continent. Herman had read many stories about this country as he always devoured history books. He knew about the Revolutionary War and the thirteen colonies' fight for independence. Stories of America's vast Western hinterland enthralled him.

He would soon be in that rugged, western land known as Oregon. And the current president! What a colorful figure Theodore

MUSIC COMES IN SPRINGTIME

Roosevelt was! Herman remembered reading about the battle of San Juan Hill and the rough riders. And he knew President Roosevelt was also a great hunter, having made several safaris to Africa.

After several days at sea, the *Pennsylvania* finally arrived in New York City. Along with many other passengers, Herman's hair stood on end as he beheld the Statue of Liberty for the first time. *What a firm, steady, enlightening figure of America*, he thought! Herman thought he saw one older lady slowly shedding tears. But the skyline from the ship was incredible. Herman had been to Berlin before and other large cities but never had he seen anything like New York. *Where does the city end?* he thought!

The day was September 19, 1907, when Herman Dressler landed at Ellis Island in America. At the age of fifteen, he arrived with only $2.50 in his pocket. Furthermore, Herman could not speak English! Not a word of it!

Although the new language barrier was difficult for him, he enjoyed the sights and sounds of New York during his short stay there. The Brooklyn Bridge, he thought, was especially grand.

No sooner had he arrived, though, than he boarded a train to Island City, Oregon. The train whistle blew, and he was off once more. He was tired of journeying and sitting so much but fell in love with the American countryside. *Louise and Emil would absolutely have loved to see this*, he thought over and over.

On the way to Oregon, he made good use of his time by trying to learn a little English. One of the passengers on board knew a little German and helped Herman make sense of a few English words.

Some words and phrases were easier than others to understand! Herman recognized that the English word *water* and the German word *wasser* had similar spelling. However, it was hard for him to pronounce words beginning with a *w* without a *v* sound as is done in German. English seemed like the most difficult language he had ever encountered, but he gave his best and eventually made progress learning it.

The train soon came to a halt in Island City, Oregon. How happy Herman felt to know this was the end of his journey! He thanked the kind lady who had helped him learn a little English. As steam gushed from the train, he exited with only two small bags in his arms. One bag was for his clothes, and the other was for a few personal belongings.

Island City, Oregon, he quickly noticed, was nothing like NYC. It was a small, rugged town in Union County, Eastern Oregon. He learned, at the train station, that the town had been recently established—having only been incorporated in February of 1904, three years earlier.

Yet at first glance, he quickly fell in love with the rugged charm of Oregon. The only thing to do now was to wait and meet his step relatives—Gerhard Heeschen and Emil Martin.

Herman sat on the dusty, wooden platform of the Island City train station for more than an hour before they showed up. They were supposed to meet him as the train rolled in but apparently were running late. Herman would have asked more people whether they were Gerhard and Emil, but he didn't know much English still and was embarrassed at his sounding out the words.

Finally, as the day drew near the end and the sunshine went down on the horizon, they finally came, headed over to him, and asked, "Are you Herman Dressler?" He said yes and shook hands with Gerhard and Emil. They looked a little rough to him, with ragged whiskers, but he delighted in meeting them. Besides, they had graciously sent the money in the first place. He owed them a lot of gratitude.

Herman got in their wagon, and they headed off to Gerhard's home. Although Herman could not speak everything in his mind because of his lack of knowing English, he tried to express gratitude for them sending the money and accepting him to come to America. He could make out that they were trying to ask him how Katherine and everyone else were faring. But he could only answer in one-word phrases: *good* or *fine*. They expressed to Herman, with simple words and hand gestures, that Gerhard worked in a flour mill. Herman then learned that Emil, or Uncle Emil, operated one of the local saloons.

They arrived at Gerhard's "house." Herman was used to the prim and proper order of German homes and communities. But this was a log cabin—with axes and firewood lying about and chickens running here and there and everywhere.

Gerhard explained, walking past the squawking chickens, that Herman was welcome to stay with him. He was to feed the chickens and attend school, where he could learn English. Herman felt thankful to have a place to rest after the long journey. Tired, he grabbed his bags from the wagon and headed into the cabin.

Gerhard lit a fire, and Herman placed his bags next to a crude-made bed that would be his own. The smell of coffee and tobacco came into his nose pungently. Emil came over, patted him on the back, and said it was good to meet him. He then headed back to his own cabin.

After eating a piece of bread Gerhard had given him, Herman undressed and got into bed. This was his second night in America! Although this bed was a little rougher than the one he had stayed in on his first night in New York, he was finally home. Finally in rugged, beautiful Oregon! He closed his eyes, all warm from the warmth of the fire and of his blanket, and went to sleep.

The next morning came bright and early. Herman rubbed his eyes, still feeling tired from his recent trip. Gerhard, already up and currently making breakfast, hollered to Herman, "Get up. You're burning daylight."

Herman arose, and Gerhard told him to go and feed the chickens; he motioned to where the feed and buckets were lying in the barn. A novel task for Herman to perform, he quickly found himself surrounded by hungry, aggressive little birds! After giving them some grain, Herman ate a light breakfast. Light because Gerhard was very skimpy and only allowed a small portion to be eaten at each meal. Although still hungry, Herman was excited because Gerhard told him he was to be starting school that day.

After breakfast, Gerhard and Herman headed out in the wagon toward the schoolhouse. They arrived a few minutes before the bell rang. Gerhard motioned for Herman to open the schoolhouse door, and they both entered the building. It was a functional, wooden schoolhouse—not too fancy but durable. A wood stove graced the middle, and rows of desks filled either side.

The teacher, Ms. Addie Hunter, was at her desk looking over the morning's agenda when she noticed the two approaching. Somewhat shy but a very attractive blond, she welcomed the two gentlemen.

"Welcome and good morning. How may I help you?"

Gerhard spoke frankly. "We would like to enroll the boy here."

"Perfect. Let me get my register. What is the name of the new student?"

"His name is Herman Dressler. He just arrived here in town yesterday. He's from Marne, Germany, and does not speak English."

"Well, we're delighted to have him," said Ms. Addie Hunter warmly. "Welcome, Herman."

At this, Gerhard headed out the door and left Herman alone with the teacher.

"You can take this seat right here." She motioned to Herman. Although he was not able to speak because English was difficult for him, he was excited to begin learning. And he already liked his new teacher! Just then, Addie went to ring the big bell. The rest of the class filed in and took their seats.

"Class, before we begin, I would like to announce that we have a new student who has joined us today: Herman. Please make him welcome."

Herman looked around at his new classmates. There were young kids and older ones as well. He was sure he would get along well with them. He couldn't wait for the day when he could actually have conversations with them—in English!

The day passed by quickly. Addie gave most of her attention to Herman that day. She gave Herman two books that would help him study English. Tired, he walked back home.

However, Herman came home to Gerhard standing angrily at the door.

"Why did you give the chickens so much grain? You wasted a ton unnecessarily."

"I'm sorry, Gerhard. I not know how much to give them."

"Let it not happen again!"

Gerhard was in an angry mood for the rest of the night. He made Herman wait on him at dinner and afterward do the cleanup.

MUSIC COMES IN SPRINGTIME

As Herman lay in bed that night, he could not figure out why Gerhard had been so mad at him earlier. *Sure, I made a mistake, but I did not think it as deserving of such treatment.*

The next day, he again went to school as Gerhard headed to work at the flour mill. Ms. Addie showed him more vocabulary, and Herman devoured it. He was excited to be learning more of the language around him.

Gerhard treated him poorly over the next several days. He made Herman do many chores and also made him his servant. Herman had to do every menial task he demanded, or else, his anger would explode. In return, he gave him little to eat, and what he did give him was practically junk.

One day, Herman came home from school, and there again stood Gerhard yelling at him. Herman had had enough of it. The fight was on, and the blood boiled hot. When it was over, Gerhard had somehow managed to get Herman's head under a cook stove! Herman, still sweating and panting, packed his bags and immediately set out for Uncle Emil's.

Uncle Emil let him stay. In return, Herman was to cook the food for the chickens, feed them, and clean his saloon. He soon got into a daily routine of doing chores and going to school. School brought him a lot of fulfillments in life. Often, he missed his family. But doing his best at school gave him a sense of accomplishment; he knew his family would be proud.

Life was going pretty well. Then one day, Herman awoke and found Uncle Emil drunk. He irrationally shouted to Herman that he needed to stay and help work in the saloon instead of going to school. Alarmed, Herman said, "No," and began getting ready for school. So Uncle Emil kicked him out of his house.

Herman packed his bags, again, and headed toward school, with discouragement in his heart. *What does life have in store for me now?* he thought. *I came here to America to stay with them, and now both have kicked me out.* His head hung low as he entered the schoolhouse.

After school, Ms. Addie asked to have a word with Herman.

"Herman, I can sense something is troubling you. All day, you had a sort of dazed look. Is everything all right?"

23

"To be honest, Ms. Addie," he stammered, "only just today, I was kicked out of my stepuncle Emil's house. He was drunk and told me to stay home and work. I told him I was going to school, and so he kicked me out. It was not that long ago I had to leave Gerhard's house too. Ma'am, I might have to leave school. It's been fun and all, but I need to find a job to support myself. There wouldn't be enough time left to study."

At this, Ms. Addie became very thoughtful. After a few moments, she spoke up. "Herman, I want so badly for you to receive an education. You are learning and learning well." Her voice was soft and kind. "It would be a shame for you to give it up when you have the chance. Would you consider coming to live with my mother and me? In exchange for room and board, you could do the chores. There's a lot to be done around our house. It would mean a lot to me. Would you consider the proposition?"

Herman beamed. Yes, he would be glad to stay with Ms. Addie. He was drawn to her cheery disposition and knew he would get along fine with her mother as well.

That afternoon, Herman went home with Ms. Addie in her buggy. He met Addie's mother, Sarah, who welcomed him in with open arms. She showed Herman his room—which had a desk and a lamp so he could study late at night. Afterward, Ms. Addie showed him the chores that needed to be done.

"Could you start by milking the cow? You will need to milk her twice a day—once in the morning before school and also in the evening. Your chores will also consist of feeding the chickens and splitting and stacking firewood for our woodstove."

She showed him how to milk the cow, and then he got right to work. He was warned, however, to not let the cow become startled because the bucket of milk might spill. *Milking a cow is quite the smelly job*, he thought. Growing up in Germany, he had lived in the city. This whole farm life was quite new to him! However, after a few days of this, he got into a routine, and the smell did not bother him at all.

Herman soon became quite at home with Addie and her mother. They both treated him well and were glad to have a man in the house who could protect them. Addie's father died when she was young, and life had been hard on her mother. However, having Herman with them seemed to cheer her immensely.

Herman continued to study English at school and then at home as well. Sitting around the fire at night, Addie would quiz him on vocabulary. Herman thought it was great fun to try to teach her a little German. She told him later that she had a new appreciation for anyone trying to learn a new language!

In the spring of 1908, once school had let out, Herman found a job driving a meat wagon for Bob Smith in Island City. He enjoyed working with the various types of meats, and Bob Smith taught him a lot about the trade. As fall rolled around, he once again went back to school.

The next several months and years sped by quickly for Herman. He was working whatever odd jobs came his way—from helping to chop down trees to working on building a neighbor's barn. He became acquainted with many of the folks in Island City and came to appreciate the ways of small-town life. In the spring of 1910, he happily finished his education at the school. Ms. Addie and Sarah both expressed their pride in him. They had seen him studying late into the night and knew that learning English was one of Herman's biggest goals. He still had a ways to go, but by now, he was talking more fluently.

As school let out, Herman wondered what life had in store for him now. He was eighteen, and although he appreciated the happy years with Ms. Addie and her mother, the time had come for him to move out and make his own way in the world.

Where would he go? The answer came a few days later. Herman's school buddy, Ray Simpson, invited him to go to Portland to find work. Herman accepted the proposal, and within a week, the two of them were headed on the next train bound for the big city.

Herman said goodbye to Addie and Sarah and several of the good folks he had met in Island City before climbing to board the train. Herman was sad to leave Island City. He had met a lot of great people and had really grown up there. However, going to find work in the "big city" with his friend beckoned like the call of an alluring adventure.

Once in Portland, Herman found employment at the Union Meat Company (later to become Swift and Company). This operation was much larger than the one in Island City, and Herman found himself already quickly occupied by the task of learning the trade. He soon got settled into the job, finding the task of cutting sausages quite fulfilling.

Herman's friend, Ray, however, could not find a job. He spent his time looking through the "help wanted" section in the newspaper while Herman was out making money. This made Ray slightly envious; he suggested they go instead to San Francisco to find work!

Herman already had a decent position with the Union Meat Company; however, he decided to go with his friend and look for new employment opportunities in San Francisco. Both of them hardly had any money, so they found the only available option—"storage passage"—on board a boat called "The Bear."

Both Herman and Ray enjoyed the weather and sights of San Francisco—which was much different from anything Herman had seen in Oregon before. However, the only jobs available were temporary. After completing these fast jobs, they were both laid off! Herman had no money left whatsoever and sold his new overcoat for money to buy food. Finally, he had had enough of this travel-to-find-any-job escapade and decided to leave Ray for good. Herman found an ad in the local paper the next day for needed construction workers in the Sacramento Valley. Upon arriving there, a construction company hired him. His jobs included building dikes and planting vineyards along the Feather River.

Although vastly different from slicing sausages, he came to enjoy the satisfaction of working to build and plant with his hands. His employers treated him well, and he was even able to find an apartment to rent. However, after only a month, he contracted malaria. Sick and barely able to move, he bought a bag of oranges for nourishment as well as a ticket back to Portland.

Upon arrival, he again found employment at the Swift Meat Company. But then in 1911, he decided to move to LaGrande,

MUSIC COMES IN SPRINGTIME

Oregon—on the other side of the state—to work for a meat company there. After one year of working at the Grande Ronde Meat Company, Herman again moved, and this time to Enterprise, per a butcher friend's request. He worked for Sam Combs' butcher shop until 1914 and then decided to move to the small town of Joseph—working for Platzoeder and Christiansen in the meat market.

It was on July 4, 1914—at a dance in Joseph's old Roup Hall—that a girl named Nannie stole Herman's heart. Herman asked to take her home from the dance that night, and this became their first date! All of a sudden, Herman, who had traveled more times than most people, found himself in love with a county girl from Eastern Oregon.

CHAPTER 4

Rugged Travels to Oregon Country

My mother, Nannie Sweet, was born on October 20, 1897, in Laurel County, Kentucky. She had one older sister named Ellen, who was born the year before. Barbara Hammack and David Sweet had married on November 2, 1895, yet sadly in June of 1898, David died of typhoid fever, leaving Barbara with two small children.

Barbara married Steve Hodge in June of 1900, and they had several more children together. In fact, between both marriages, there were a total of twelve children! The first of this "second batch" of children was Charlie, born in 1901, and then Estella, in 1902.

August 1, 1902, would be a day for the family to remember. Mother and father, with four children—Ellen being six and Estella only four months—along with an uncle, aunt, and five cousins, left Lily, Kentucky, to head for the great country of Wallowa County, Oregon. Grandpa Hammack (Barbara's father) had moved there with his second wife, Fannie, about a year prior, and he wrote to his remaining family about the amazing opportunities out in Oregon.

Five-year-old Nannie remembers traveling first to London, Kentucky, and spending a night with friends there. After breakfast the following morning, they took the group to the train station.

"After breakfast, they took us to the train for the trip that was to take five days and nights sitting and lying in the day coach seat," she later recalled. "We had our lunch packed in an old-fashioned blue box suitcase. Mother also had a small bag she called the 'grip' that contained clothes and diapers for the little ones. This was an interesting trip for Ellen and me as we had our four cousins [Jim Hammack's children] to play with. However, for the mothers, it was real hard because there were nine children, the oldest of them being seven."

Finally, the train reached its primary destination: LaGrande, Oregon. The next morning, they boarded another train that took them into Elgin, in Wallowa County. But to get to Enterprise, the family had to take the stage—a ride through the cold, mountain snow.

"The stage was a bobsled with straw in the bottom, quilts, and a big cowhide to cover us. They called it 'hair.' It snowed on us going over. We stopped at the boarding house someplace in Wallowa Canyon between Minam and Wallowa to spend the night."

At long last, they made it to Enterprise, where one of Barbara's cousins—Joe Weaver—met them. He brought with him another bobsled to take the family to Grandpa Hammack's shack—six-and-a-half miles southwest of town.

Grandpa's shack wasn't much to look at. Then again, the family did not expect it to be a palace; it served its purpose, humble though it appeared. How good it felt to finally have arrived at the end of the journey. Oh, how there were so many aches and pains to get there! And to see Grandpa Hammack! It had been over a year since he had moved away to this faraway country.

Because of the shack's small size and the enormity of Nannie's family, they were not able to stay there. Uncle Jim Weaver graciously allowed them to stay in a cabin he owned over on "Alder Slope."

Barbara felt grateful to have a covered place where she could lay her head at night. This shack was not much different from Grandpa Hammack's, with only the bare essentials. But they, like any other family in Oregon, made do. There was no place for selfishness and vanity out here; if one wanted to survive, he had to make it on resourcefulness and gratitude.

To Nannie, the whole thing was an exciting adventure. She loved the new scenery and the view from the shack on the slope—with all the snow-covered trees. It was cold inside, terribly cold. However, it had a sheet-metal heating stove inside. Nannie recalled, "We almost had to sit on top of the stove to feel any heat, but we managed."

Although the property had a well, squirrels had decided to make it their home. So during that first winter, the family melted snow for water. Ellen and Nannie would sometimes enjoy simply eating it like a snow cone! How the little girls loved to play in the snow—making little dugouts and endless snowballs.

While the girls played in the snow, their mother stayed indoors trying to stay warm and care for the two babies, and their father found work to accomplish. First, he split firewood for Uncle Jim and Grandpa and did whatever odd jobs he could find. Sometimes he would work with Mr. Runstaddler. The Runstaddler family lived closest to the shack, and the two families became fast friends. Nannie and Ellen often spent hours playing alongside their young children. Mrs. Runstaddler was a very caring friend—bringing milk and fruit to the family and trying to make life easy for the new settlers.

After living in this shack for some time, they moved to another home not far away where baby Fred was born on November 28, 1903. And then one year later, they again felt the urge to find a new home.

Two miles from their location, Steve Hodge filed a claim to an eighty-acre homestead on Alder Slope. Not long before, he had excitedly acquired his own wagon and team, and the whole family was thrilled to finally be moving to their own homestead.

But the property was bare. Before they moved, they had to build the cabin. Although their mother still had many young children to care for, she and her nephew, Newt Sasser, went daily to the property to cut down trees for the new cabin. It was hard labor for her, but she persisted. Additionally, they cut wood to be sold in town, so they could buy food, clothes, and supplies.

Their father and mother worked tirelessly building the cabin—even with many children who needed attention. But to them, this finally felt like the start of a new life. They owned their own home, eighty acres, and a good wagon and team. What more could they want?

Finally, in the summer of 1904, the family moved into the cabin. It had one room and measured fourteen by sixteen feet, with no door, floor, or windows. And all this would have to sleep a growing family of seven!

There was little privacy or room for "me space" here. Nannie, an almost seven-year-old girl and the second oldest, learned to become a responsible daughter and older sibling. She tirelessly helped her mother with chores and caring for the younger babies. Most of the day, their mother was gone, and she had to take charge. Their mother and Ellen would be outdoors helping to saw wood by hand, and their father would split the wood. The girls would then help load the wood, and their father would take a cord at a time into town to be sold for groceries.

One of the children's favorite memories of this time was when their father returned from town. Upon selling the wood, he always remembered to bring back a sack of hard candy! What a treat. Everyone would gather around their father as he carefully divided it evenly among the children. Nannie laughed each time she saw three-and-a-half-year-old Charlie trying to bite into a hard candy! What a mess he made!

It was in the fall of 1904 that their father sat down in the little cabin with the rest of his family for a meeting. "Your mother and I have talked it over, and we have decided to add another room close to the cabin. This house is just too small, and our family is growing like weeds." The family affectionately called the new room "the big house." This new cabin was a few yards from the old one, and their father made sure to put in a floor, door, and windows! He made two new beds for the cabin, and these lay along one wall. The other side housed a heating stove. To make it as warm and snug as possible, their father papered newspapers all around the interior.

Everyone, especially their mother, adored the newer, better cabin. She had appreciated the old one, but the lack of space and comfort had been difficult at times. As the winter of 1904 was coming, it would be nice to have a cozier place for the younger children. Having an actual floor also meant that the younger ones would not try to eat and make a mess of the dirt! In the evenings, the whole family would gather around the stove in "the big house" to tell stories and try to stay warm.

Nannie and Ellen still had to sleep in the old cabin. Vividly, Nannie remembers the icy winters. Because the cabin was not sealed on the inside, when the deathly cold winds blew, their beds would be covered in snow! She would wake up in the mornings shivering, with a blanket of white all around her. As hard as the cold was for her, however, she chose not to complain. Her mother and father already had a lot of hardships—trying to find any work that would come their way and feed their large family. Everyday life could be challenging, such as having to walk a quarter mile through snow one way to fetch water. Complaints would only add to their troubles. And so, though the situation may not have been perfect, they felt content and grateful to have their own piece of land on Alder Slope in Eastern Oregon.

CHAPTER 5

Raised Rural

As the family became settled in their new way of life here, the idea of school became a reality. Nannie and Ellen attended the local Hurricane Creek School, but first, they had to walk two and a half miles to get there. Many mornings, it truly was "over the river and through the woods, off to school, we go."

"Mother would wrap our feet in burlap sacks over our shoes to keep them from freezing," recalled Nannie. The schoolroom was one room made of crude boards. A wood stove stood in the middle, with little desks surrounding it. The girls had never attended school, but they grew fond of learning. As much as they enjoyed learning, however, daily attendance could be irregular, especially because of the difficulty in making it on time.

This is the only school where Nannie ever received a whipping—and for an odd reason. Teacher Mable Wilson whipped her because she failed to spell the word *cruel* correctly. (Doesn't that sound like something that should only happen in the movies?)

Her mother had made Nannie a beautiful white dress with small black dots to be worn at school. On the first day, Nannie wore the dress, she spilled her entire bottle of ink all over it! The school kids laughed and made fun of her, and she went home distraught. *I feel so bad about ruining Mother's homemade new dress. Hopefully, she will let me wear something else tomorrow*, she thought. To Nannie's surprise, her mother made her wear the dress to school the next day even though it was still covered in ink. She recalled the reason: "to teach me to be more careful."

Neighbor kids also attended the school with Nannie and Ellen, and they became fast friends. Two older boys, Lester and Earl Emmons, especially were kind to the girls and made them feel welcome. They often walked to school together, talking about their families, or what so-and-so said at school the other day. Although there were many other nice boys and girls at the school, some were not so—such as Sam Shiner.

One day, as Nannie exited the schoolhouse door to head home after school, Sam crept up behind her and shoved snow down her back! Ellen screamed to try to warn her, but it was too late! Nannie almost started crying, but she fought back tears as Sam jeered at her. Just then, Lester Emmons came out of the schoolroom. Ellen told him what Sam had just done. This immediately irritated Lester, so he laid his books down on a log, jumped on Sam, pinned him down, and gave him a snow bath!

Nannie seemed to be extra nice to Lester after that! Both girls were very glad to have "older brothers" to come to their side when needed.

Back at the cabin, new excitement filled the air. Their mother had given birth to another baby, Steve, on January 24, 1905. Nannie was old enough now to really enjoy new babies, and she often loved to sit by the stove and snuggle with baby Steve to keep him warm. Lots of hands volunteered to hold the new little one.

Their father continued to split wood and sell it for the family's needs. He had a few problems of his own, such as having one too many whiskeys every now and then, but he really strove to provide to the best of his ability. Most meals at the house included vegetables raised in their own garden and, whenever possible, quality meat.

The winter of 1904–1905 turned into spring, and spring, into summer. Their father then worked in the hayfields, helping to load the dusty, dirty thrashing machines. He also helped to maintain the local roads in and around Enterprise. Mother and Ellen would continue to cut wood and pick raspberries to be sold in town. While they picked raspberries, the other children busily picked huckleberries, which grew freely on Alder Slope. Amazingly, a ten-pound lard pailful of huckleberries only fetched fifty cents. Much picking happened that summer. Their mother occasionally made jams and pies, but sometimes, everyone would feel sick from eating too many berries!

It was Nannie's job to look after the younger kids and babies. Sometimes she would take them picking as well. Occasionally, to everyone's disappointment, baby Steve would get ahold of the buckets and dump everything out! Young Fred was not too happy about that!

Another baby came on August 11, 1906—baby Bill. Neighbor Mrs. Mahon came over to help mother with the delivery as she had for the last few. The Hodge family now had seven children in the household.

*****

Life passed. When Nannie was eleven, in October of 1908, something exciting occurred. The railroad was coming through Wallowa County! One morning, their father and mother led the kids outside to let them see a trail of smoke from the new, nearby train. To see the smoke from a train—oh, it was exciting! The county welcomed the train and tracks as this meant that goods could come and go more easily.

On many mornings, the children often loved to step outside the door of the cabin to watch the billowing smoke in the distance. Sometimes, one of them (usually young Fred or Steve) imagined they could even hear the train whistle!

The children also enjoyed playing in the pine trees on the slope. They would be gone for hours, pretending to be pioneers in the new frontier. Dressed in "frontier" clothes, they would imagine themselves gone hunting or cooking over an outdoor fire. One time, two-and-a-half-year-old Fred was bored, and so he wandered back toward the house. He wandered off by himself! And he went the wrong way!

It took a while before Nannie and Ellen realized he was gone as they assumed he had been with the other kids nearby. Once they found out, they almost panicked. Ellen raced home to tell her mother, and then they began looking. Nannie went in the opposite direction to search for him.

"Fred, oh, little Fred, where are you?" they called, their voices starting to strain. Nothing. Ellen leaned up against a pine tree exhausted and panting. She had been playing in the woods with her younger siblings all day and now had been running through those same woods for the last two and a half hours. *How could I have been so irresponsible?* she dared to think.

But just then, she heard a small cry. She ran toward the sound and found Fred caught on a rail fence by the belt! Fred almost started crying when Ellen came to the rescue.

"I thought you would never find me," he wailed.

"Of course, we would come for you, Freddy! We love you!" Ellen reassured him lovingly.

Fred had wandered over a mile and a half from Hodge's property! The whole incident shook the family a little, but they learned even more so to keep an eye out for one another.

Nannie had many fond memories of their neighbors and playing with their neighbors' children as well. One family, the Daggetts, was particularly kind and generous. They always seemed willing to lend a helping hand. On many occasions, the Daggetts gave them fruit, honey, butter, and apples from their small orchard. The kids especially loved the fresh honey! And mother always appreciated the butter and fruit.

On Valentine's Day, 1908, their mother gave birth to a baby girl, Visa. She gave her the middle name "Marilla" after these kind neighbors.

It was the Daggets who introduced the family to something new during the winter of 1908—a Christmas tree. One cold December evening, the families had a get-together at the Daggett's home, and Mr. Dagget promised the Hodge children that he had a surprise inside.

"This surprise is big and shiny. Cover your eyes, and then once you step inside, you can look," he told the children.

Sure enough, to the children's awe, there stood a magnificent tree decorated with tinsel. Nannie, Ellen, and the other children had never before seen a decorated tree! But they fell in love with the idea at first sight. The younger boys wanted to play hide-and-seek in the tree, but their mother firmly objected. Both families had a fun time of games, food, and laughter that night, but the tree outshined them all as the biggest joy for the Hodge children to experience.

"It seems a little silly that grown-ups would decorate a tree, right? But I think it's amazing," eight-year-old Charlie exclaimed.

"Who knows," Nannie replied, "we may have our own tree next year!"

And that they did!

*****

Out in Oregon in 1909, a family had to survive by their wits. Life came with much joy and happiness, as well as sorrow and grief. To those who wanted to survive, they had to choose to press on no matter if in the mountain peaks or valleys of life.

One hot summer day that year, four-and-a-half-year-old Steve played outside with the rest of the children. He walked barefoot like the rest of them. No one in the family thought anything of walking barefoot during summertime. Suddenly, Steve stepped on the neck of a broken beer bottle and started screaming. Blood gushed from his feet.

Nannie panicked. But if her brother wanted to make it through, she needed to find help, and fast. Despite not wanting to leave her brother in agony, she raced toward the Daggett home. Her mother and father went to town for the day and would not return until the evening. She arrived at the Daggett home out of breath and was not able to communicate what is wrong. Sensing something was not right, Mrs. Daggett immediately followed behind.

Meanwhile, Mr. Daggett was out cutting wood and, upon hearing the traumatic screaming, ran down to the Hodges' place. The bleeding was worse than they had thought!

Mr. Daggett immediately went for Dr. Fleenor in Joseph. Mrs. Daggett and Nannie started putting flour and dried horse manure on the wound to stop it from bleeding. He had almost bled to death before they could get it stopped.

"He [Dr. Fleenor] put seven stitches in Steve's heel. Of all our accidents, this was the worst one I can remember," Nannie recalled.

When her mother and father finally arrived home and found out, her mother broke down in tears. They were so grateful to Nannie, Dr. Fleenor, and the Daggetts for saving their little one's life. If they had been any later in helping Steve, he would not have made it alive. That night, the family sat around the stove in somberness—shocked, tired, and yet profusely grateful. Their little Steve had been spared.

*****

Summertime also meant the Fourth of July! This was one of the family's favorite celebrations, and everyone in Wallowa County made it a big deal. The people of Eastern Oregon prided themselves on being patriotic; that year, they celebrated fifty years of statehood. The Hodge family enjoyed camping at Wallowa Lake for two or three days around Independence Day. It was a big endeavor with so many children! "Mother usually had four or five days to make dresses for us, get all our clothes ready, and cook chicken, bread, pies, and all the other goodies we took along to eat," Nannie remembered.

After arriving at Wallowa Lake, their father would pitch the old tent, and their mother and the children would help bring out clothes and food. Their mother started preparing a meal over a campfire, while Ellen and Nannie took some of the younger ones swimming. How good the water felt on those hot summer days! Nannie enjoyed swimming, as well as reading by the lake. Their mother enjoyed sitting and talking to their father. Their father enjoyed smoking his pipe and being with the family. He worked constantly, and time to relax at the lake alongside those he loved was much needed.

After a day around the lake, they would gather around the fire to eat supper and dessert and tell stories. Not everyone could fit in the tent, so some of the children opted to sleep outside and listen to the steady, quiet rush of the nearby river and watch the twinkling stars as they drifted off to sleep. Little did anyone know at that time how special Wallowa Lake would become to the family or to the family to come.

The summer of 1909 also brought a new change to the Hodge house. Their father decided to build an additional room, measuring twelve by eighteen feet as a lean-to on the west side of the big house. Made from rough lumber, like the rest of the cabins, it provided more, much-needed sleeping space. Their mother was pregnant again and gave birth to baby Even on October 11, 1909.

Nannie remembered her mother going into labor that night and sending her out to fetch Eff Daggett to help with the delivery. Their mother was particularly anxious that she returned home soon. Nannie headed out the door, but darkness had fallen, and she had the most difficult time finding the right home. She got lost a few times in the woods and became worried about not being able to make it home at all. Gratefully, she made it with Eff, and the beautiful baby was delivered with no complications. Their mother had already been through this process a few times!

Their mother lived a life of frugality. For diapers, she used old flour sacks. She also believed nothing should go to waste. The children were to eat everything on their plates. And clothes were to be worn until there was absolutely no more use to 'em!

That Christmas was especially meaningful and joyous for the Hodge household! The year before, the Daggets had introduced them to something new—a Christmas tree. Now all the children could think about as December rolled around were trees.

The community on Alder Slope had a special system worked out. Certain neighbors would go to one another's homes and find out the names and ages of the children. Such a thing occurred to the Hodges one windy day. In fact, it was Eff Daggett who came over with paper and a pencil in hand to record all the kids' names and ages.

On December 23, the family bundled up into a bobsled to ride to Hurricane Creek School for a special Christmas celebration. It was, as usual, snowing. The chilly snow had already piled two feet high as the children all crowded into the bobsled. Their father had laid straw on the bottom, and then quilts would cover them to keep everyone warm.

"Everyone in?" their father shouted above the wind.

"One moment!" their mother cried as she and baby Even squeezed in.

"Let's go!"

They glided over the snow, their father guiding the horses, traveling two and a half miles to get to the school. Upon arriving, in the dimly lit snowy evening, everyone piled out of the bobsled—feeling cramped and very cold.

"Please come in. Welcome. Merry Christmas!" Mrs. Daggett stood at the door waiting to welcome them in.

The family headed from the freezing cold into the warm, candlelit schoolhouse. Many of their friends and neighbors gathered there—talking, laughing, and some singing "Jingle Bells." There, in the middle of the room, stood a beautiful Christmas tree. Decorated in tinsel and shining with candles, it stood brilliantly. And lo and behold, who else should be beneath the tree but Santa Claus himself!

"You have a Christmas tree! Yay!" shouted Fred, Charley, and Estella.

Mrs. Daggett directed the children to stand in line to see Santa. The kids did not know who Santa was. Honestly, he looked like another backwoodsman from the area. Mrs. Daggett laughed and explained all the legends surrounding good old Saint Nick.

Nannie felt excited to receive a present. The children had rarely ever received gifts, and this was a very special treat. As she stepped toward the tree, Santa asked her name and age. He chuckled and then reached down under the tree and, with his white gloves, pulled out a neatly packaged gift for her. Inside lay a beautiful little doll. Oh! And a small sack of candy and nuts. What a treat!

The younger children raced to show their mother. Now the old schoolhouse was packed with many jolly neighbors from Alder Slope. This evening beamed as a joyous occasion for everyone. A time for gathering. And a time for giving. For even if they did not have much, they shared what they could. Their mother and father could not have been more pleased to have them as friends and neighbors and to call this part of God's country in Oregon home. It was a Merry Christmas to all!

MUSIC COMES IN SPRINGTIME

The children loved being outdoors during the wintertime! Everyone's favorite activity had to be coasting down the slope. As they lived on a steep hill, the ride felt exhilarating. They would be out for hours, clamoring to the top of the hill and then sliding down the slope—barely dodging trees, rocks, and one another on the way down!

Almost nine-year-old Charley especially loved the thrill. One December day, he went out with Nannie to their favorite spot. He had gone down so many times and yet trekked back up again, thoroughly exhausted. Even more so exhausted was big sister!

"Charley, it's getting dark out, and I'm really tired. Let's go back to the cabin."

"Oh, Nannie, can't we just slide down one more time?"

"All right. We'll do it one more time," Nannie replied firmly.

They both reached the top and then positioned themselves for another daring ride down the snow-covered slope.

"Ready, set, go!"

Charley slid down the slope faster than he could breathe. What an awesome ride! The thrill of snow in your face and having to dodge everything in sight.

"Watch out!" Nannie cried.

Charley forgot to lean. He slid over a huge pile of rocks and went flying ten feet in the air! A moment later, he crashed down in the deep snow and suddenly became buried four feet below. Nannie came over, breathless, and helped her brother out.

"Are you okay in there?" she asked.

"Let's do this again!" he shouted.

(I don't even need to tell you how Nannie responded!)

*****

During the summer of 1909, their father had laid claim to an eighty-acre homestead on Swamp Creek. Now in January of 1910, the family finally moved out of the old homestead. Their father sold the place for a little over $1,000.

They moved in with the Keeler family and then later spent the summer with the Hewett's while father constructed a cabin. He used lumber from the Rankin Mill to build a two-room, rough-board cabin.

Something happened just before they were about to move to the property! Some Indians who were passing through asked their father if they could temporarily camp there. The children especially found this fascinating. They had never really interacted with Indians in their almost ten years of living in Oregon.

Nannie remembered walking with Ellen and the rest of the children over to the property one day after school. They crept up sheepishly and did not know what to expect.

Who are they, and what are they like? they wondered.

Now in the movies, usually every one, Indians and white men, could understand each other's language. That was not the case in real life, at least for the Hodge children. They entered the Indians' makeshift camp and first spotted a little boy and girl playing a game made of bones in the dirt. Fred wanted to go play with them, but Nannie hesitantly disapproved. After a moment of awkward silence, Nannie went over and introduced themselves to the boy and girl.

"Hi! My name is Nannie, and these are my siblings—Ellen, Charley, Estella, Fredie, and Steve. You are staying on our homestead."

The boy and girl looked up, trying to understand but obviously had no knowledge of the English language. Though since Nannie had pointed to each child and said their name, they could sort of make out who was who.

The boy and girl, in turn, said something which sounded like gibberish to the children. However, even though there was a language barrier, children have a way of understanding one another. Through their body language and kind expressions, the Hodge children felt welcomed by the Indian children. They invited them to join in the fun and play the game with the bones.

This is a neat setup, Nannie thought. Round wigwams gathered around a central fire for cooking and staying warm. The children were not too far away from the fire; it was cold out that day.

MUSIC COMES IN SPRINGTIME

After a few minutes, one of the Indian women came over and offered them dried huckleberries for a snack. This everyone ate heartily as they laughed and continued playing. After a while, the Indian children invited them to come and see inside their wigwams. The structure stood round and roughly made, but it served its purpose of keeping the family dry and warm at night. The Indian women were gathered in a circle on the floor beading moccasins as the children stepped inside.

"What colorful beads!" Nannie exclaimed.

The women let her and the rest of the children observe and touch the ornate shoes they crafted. They watched in awe as the women quickly yet carefully went about their work. For the Indian women, it was a time for socializing and for getting work accomplished.

The Hodge children enjoyed their time with the Indians and appreciated how friendly they were to them. As a parting gift, one of the young women gave Estella a pretty string of colored beads. She heartily cherished the gift.

*****

Finally, in the fall of 1910, the family moved to their new cabin on Swamp Creek. Until the barn was completed, in the spring of 1911, the animals had to be kept at the Hewitts' place. They would trek to their property every day to feed the horses and milk the cows.

Excitement brewed in the new, two-room cabin! Their mother gave birth to baby Joe on April 24, 1911. As usual, everyone was excited to welcome the beautiful baby boy into the world. Sadly, however, soon after giving birth, their mother fell terribly sick.

She was in pain and had to lie down for many hours of the day. She wished she could simply be a mother and take care of her new baby.

"Mother, you have lovingly given birth to all of us. You are a great mother. Lie down now and take your rest," Nannie reassured her.

As one of the older girls, Nannie took it upon herself to watch after the children, cook meals, and hold baby Joe. She would rock the baby in the chair, sing songs to quiet him, and pray that her mother would soon be well.

A huge blessing to the family at this time was their friend Mrs. Barnes. She came over to the cabin daily to check on their mother and take care of baby Joe. The children loved to see her, for she was very kind to them. To her, the fact that their mother might not make it was something not to be discussed with the children. Mrs. Barnes only hoped and prayed for a miracle.

After ten days, mother finally began to show signs of improvement. The whole ordeal made everyone realize just how thankful they were to have a great mother. Nannie especially felt truly grateful for her mother's dedicated persistence and love for her and the rest of the family.

The coming of summer meant more berry picking! Their father, mother, Ellen, Steve, Estella, and Joe would go over to Alder Slope to pick huckleberries. The family picked berries by the hundreds and sold them in town. They pitched a tent on the hill and sometimes would be gone for several days. Nannie's job included watching Charlie (ten), Bill (five), Visa (three), and Evin (almost two) back at the cabin. Nannie, at only thirteen, proved to be a responsible babysitter.

Milking the cow and making sure it received water was one of Nannie's chores back home. The cow gave about a quart or more every day. She felt scared of the cow, though, and knew the cow knew it! Since water was scarce on their property, she drove the cow over to a neighbor's place for water. It was on one of these trips to let the cow drink water, however, that Visa lost the beads given to Estella by the kind Indian lady! (Estella was beside herself after finding out about this.)

Still, the children loved one another and enjoyed spending many hours outdoors playing. The Hodge's had a fourteen-foot well on their homestead. It contained little water. Nannie climbed down the rocks into the well and would take a cup to fill a pail full. Charlie stood ready at the top to pull up the bucket. Obviously, the worst was when Charlie got careless and spilled the precious water back into the well!

MUSIC COMES IN SPRINGTIME

One time that summer, the family camped out on Alder Slope and picked huckleberries for thirteen days. That was a long time for a thirteen-year-old girl to keep four rowdy kids occupied. Yet Nannie enjoyed being in the kitchen and cooking. She especially enjoyed making hot cakes out of only flour, salt, and water. Of course, the boys loved them—even if they weren't that great! The boys often tried to "help" in the kitchen, but sometimes, this became more trouble than it was worth. Nannie sent them outside to play.

Back in 1911, most children out in Oregon did not have many toys! During the long summers, they had to use their imagination and make anything out of sticks or stones. Charlie loved building forts out in the woods. Bill, Visa, Evin, and he spent many hours in their makeshift hideout made from sticks and leaves and a little mud. Nannie only let them in the house and eat her piping hotcakes if they cleaned themselves up. She became an expert on only rewarding good behavior.

She herself thoroughly loved the outdoors. The beauty of Eastern Oregon captivated her imagination. She loved studying the trees, flowers, and birds that swept past their homestead. With lots of responsibility, the outdoors was a place for her to rest, relax, and feel rejuvenated. A small journal sometimes accompanied her walks through the pine trees on summer evenings. In it, she recorded thoughts on life, the beauty around her, and her hopes and dreams in life. Obviously, one day, she dreamed of being married and having children of her own. Sometimes her thoughts would drift off in imagining who her future husband might be.

Summertime came to a close. Once the family reunited again, their mother let the younger children who had remained home eat a pail of huckleberries. This they devoured! The rest of the picking crew by that point had eaten their fair share of berries.

Fall came again, and the children would be going to school. This time, they only lived a quarter of a mile away. This seemed like a short jaunt compared to the last school. Sylvia Graves, Eula Russell, and Mrs. O'Neil were some of their teachers over the years at Keeler School. Nannie enjoyed learning there. There were, however, few older boys who attended as the teachers couldn't handle teaching them. Most of the students were young children, and the level of education taught was not at all advanced. In her own words, Nannie recalled, "I was fourteen years old, shy and bashful."

Change occurred around this time as the family once again moved, now into Enterprise. Nannie was in the fourth grade. After this move, the children began attending school more regularly. In seven months, Nannie only remembered missing one day. This was a significant improvement from previous years!

In the spring of 1912, after their move, their mother and a few of the younger children went back to the homestead. They needed to stay a little longer in the cabin to fulfill their "required time" at the homestead and thus receive their final proof on the claim. Their father and the rest of the family remained at their new home in Enterprise because the children were still in school.

On one stay, which lasted over two weeks, their mother had a serious problem. She thought she had packed enough but obviously had not: They ran out of food! At first, she contemplated going out into the woods and killing game by herself. Then she realized what a ludicrous idea this was with small children to look after. Finally, she made up her mind: They were to start walking back to town, an eight-mile journey, at once. The children needed food! They couldn't just stay out there and starve!

It was a cold spring morning and over hills, carrying a one-year-old on her back when she trekked back to Enterprise. Their mother was very strong-willed, and on this occasion, she made up her mind to return in time before the younger children started saying, "I'm hungry."

Well, needless to say, she did not make it in time. Little hands started clawing at her.

"I'm tired, Mother, and I'm hungry."

This is ridiculous, mother thought. *How could I have been so dumb and irresponsible as to not have brought enough food? Oh, my knees are killing me!*

Now normally, their mother was not one to complain. However, this occasion may have been one exception. When Nannie saw their tired mother walking up the path, with disheveled hair and children clinging to her, she realized something went wrong.

"I am never returning to that place again!" she shouted.

Their father, Ellen, and Nannie immediately came out and helped their mother and the children. They brought them inside and gave them a warm meal. Mother soon fell fast asleep.

With a bit of humor, their father said, "Well, that's a side of your mother you don't get to see often!"

*****

The family enjoyed living in town. Conditions here seemed much better than had been the case on the homesteads. The children loved being with other boys and girls their own age. Their mother became well acquainted with several ladies in town. And their father found more work opportunities here. During that spring, the first elk had been brought to Wallowa County, and he helped drive them down to Billy Meadows. What an exhilarating job this must have been! And a little dangerous trying to herd dozens of elk!

That Fourth of July, the family celebrated in the nearby town of Wallowa. They camped near the train depot for three nights. This was a particularly exciting year! Besides the usual red-white-and-blue banners, delicious food, and folksy music, Wallowa hosted a big bright balloon! The younger children were mesmerized by its size and by how high in the sky it could go. They clustered on the grass to watch it slowly go up and then gently come down. *What a thrill,* they thought, *to go flying up in the sky and see people look like ants down below!* Unfortunately, they did not get to ride the balloon that year but maybe someday, they resolved.

For Nannie, the highlight of this year's Fourth of July celebration was an experience she would never forget. Their father had hired a man to take them on a ride in his Buick car. None of the family had ever ridden in a car before! Exploring the rolling hills of the surrounding area was on the agenda that day. They passed several people on the road, and Nannie and Ellen waived proudly.

I do hope someday I might be able to have my own car, Nannie thought.

Practically hearing her thoughts, the driver said, "Cars are soon to become essential. In a few years, everyone will be driving one!"

They rounded the last corner, and the enticing tour came to an end. It had been a very bumpy and dusty ride but well worth the experience.

During the fall, after having lived in Enterprise for only half a year, their father decided to move the family to the nearby town of Joseph. They moved just in time for the children to begin school. Ellen and Nannie had mixed feelings about leaving; they had moved many times, and moving is not that easy. However, Nannie fell in love with the new school and especially the teacher, Ms. Koelewyn. The school was a beautiful three-story brick building, and Nannie started the fifth grade there. At least at this school, which was completed in 1910, there was more space for everyone. (Sadly, though, during the winter of 1918, a cold wind blew off the third floor! Instead of repairing the third floor, it was decided to turn it into a second-story building.)

Arithmetic seemed very difficult, like a foreign language, to her; however, she thoroughly loved writing. Ms. Koelewyn was a very strict teacher but also loved her students. She only wanted them to grow and exceed in life. Nannie felt the strictness at times. Yet she diligently applied herself and made much progress.

Her brother Fred, however, really enjoyed math! Nannie couldn't understand how he would come home and actually enjoy scribbling a bunch of crazy numbers on paper and solving them. *Everybody is good at something, I guess*, she thought. *But my passion is not with numbers, it lies in words.*

Following the school year that summer, father found work cutting and hauling hay, as well as repairing local roads. He would be gone from sunup until sundown, trying to use each moment of daylight to accomplish something. Their father was strong, and bucking hay bales all day made him even stronger. To be perfectly honest, it was not his favorite job. But he did it because he knew he needed to provide for his family. The long summer days were hot, dry, and dusty as he would be out in the fields cutting hay. He often worked up a huge sweat which left his clothes soaking wet.

Though a strong, tough man who worked hard, he was kind and thoughtful as well. He enjoyed talking to his fellow coworkers as they bucked bales of hay onto the wagon. During what little break times they had, he would sometimes start humming or singing a folk tune—the other guys sometimes joining in with him.

He also loved to be working with his family. Even until nine or ten o'clock at night, the family could be found sawing wood together, as their father had brought yet another load of logs. Nannie, Ellen, Estella, Fred, and Steve worked beside him. Mother would be sitting on a wood bench with the rest of the children in the dim light of the woodshed. This was family time. Sometimes it meant resting by the fire indoors and at other times working hard together.

The school year of 1912 was the last one for Ellen. She had had all the schooling necessary for her grown life in Eastern Oregon. Now she did housework for many of the ladies in Joseph. Ellen had a pleasant personality and won the hearts of many ladies and children while cleaning their homes. It seemed she had many "adopted" families.

On April 13, 1913, baby Lily Alice came into the world; she was a sweet special baby. Although it seemed there would be no end to the Hodge children, their mother and father loved them all very much. They knew that, possibly, Lily might be their last one. And so, they cherished those crazy yet profoundly beautiful days of having a young baby in their lives.

At eighteen months old, she was still a healthy, vibrant little girl. However, she soon contracted measles as well as pneumonia. Today, something like this could be treated. But in 1914, this condition could mean life or death. Mother sat beside herself as she gazed at little Lily in her bed—her head and body burning up. What would become of her little baby!

For several days, the routine stayed the same—watch over Lily and see if she has made any progress. At times, it felt like the world was coming to an end. This baby just could not die.

With grateful hearts, after several days sick and near death's door, Lily finally began to recover. It was yet another miracle and something to be grateful for for the Hodge family.

The children went to school again in the fall of 1913. Again, it was another great year of progress for Nannie.

In the summer, they had an opportunity to work for a fellow named F. D. McCully. He was a farmer and wanted the kids to pull Jim Hill mustard from the wheat fields on Prairie Creek. So that meant Nannie, Charley, Estella, Fredie, Steve, and William spent most of their summer in the blazing hot sun pulling weeds from a wheat field! It was hard work, and sometimes, the children wanted to quit. But Nannie would not hear of it. She pushed them harder and harder as they brought buckets upon buckets of weeds to the dump pile. Sometimes, the children would eat some of the wheat kernels for a snack, or Fredie would sometimes put a straw of wheat in his mouth as he worked away at those nasty weeds.

Meanwhile, their mother tended to the garden. She kept one each year and enjoyed all the fresh produce it produced for her family. Onions, sugar beets, and tomatoes were among her favorites to grow. She spent many hours meticulously weeding the garden beds. For her, it was satisfying to keep the garden looking pretty and reap the benefits of harvest.

Even with a good-producing garden, it still did not produce enough to fill the needs of a large family. Their mother and Father went every fall to the town of Imnaha to bring back a wagonload of fruit. The family loved eating fruit and could only enjoy it when it was in season.

Their father also would go out to Wallowa Lake during the fall to catch fish. He often liked bringing Fredie, Steve, or William out with him. Back in those days, there was no limit on how many fish one could catch or even a restriction on the method of fishing.

Father enjoyed fishing immensely as it provided a time for him to sit and think quietly beside the lake. After busy summer days, this was just what he needed. He also liked to show his boys the best fishing practices but normally sat quietly while waiting for the fish to bite the bait. Fredie soon picked up on his father's fishing advice, and he became an excellent fisherman.

Sometimes, after many patient and long hours of fishing and filling several tubs full, they would go swimming. Sitting in the hot sun all day had taken its toll; it was time to get wet! How that water felt good!

It was during the spring of that year, once school had finished, that Nannie went to work for Mrs. Christiansen. With her education now over, she cleaned and cared for this family's two young daughters—one fifteen months and the other three months old. They gave her $3.50 a week for her help.

Nannie soon fell in love with the Christiansen family. She often sat for many hours talking with the missus about various things in life. The two babies were a lot of work, but Nannie enjoyed taking care of and playing with them. Sometimes, she would rock them, one on each knee, and read children's stories. Mr. Christiansen appreciated Nannie investing in the lives of his two young girls and made Nannie feel she was a part of the family.

As Nannie cleaned the house and took care of two busy babies, she noticed a man passing by daily. Apparently, he was on his way to the slaughterhouse and had to pass by the Christiansen residence to get a horse to ride to work. Not only did he butcher at the slaughterhouse, but he also worked at the meat shop, which was only a block from the Christiansen's home.

Nannie would be about her business and then suddenly stop to watch him pass by through the curtain windows. *Who is this man? I wonder where he came from. He is a handsome fellow!* she thought.

After a few days of wondering, and perhaps daydreaming, she asked the Christiansen family more about him.

"Yes, yes, we know Herman. He's been in the area for a little while now and is a hard worker. He does quality work and is one of the best butcher men around," Mr. Christiansen stated.

This is how Nannie Sweet met Herman Dressler. The two of them had wildly different stories—wildly different backgrounds—but they met.

Nannie was no longer a little girl. She would be turning seventeen that October and had finished her schooling. However, she had been grown-up for many years now. With several young children to look after, meals to be made, and chores to be done—she had learned to be a responsible young lady. "We could not have made it without you," her parents had told her. Lovingly caring for her own siblings and for the Christiansen girls had prepared Nannie for one day being a mother. She also greatly desired to meet a kind, strong man who would look after her and protect her. Why not this handsome man who passed by every day?

Herman, who as you know from earlier in the story, had recently come to Joseph to work for Christiansen and Platzoeder in the meat business. Yes, Mr. Christiansen was who both Nannie and Herman worked for!

Herman had grown up in Germany. His story includes many hardships as he sailed across the Atlantic to Oregon and tried to make it on his own. It was around the time he moved to Joseph that a longing in him developed. He knew he wanted to one day be married—to find a wife to share life with. He wondered whether that special person might be there in Joseph for him. After a lot of heartbreaking times with his father and stepmother, he desperately wanted someone to love him. Could this charming country girl be the one?

CHAPTER 6

Better Together

On the Fourth of July, there was to be a dance in town at the old Roup Hall. Both Nannie and Herman attended, although not together. For a few of the first numbers, Nannie danced with a few strangers or stood slightly awkwardly against the wall, sipping punch and spying on the crowd. However, on one of the last numbers, Herman made a move.

"Miss, may I have this dance?" he excitedly asked.

"You may, kind sir," she said as she bowed.

Nannie wore a simple, yet beautiful white dress with two ruffles around the neck that night. Herman was dressed in his nicest suit. They danced to the cheery fiddle tune, with the old wooden floor creaking beneath them. After a moment or two of awkward silence, Herman introduced himself.

"My name is Herman Dressler."

He told Nannie a little bit more about himself and how he had ended up in Joseph. Nannie was enthralled to finally meet the man she had seen pass by every day. She listened with fascination as Herman recounted his journey from Germany and ended up working in the meat business.

Herman also asked Nannie where she was from. Nannie shared part of her story—how she had moved from Kentucky to Oregon and had homesteaded in two places and then later moved to the town of Joseph.

The number ended, and then came the last dance for the night. However, Nannie was too excited to dance. She quietly slipped back to the punch table to grab one more glass to think and watch the rest of the thirty or so couples in the dance hall.

Can this be the one? she thought, her cheeks flushing red.

When the last dance had ended, Herman walked over to where Nannie stood.

"May I walk you home, Nannie?"

She accepted, and the two of them walked out of the bustling dance hall into the quietness and stillness of the night.

Again, for a moment there was an awkward silence as Herman thought about what he should say to this girl he had just met. Finally, he asked her more about her family and what life was like back home.

"I come from a very large family," Nannie said with a smile. "There are eleven of us children in total, and Mother is pregnant with number twelve."

Wow! Herman thought.

"Growing up in a large family, I have had to learn to be responsible from a very young age. As my mother often picked berries during the summer, I would be left in charge to watch the young ones for several days at a time," Nannie shared. She may or may not have been trying to say, or at least hint at the fact, that she was, indeed, old enough for married life!

As they rounded the last corner of the dusty street where Nannie lived, Herman took one last glance at her and said, "It was delightful to meet you, Nannie! I am sure we will see each other again sometime soon!"

Nannie almost blushed as she humbly and politely smiled and waved goodnight and opened the door. Herman impressed her as a kind and gentle man. *I wonder, just wonder...*, she thought.

She told her parents about Herman. Ellen attended the dance, too, and had noticed the way Nannie had looked into Herman's eyes. But she was a loyal sister and would never say anything to her parents before Nannie had the chance.

Their father and mother approved of the new relationship and wanted to meet him. Of course, the culture in 1914 maintained that a girl should be married young. Nannie was almost seventeen, so her parents had been in the expectation that, at any time, she could be married.

The Christiansens, however, made a big fuss over Herman walking Nannie home on that first night. Mr. Christiansen let Herman know at work the next day how he felt about it: He thought it was hasty and inappropriate.

Yet from then on, Nannie and Herman spent each Sunday together, sometimes going on walks or even sitting on logs and simply chatting. On warm summer Sundays, they enjoyed each other's company by walking around Wallowa Lake. The lake setting was very peaceful and idyllic—the crystal blue waters surrounded by soaring ponderosa pine trees. The birds sang in the trees, and the squirrels scurried about.

After a few jaunts around the lake on Sundays, Herman, who did not own his own horse, hired a buggy for the two of them to ride around the lake. On one occasion, he wanted to treat Nannie to an extra special ride. It was a long buggy ride; they rode as far as the road went around the west side of the lake. There they stopped, and Herman helped Nannie out of the buggy.

The two of them walked a short distance, hand in hand, as Herman carried a picnic basket in one arm. They found a nice log with a good view of the lake, and then Nannie began preparing a nice Sunday dinner. Sitting there on a log, Herman asked, "Nannie, would you consent to be my wife? I love you, Nannie, and want to spend the rest of my life with you."

He almost choked up as he said this. Nannie, pouring a glass of water, suddenly stopped and gazed into his eyes. She instantly beamed. "Yes, yes, I do want to marry you!" She, too, had a tear in her eye. Herman gave Nannie a side hug as Nannie gasped for breath. Happily, they were to be married! They were to be husband and wife!

In Nannie's own words, "When I look back on the clothes I wore and the home I came from, God must have had something in His plan that didn't show on the surface. Things went faster than we had planned. We got married on August 29, 1914, in my folk's home at about eight-thirty on a Saturday night—just eight weeks after our first date."

Family and friends crowded the little home that night as Herman and Nannie said, "I do." Nannie wore the same dress she had worn to the dance, and Herman wore the same suit. Algott W. Holmes, who worked with Nannie's father, married them. The wedding was no "fancy affair" but a simple setting, with simple clothes, simple food, and a simple ceremony. Yet Herman and Nannie loved each other deeply, and that was all that mattered. Herman Robert Fritz Dressler and Nannie Sweet Dressler were married.

As happy as they could to be together, life still happened. There was no honeymoon for the new couple as Herman had to be at work the very next morning. Nannie's parents also had left after the wedding for Imnaha as they needed to gather another wagonload of fruit. Even though a new bride, Nannie was left to care for the eight children who were left at the house. Normally, she could keep order and maintain their cooperation. However, the older children resented Herman's help. (Imagine what this must have been like for Herman. Here he is, newly married and trying to care for his wife's eight siblings who he barely knows!)

As if this was not enough, three of the children came down with red measles. Little four-year-old Evin became sicker than anyone else. He cried, "I itch and itch." As the rest of the family was confined to the house during this time, they sort of had a breakdown and at times lost it with each other.

On the way to Imnaha, the wagon overturned, and mother hurt her leg badly; she was seven months pregnant at that time. This really shook her up. Some friends passed by on the road and helped their father and mother get the wagon back on the road. Although stunned by the accident, they pressed on to Imnaha for the fruit.

Their father and mother left for a week, but it had seemed much longer than that. A few weeks after their return, Nannie also came down with measles and felt terrible.

Only after Nannie was beginning to heal from her case of measles, Herman got into a heated argument with Mr. Christiansen and quit his job at the meat shop. It seemed like one bad thing was happening after another. However, this change may have been for the best.

Herman decided to go to LaGrande for work and found employment at the LaGrande Meat Company. He stayed only a short time because a better opportunity presented itself. In Imbler, he started a small meat shop. The meat he sold came from LaGrande.

Herman worked hard to start his meat shop. He obviously realized running a meat business took more skills than simply the butchering aspect—many business skills he, at first, lacked. However, he was a fast learner and was not afraid to ask for guidance and wisdom. He had no money, but he persevered.

In the beginning, Nannie remained back in Joseph. After a little while, she moved to Imbler and helped by watching the shop and dealing with customers while Herman did the cutting. At this time, Nannie was pregnant with their first! Time seemed to have whizzed by. Already they owned their own business and were soon to be a family of three.

They worked hard to make their business run smoothly. Herman worked long days cutting meat and also fixing up the shop. Nannie helped repaint the interior and tried to make it an attractive store.

After a short time, people in the community of Imbler began to appreciate the honest ways and quality meats of the shop. Herman knew he needed help as business continued to increase rapidly. He asked Ray Simpson, a friend from LaGrande, to come and help the budding business.

In the spring of 1915, Herman purchased a 1910 Buick and built an icebox on the back of the truck to haul and deliver meats to farmers during the harvest. It became Ray's job to drive the truck, deliver the meats, and accept the payments.

On June 17, 1915, Nannie delivered a baby boy. How excited they were to have their very own child! Sadly, the baby was stillborn.

Nannie had no family in the immediate area and had to face this severe trial alone with a few friends they had recently met in Imbler. The teen mom broke down in tears and struggled to see the meaning in life.

"Why has life been so hard?" she screamed and cried.

Herman built a small casket and carefully lined it with material from Nannie's wedding dress. The local sexton, Herman, and Ray laid the baby to rest at the Summerville Cemetery.

What a loss for the young couple! They had much been looking forward to having a little one around the house. Nannie had dreamed so often of having her very own children. She loved young children and had spent most of her life caring for her younger siblings.

"Dad [Herman] was so wonderful to me. He tried to do everything to help me. Money can never buy such love and kindness. Something I'd never had before in my life was 'understanding love,'" Nannie later recalled.

*****

Herman greatly trusted Ray as both a business associate and a friend. However, after all his delivering meats and gathering the payments, Ray stabbed Herman in the back and escaped with the money. Devastated, Herman and Nannie now stood deep in debt.

Nannie recalled, "All we had left by now was a valuable experience, and we were several hundred dollars in debt." Through this action, the business ceased its success, and the couple had to work hard to make it survive.

They had been through much already in the last year. The only hope Nannie had was that they were doing life together. It didn't matter what the future held as long as they could do it hand in hand. Nannie now felt she understood what real love meant. How grateful she was for her husband, Herman! And how grateful he was to have her at his side. Somehow, they knew they were going to make it.

Eventually, Herman had to close his doors for good. That was a sad day for both of them. They had invested so much into the little shop. The locals in Imnaha were also sad and disappointed in seeing them close down. However, with so much debt and Nannie being pregnant again, it seemed inevitable.

The next season of life began in LaGrande. Herman went to work for the LaGrande Meat Company in the fall of 1915. As he proved himself an invaluable employee, the company was glad to have him. Although dismayed by the closure of his own shop, Herman appreciated the employment in LaGrande.

The winter of 1915 blew cold and harsh. This was a time in their life when Herman had to walk to work. Those walks sometimes felt like death marches. One morning, he trudged through more than four feet of snow! It took him several minutes to "thaw out" before he could even begin work once he arrived.

Meanwhile, as Nannie was pregnant, she remained at their little home in LaGrande. She picked up a new hobby—crocheting. Sitting by the fire, she enjoyed trying her hand at making clothing articles, such as a hat for the new baby or a scarf for Herman. The first few weeks in LaGrande were lonely for Nannie. *How I miss my family*, she thought. Her whole life had previously revolved around them. And now she sat alone in their own home away from that family.

The loneliness did not need to last long, however. With Herman working at the meat company and meeting many new people, Nannie soon found a company in some of the other employees' wives. She enjoyed having them over to their house, which was not large or fancy, but Nannie knew how to make people feel welcome.

Herman (whom Nannie affectionately called "Dad") worked long hours at the meat company yet would come home and still have time to talk with Nannie. As they had when they were dating, they would sit and talk by the fire for hours about everything and anything in life. There was a small old woodshed only a few yards from the house, and Herman often found delight and rest by working with wood. Before long, he became excellent at building many things out of wood: tables, kitchen cabinets, and even later dollhouses. Herman enjoyed working with his hands; he valued creativity and craftsmanship in his products.

Nannie and Herman loved the community in which they lived. Out of an abundant heart, Herman enjoyed making chairs, for example, for those of their neighbors who needed one. The process of creating a quality chair was quite tedious, but he did not mind. Giving to those who were in need was something important to them.

Before long, a better job opportunity presented itself, and Herman went to work for the Grande Ronde Meat Company there in town. The slaughterhouse where Herman worked was much closer to their house than the previous job had been. After days at the slaughterhouse, Herman would come home covered in blood! Nannie, of course, appreciated his cleaning up before staining the house red.

The couple looked forward to their little one's arrival. After having experienced the travesty of a baby stillborn, they hoped and prayed for a healthy baby. They knew that once they had a baby in the house, life would never be the same for them. But both of them were used to being around younger children. Nannie certainly was qualified enough! Still, taking care of someone else's child was one thing. It was an entirely different matter to care for one's own!

Herman had struggled with feelings of acceptance as a young teen. He expressed to Nannie over supper one evening his desire for their children.

"Nannie, I want them to feel loved and appreciated. I want them to know that they belong. Our family would be incomplete without each child that we are gifted with," Herman stated.

"Yes, I fully agree, Dad. May our family and home be one our children look forward to being a part of."

Herman slipped out of his chair to wrap his arms around Nannie. "Though life has given us challenges, music comes in springtime."

Nannie thought about that and then suddenly realized the meaning of his statement. After a hard winter of life, so to speak, the sun would soon shine—music would come in springtime.

On June 4, 1916, Nannie gave birth to a boy—Herman Jr. How excited the new parents were upon seeing his sweet, innocent face. The boy looked a lot like his father! Nannie carefully wrapped him in her arms and put him in clothes she had made herself.

Nannie's mother came to stay with her for a week and a half following Herman Jr.'s birth. Little Joseph, Lilly, and Albert Hodge came along. Albert, the youngest and the final baby of the Hodge family, had been born shortly after Nannie's wedding in November of 1914. The Hodges had had twelve children in total!

Nannie's mother set about helping Nannie in any way she could—cooking, cleaning, and holding her dear grandchild while Mama got some rest. Joseph, who was only five, was infatuated with his new little nephew. With Nannie's approval, he held him ever so gently in his arms. "We are going to be buddies," he said to baby Herman.

Nannie appreciated her mother coming to help. She had not anticipated how tired she would be after having a baby. Mother was well experienced with such things, however, and Nannie asked for her guidance and wisdom in being a new mom.

"Love 'em, Nannie. Make them feel loved and a part of the family," she said.

Maybe it was homesickness or the need for another change of pace; however, Nannie, Herman, and baby Herman Jr. moved back to Joseph. Herman went and again found employment working for Platzoeder and Christiansen.

They thoroughly enjoyed being home in Joseph and closer to Nannie's family. However, this pleasant life did not last long. Mr. Christiansen had a bad habit of sticking his nose into people's private lives. Even while Herman simply tried to quietly work hard, Mr. Christiansen attacked him for all the things he was not doing "right" as a husband or as a father. Although it would be hard to leave Joseph, Herman felt he could not stand another minute of his bosses' abuse. The day came when Mr. Christiansen was giving his all too common "advice to the young man," and Herman simply walked out of the building with him shouting to get back in there! Herman never returned; he packed his bags and moved the family right back to LaGrande.

Herman, however, was known for being a hard worker and for doing a quality job. Around the time of Herman Jr.'s first birthday, in 1917, Platzoeder and Christiansen purchased an even larger company than their own in Pocatello, Idaho. Mr. Christiansen sort of "apologized" for his rude behavior and offered Herman a job in Pocatello. The opportunity seemed promising. Herman again said goodbye to LaGrande and then hello to Pocatello, Idaho.

Time moved quickly, and in no time, they became quite settled in their new community. Herman went to work and enjoyed the challenges and thrills of the recently acquired company. Nannie stayed at home, trying to keep up with one-year-old Herman Jr. The kid had faster legs than she realized! Fortunately, he also liked to snuggle with mommy, and Nannie became accustomed to taking naps with him in her arms.

On a broader level, in 1917, America had become caught up in the Great War. The Dresslers did not have their own radio, but one of Nannie's friends in Pocatello had one. On blustery days, she would sometimes sit with her friend and listen to the radio about what went on across the Atlantic.

After one year in Idaho, Herman received a letter from his friends at the Grande Ronde Meat Company. They wanted him back! And, of course, the plan was to pay him more than his current job's wages.

Again, the small family moved back to LaGrande in September 1918. However, the war ended in November of that year. The return of American heroes meant that they could return to what jobs they had held before the war. So Herman found himself out of a job as many young men returned to LaGrande. This was a difficult time for Herman. Not only had he suddenly lost his job, but American sentiment toward German people was quite low at that time. Now finding employment seemed a difficult task. And he needed to provide for his family.

Herman had been in America now for more than eleven years. He respected and honored the country dearly and had fallen in love with its high ideals. Ideals such as freedom were precious gems to the American people, and he found himself longing to be a part of this great country. He had not yet become a citizen of the United States as he only had a first declaration for citizenship. With the help of his friend, Judge Knowles of LaGrande, Herman became a citizen of the United States of America in 1920. The process of waiting was long and grueling, but finally, after thirteen years in America, he had been granted the privilege of becoming a citizen.

Nannie remembers quite well that day. How proud Herman was of his citizenship papers! He took being a citizen of the United States as a duty. To him, he had the responsibility to work hard and to love and better his nation. He did not take this lightly.

"I am so very proud to now be an American." He spoke.

MUSIC COMES IN SPRINGTIME

A blessing came later that year. Herman found a job and soon began working for Mountain Meat Company in Enterprise. This meant another move, but it was worth it! Both Herman and Nannie had spent time in Enterprise and knew several of the townsfolk. This made moving easier; it is always nice to have friends waiting for your return!

Again, the family settled into a routine. They lived a quiet American life—plain and simple. Mountain Meat Company had heard great things about Herman and was very glad to have him. Employees there welcomed him aboard. Two gentlemen he became fast friends with were Roy McElroy and J. W. Henderson.

Often on lunch breaks, the three men would sit together—all sweaty and messy from working with meat. A camaraderie developed, and Herman trusted he could share personal things with them. Roy and JW opened up with Herman as well and also invited him to church. They both attended the local Church of God.

Church? Herman had grown up a Lutheran, but the idea of religion had sort of died away over the years for him. Nannie also had not grown up knowing anything about Christianity.

Then, one Sunday, a friend of six-year-old Herman Jr.'s invited him to attend Sunday school with him.

"Come with me, Herman," his friend pleaded. "You will really enjoy hearing the Bible stories."

Herman Jr. went to church for the first time that day and, indeed, found the Bible stories to be quite fascinating. However, upon coming home, he told his mother something that bothered him.

"Mom, they prayed, and I didn't know how," he admitted.

Mother had already heard of her husband's friends who attended the church. They seemed like respectable people. After hearing her son out, she decided to visit the church the next Sunday with him.

The following Sunday morning service came, and Nannie found the people there to be very friendly and genuine. She herself had no knowledge of anything "church," so this was a completely new experience for her. Although she liked what she saw, her heart remained unchanged.

Nannie and Herman attended the church with their two children every so often. The beautiful building housed a warm and welcoming congregation. The couple found that these people loved and cared about them.

Soon, the church hosted a weeklong revival meeting. As Herman was intrigued by the genuine kindness of his two friends, he took his family to the meeting.

The preacher preached powerfully that night. Amidst the crowded building, it was here that GOD began to work in the hearts of Herman and Nannie Dressler.

In November 1920, Nannie went to church alone on this particular Sunday. After hearing a passionate sermon on the unending grace of GOD, she came to the altar. Tears streamed down her eyes as she realized the power of GOD and His saving grace and mercy to forgive her sins. She accepted Him as her Lord and Savior and—at that crude altar—immediately had a quiet peace in her heart.

"When I came home, I told Dad, and he said I seemed happy," Nannie recalled. "So just three weeks later, he got saved too."

Nannie said it was at the revival meeting where she had first heard the gospel preached. Before, she had had no knowledge of Christianity and, frankly, said she was as ignorant as a "hottentot," which is vernacular for a heathen.

Could it be? Both Herman and Nannie had grown up very traditionally—instinctively knowing right from wrong. But just now they were not playing religion. The two of them had simply put their faith in the Lord Jesus. He would now be the King of their lives, and they would follow as He led. The joy and peace they felt were beyond compare. Herman Jr. would grow up in a Christian family, and he would be taught straight from the Bible.

"We lived very happily in our new life," Nannie stated.

And another blessing came their way in September of 1922. When Herman Jr. was six years old, he became an older brother! Baby Bob arrived.

With two children, a steady job, and a caring church, the family remained grateful for all blessings. Those who attended the Church of God, such as Roy, Brother JW, and the pastor, Brother C. K. Chapman, became godly influences to Herman and Nannie.

Pastor C. K. Chapman came to their home weekly, teaching them personally from the Bible. The young family had many questions, and Brother CK loved watching them grow in their faith. Beyond a pastor, he became a close, personal friend.

"God did wonderful work in both of our lives," said Nannie. "We learned to love the church and the people. There were about seventy in our congregation."

For Herman, one of the most wonderful things to learn was how God could be his heavenly Father. How he had longed to have had a closer relationship with his own father! Yet the love and compassion of God provided him with a great sense of peace. Nannie especially loved learning about God's sovereignty. To think that God was in control even with the many challenges of life felt amazing.

After living happily for what to them seemed like a long time, in Enterprise, something happened that would require them to move yet again. In January of 1924, Herman lost his job as the Mountain Meat Company had been bought by another company. After prayerfully considering their options, they decided to move from Eastern Oregon to Portland—in the northwest section of the state.

The move was especially difficult for Nannie. Not only had she grown very fond of her newfound friends at the church in Enterprise, but she had also spent most of her life in Eastern Oregon. There would be so much to miss! Family, friends, and God's beautiful creation were all things that had meant so much to her.

Herman headed out to Portland first that January, and Nannie and the kids followed along with her sister Estella in February. She was glad to have the extra month to say final goodbyes to all her friends and family. Saying goodbye to her father, mother, brothers, and sisters was especially hard for her. There were just so many good memories and good people in Eastern Oregon. Forever, a piece of her heart would remain there.

Herman found employment fast in the bustling city of Portland. He soon began working for Schlesser Brothers Meat Company. In February, Nannie, Herman Jr., Bob, and Estella boarded a train westward bound. Seven-year-old Herman Jr. enjoyed the ride! He had never been this far west before. As two-year-old Bob squirmed in his aunt Estella's lap, Herman looked out the window and asked Nannie a hundred and one questions about what Portland would be like!

Herman had traveled extensively as a young man and had lived in Portland working for a meat company for a short time. Nannie, however, had visited a few "big" cities. She worried that this new "city" life may affect the way they wanted to raise their two boys. Herman had been free to play in the woods; Nannie had grown up doing the same thing. She simply wanted them to be free from the cares, fears, and temptations which sometimes accompanied the bustling cities.

The train stopped, and the four of them stepped out onto the platform at the Union Pacific Railroad Station in Portland. Herman stood waiting to greet them. Nannie ran right over to him, and the two embraced.

"I am glad to see the four of you made it safely," he said, with a fully caring and half-worried look.

"The train ride felt long, but we enjoyed it. Herman especially liked looking out the window at the new scenery," she said smiling at her son.

"Herman, did you know I lived here for a little while before I met your mother?"

"You lived here?" His eyes widened.

"I did, indeed. But hurry, we must not remain on this busy platform. I want to show your mother and you all our new home."

They lived in a sweet, small cottage with two bedrooms. There was work to be done to fix up the house and make it feel like home. Yet Nannie felt blessed to be living there. It was especially good to have Estella living with them to keep her from being homesick. While Herman worked most of the day, Nannie and her sister and the kids enjoyed going for walks in the city. There were so many new things to see! Buildings that towered into the sky, hundreds of cars, and everyone racing quickly to get to their destination. The people here were different from what they were used to but still friendly.

MUSIC COMES IN SPRINGTIME

In the evenings, the family sat around the fire, as had been the tradition back where they had come from, and talked and read books. Only now, they not only had the glow of the fire but also the glow of the lights of the city! Truly, they felt, Portland was to be their home now. It might take a while to adjust to the new pace of life—much quicker than they previously knew. But life was an adventure. And this city was where they had been called.

Estella went back to Eastern Oregon in July. Before she left, Nannie had a little surprise to tell her. She was pregnant again! Estella had very much enjoyed being with her sister, brother-in-law, and sweet nephews but was also ready to get home to the rest of her family. Herman rode the train out with her and then drove back to Portland in their old 1915 Maxwell, which they had left with Nannie's parents.

Herman returned home with a little surprise for Nannie. Sister Henderson, JW's wife, had come out with her two children for a visit. How happy it was for the two friends to meet again! They both went with their children for the first time to the Oregon Church of God camp meeting held in Woodburn, which was about thirty miles south of Portland.

The two ladies had a wonderful time reconnecting and sharing about all the changes that had taken place in life.

"We have been attending the Failing Street Church of God since around the time we moved out here. The people here are very kind, and the pastor preaches wonderfully," Nannie shared. Ironically, though, both ladies were pregnant but did not tell each other!

Nannie loved attending her first camp meeting with her close friend. It filled her heart with joy sitting in the large tent and listening to the powerful speakers. And the music! Hearing thousands of other believers singing hymns such as "Amazing Grace" almost made her shed tears.

When services were not in session, while Herman Jr., Bob, and the other kids were out, Nannie and Sister Henderson helped the other women prepare meals for the large gathering. As can be imagined, it took a lot of food! Nannie enjoyed meeting many wonderful new friends that year at the camp meeting.

BETTER TOGETHER

The summer passed by, and soon came fall. Herman attended Peninsula school that year, and Nannie stayed home to care for two-year-old Bob. She was pregnant and excited to bring another child into their lives.

CHAPTER 7

Yet Another Story

"I, Carolla Emmogene Dressler, was born December 7, 1924." Our family lived on Willis Boulevard in Portland at the time, and I was born at Emmanuel Hospital. (I am the narrator of the book.)

Mom, Dad, Herman, and Bob were all very excited to have a little girl in the home—especially Mom. Dad would come home after work and hold me gently in his arms, singing in his deep German voice.

It was during the winter of 1924 when Mother had both tremendous joy and sorrow in her life. Giving birth to me was the joy. However, her own mother experienced a physical trial that would remain with her for the rest of her life.

This is the story. My grandmother (Nannie's mother) was walking over to the Eastern Oregon Lumber Mill, where several of her sons worked, to bring them a warm lunch. While walking, she suddenly felt a sharp pain in her head.

Oh, maybe it is just from the sun. Its brightness is reflecting off the snow and giving me snow blindness, she thought.

However, this was the beginning of the end. She was going blind. By 1932, at the age of sixty-one years old, she had become completely blind.

These years were hard for her to accept, but she chose to bear them with as much joy as possible. She had been a very ambitious person. After having twelve children, she understood how to get things done—and quickly. But the blindness slowed her down. No more could she run to and fro as she used to. The physical darkness she saw was very difficult at first, but she chose to "look" at the things surrounding her. These were what really mattered. She could still hear her children and husband—talking, laughing, and singing. Although longing to see them, she accepted her blindness and made the most of it. There was still much to be grateful for. She could still cook and crochet; it just took a little bit of extra concentration now. Life still went on, and she felt blessed.

*****

One of the things I most enjoyed about attending the Church of GOD on Failing Street as a little girl included Sunday school. I sat there in class, in the short dress mother had made for me, listening intently to all that the teacher had to say. After graduating from the "Cradle Roll Class," my teacher taught us this song:

> *I have ten little fingers and ten little toes,*
> *Two blue eyes and one bud nose.*

We moved to another home in Portland when I was still young. Two of my friends were Joyce and Violet Daniels. What times we had together! The three of us girls could easily get into mischief; we could be a wild bunch. At other times, I simply enjoyed going over to their backyard and playing ball or maybe playing in the dirt. None of our families grew up with many toys, so we had to improvise outdoors.

Two other neighbors were a huge blessing. "Auntie" and "Uncle" Nelson did not have any children of their own, but they enjoyed making all of us kids feel special and loved. Auntie Nelson always welcomed me into her home. The cookies on her counter could have been one of the reasons why I loved going in and saying hello!

Herman attended Jefferson High School for a time while Bob, in the first grade, attended Ockley Green. On one occasion, the school hosted a movie! That was big stuff—especially back then. I hopped in the car with Dad to pick up Bob. However, when we got to the school, he realized I was wearing my old dirty playclothes dress and would not let me out of the car! He went to the school to pick up Bob by himself. *Where is he?* dad thought as he looked down several halls. Finally, he saw a sign pointing into one of the rooms: "Movie showing today." He decided to check it out and ended up enthralled by the movie, staying for the whole thing—forgetting about his young daughter in the car!

It was in 1930, when I was five years old, that one of dad's friends from Enterprise, J. W. Henderson, came to Portland for a minister's meeting. We had him and his wife stay at our home. What a feast Mother prepared for them that night! It was so good for them to reconnect. After us children had been put to bed, JW had a talk with Dad around the fire.

"Herman, I want to invite you to become a partner with me and to buy into the Community Meat Market back in Enterprise," he offered.

"JW, I will definitely pray about the offer," Dad replied.

Mom and Dad talked quietly about it in bed that night. Should they pack up and leave yet again? Should they leave the city where they had become quite accustomed to by now?

Moving to Enterprise would mean leaving all of the special friends and neighbors they had learned to love here in Portland. Yet Dad was drawn to JW's offer, and after praying about it, he decided to accept the proposition. After having lived in Portland for six years, he decided to move the family of five back to Enterprise.

"It was hard for me to leave Portland," Mom said. "I had learned to like the people and city life. When we got back up there (to Enterprise), the place looked so small and shabby—unkempt—just like shack town. But it didn't take long until we really enjoyed living there with my folks, many relatives, and friends. The kids liked the school, and the snow in the winter was fun. We felt needed in the congregation."

I reveled in the new scenery! The town was, obviously, much smaller than Portland. Mom and Dad pointed out place after place where they had some fond memory. After arriving at the train station the day we arrived (this was my first train ride), I met several of my aunts and uncles. Some of them were not much older than me!

We soon adjusted to our new life in Enterprise. Dad thoroughly enjoyed working with JW. They both had niche positions in the Community Meat Market. JW cut meat as well as sold it over the counter. Dad kept very busy! He purchased cattle, butchered them, and made sausages. As a five-year-old girl, I loved it when Dad would bring home freshly cut sausages!

Here in Enterprise, I began the first grade. The schools here were much smaller than the ones in Portland, which I felt delighted about. I was not really into school, the same way my older brothers had been. Who needed all that knowledge anyways? Studying live critters—like ants and spiders—was my kind of "learning."

Our schoolhouse stood on the top of a hill, and during the winter—with the land blanketed in snow—we enjoyed sledding. I would drag my sled to school, along with my books and sack lunch. Once the last bell rang, I usually ran out the door first. Sometimes I sledded all the way to the library, which was three blocks away. One time, I almost hit a lady coming out of the grocery store, but thankfully, I dodged her just in time.

My sledding partner became one of my fast friends: Zelpha Henderson. Our families were already friends, and we had a lot in common, such as both of us being the youngest in our families. We enjoyed each other's company, even getting into some good fights every now and then.

As my mom had many brothers and sisters living in Enterprise and the surrounding area, I always had many cousins to play with. Trips to Grandpa and Grandma Hodge's home were common. Grandpa stood outside the door waiting to welcome Herman, Bob, and me into the house to sit and listen to a story. Grandpa told stories like no other! My spot was always on the white kitchen stool, putting my shoes on the nearby woodstove. I giggled and laughed often, but one time, he told me about the adventures of Robinson Crusoe, and I sat intrigued. Without realizing it, as I sat imagining the tall tales, I burned the soles of my shoes on the wood stove!

MUSIC COMES IN SPRINGTIME

While Grandpa told stories, Grandma would start making biscuits for us. By now she was blind, but could still tell who we were by the sound of our voices. After the story, she let us take the dough and roll it into circles to cook on the top of the wood range. Sometimes they tasted bad because the milk would be too sour, but it was fun. What wonderful grandparents I had!

At this time, Grandpa owned a team of horses and a wagon. He found work by not only cutting and hauling wood but also by operating a garbage route behind the stores in Enterprise. Whenever Mom let me, I hopped up on the rickety old wagon with Grandpa. What a sight it was to see the back of the wagon covered from top to bottom with old barrels, crates, rags, clothes, and whatever else! After covering the route, he would let me help water the horses a few blocks from their house. Everyone loved Grandpa!

At ten years of age, in 1935, I sat on a bench in our house with a catalog in my lap. It was the *Montgomery Ward* catalog. Dad and Mom had agreed to purchase a bicycle for me! Herman already had one—a twenty-eight-inch small-tire bike. They enjoyed putting me on the thing, giving me a push, and watching me buzz down the street. Of course, falling was the only way to stop! The time had come for me to have my very own bike.

Zelpha ordered one as well, and the two of us rode all over town. We thought we were hot stuff! During the summertime, we could be out biking nearly all day.

The summer of 1935 seemed to fly by, but there were so many fun things to do. Not only did I have my sweet bike, but I also learned how to roller skate. The town also put in a swimming pool. Dozens of us children would be out there enjoying the water—although it was freezing.

There is one particular day at the pool I remember quite well. Some "big" rowdy boys, probably about Herman's age, thought it would be fun to throw Bob into the pool. We had just arrived and were taking our shoes off when they came over to Bob and whisked him off—two boys hauling his arms and two hauling his legs.

"Stop, let me go!" Bob cried.

I ran over to them and started screaming.

"Three, two, one!" They laughed and were just about to throw him in. I became distraught and started threatening to tell on them. For some reason, they listened to me. Bob was released, but then, to my horror, they picked me up instead! As I started yelling, Bob did not even try to help me. They threw me in—laughing the whole way. After finally making it out of the chilly water, I ran home crying. How dare those boys! And what a loving brother Bob had turned out to be!

My oldest brother, Herman, carried himself very maturely. He graduated in Enterprise: a National Honor Student. Unlike me, he actually had a passion for learning and excelling in school. I remember seeing him studying books for hours at the kitchen table. He always had some amazing facts or discoveries to share with the family around dinner. Interestingly enough, Herman and one of his friends excelled to such a high level in math that the high school created a special class just for them! I was proud of my oldest brother!

Upon graduating, he found work at the Community Meat Market: working alongside Dad. However, he missed school so much that when the first day of school came, he headed right back! I was shocked! *How could anyone want to go back after tasting freedom?* I thought.

I was a spirited young girl who often got into trouble. We lived in six different houses in Enterprise for six years. We lived by a creek one time, and there was an island behind our house. The island had a bridge to get to it. We played there on the Fourth of July. I thought it would be nice if my firecracker had a longer "sizzle," so instead of breaking the firecracker in half and lighting the middle, I pulled out the fuse and lit the end. It nearly blew my head off! Did my ears ever ring! (That wasn't too smart). At the same house, I dangled my feet over the water and lost one of my new shoes. It was "long gone," and we never did find it. I also cut my leg on a barbwire fence. It got infected so I made the bandage bigger to cover the boils. Mom noticed the size of the bandage and investigated the problem. She put a piece of bacon on it and the boil came to a head. What a childhood!

I grew up during the Depression era. My folks, like most people in America, did not have much money. Yet we were grateful for what we had. Complaining was not allowed in our household. One had only to glance at the headlines of the papers to realize the difficulties of those around us.

Our family was blessed.

Church stood at the front and center of our lives. It was here that we had worship and fellowship with our dear friends. Some Sunday sermons were especially long, but Dad and Mom always made sure we paid close attention. I admit, there may have been times when I daydreamed about how fun it would be "right now" to go bike riding or swimming. Yet I knew church was where I belonged. The services set a certain precedent for our week ahead: They helped our family realize what truly was important in life.

Many times, I watched my dad come home after work—dirty, sweaty, and tired. Yet he would not so much as take the time to eat but promptly cleaned himself up and headed to the prayer service on Wednesday nights. Occasionally, I went with him; and even as a little girl, it shook me to see my dad pray. The floors we kneeled on were stone-cold, but the atmosphere in the room was as warm as ever.

Our church family felt very close. Only three families attended, in addition to some kids who came for Sunday school. During Christmas time, we lent our lights to the church for their tree. Following the service on Christmas Eve, I excitedly took the lights off the tree to bring home for our own. Even after arriving home, we still had to wait to celebrate. By this time, Herman had become well acquainted with a lovely young lady named Ruth. He walked her home after the service before coming back to the house. How I loved Christmas trees! Mother had never had one in their home growing up; she had only seen them at parties and at friends' houses. However, dad—being from Germany—had grown up with the merry tradition.

Life went well in Enterprise for the family during the mid-1930s. Dad worked at the Community Meat Market, of which he was part owner. Herman had, by this time, "officially" ended his school career and joined Dad as a budding butcher. J. W. Henderson, a close family friend, explained his vision for the business to Dad.

"I want this business to be a place where we can train our sons, so they can have the proper experience when they take over after we have left," he stated passionately.

Dad shared the same vision; he had his son working alongside him. JW also had recently hired a relative, Kenneth, to begin working with the team.

Kenneth had no experience in the meat business but was eager to learn. As Herman had been trained by his dad, he knew the trade very well at this point. However, an argument over these two boys resulted in a drastic change for both of them.

JW approached Dad at work one day while cutting sausages to share his new "proposition."

"Herman, you know I recently hired Kenneth to come help us in the business. Well, he has a wife and two children to support, and I believe he should be paid more than Herman. I have nothing against your boy. It's just Kenneth has a family to take care of."

Dad couldn't believe his ears. "Why don't you raise both of their salaries then, JW?" he asked frankly.

"Why, don't be ridiculous. Our small business could not afford to raise both of their salaries," he argued.

"JW, this is wrong. Of course, Kenneth should be paid fairly, but it would be unfair to pay him more than Herman—who already possesses the necessary skills and has proved himself invaluable."

JW stormed off. The conversation had obviously not gone as planned.

Dad went home that night feeling disgusted. At this time, he hid it from the rest of us, only telling Mom once we had gone to bed. She, too, felt this arrangement ridiculous and wrong. They prayed about it together around the dinner table and then ended the conversation for the night.

The Community Meat Market was co-owned by three people: JW, Herman (Dad), and a lawyer named Jordan. On the following day, JW again approached Dad; but this time, he brought Jordan as well. Dad seemed confused. The three only met like this for important meetings and other such occasions.

"Greetings, JW and Jordan. Is everything in the business all right?" Dad asked.

Jordan spoke in a sort of timid manner. "Herman, how would you feel about selling your share of the company to us?" The two men's body language showed they were only willing to accept yes as an answer. Dad had no other choice. What could he possibly say? The two of them were against him.

JW presented Herman with an "offer" for his share of the company. As Dad had a thorough knowledge of the company and where it stood financially, he knew this was not a fair price. Why they would even suggest such a low offer, he never understood.

It took all the strength from GOD to simply accept their terms and walk away quietly. Tears streamed down his face as he thought of how his "friends" had treated him.

What am I to tell Nannie? He thought driving home. The drive home went faster than he wanted it to; he dreaded having to tell his wife.

Mom took it as best as she could. She had grown up with many hardships, and this was simply another one in the story of her life. The worst part of it for her was not Dad being out of a job but how Brother JW and Jordan—their dear friends—had spitefully treated them.

The word spread fast although Mom and Dad tried their best to cover up what had been done to them. Grandpa and Grandma talked to Dad about staying in the area to "pick chickens and do odd jobs," but Dad was a skilled butcher and sausage maker, and he wanted to do his trade and support his family.

Shortly after the incident, on a cold morning, Dad went alone to church—not for service but to simply sit alone and pray. He sat there on the rough benches, head humbly bowed down, as he asked for guidance from the Lord. Brother D. P. Schmidt, the pastor, came into the room and prayed with Dad. The pastor agreed that what had been done to him was wrong. He offered to help Herman in any way he could.

"The Lord sometimes allows us to go through hardships," he said softly, "to teach us how to love Him more: to solely rely on Him for our daily bread."

"I hear and believe what you are saying, Brother Schmidt. It's just that—trying to rely on Him for everything seems beyond the strength I have."

"You don't have to do it in your own strength, Herman. Only trust and believe. He will give you His strength."

Having Dad lose his job at the Community Meat Market would mean a new chapter in the story of our lives. It ultimately meant relocating to Southern Oregon in 1936 to a town called Medford.

What my parents' dear friend Brother J. W. Henderson did to them in business was devastating because he had been such a spiritual mentor. But through it all, they never lost their faith in GOD or their love for the church.

Before moving, however, our family had one major joyous celebration. Herman and Ruth were getting married! It was hard for me to accept the fact of my older brother was old enough to marry. But he was over eight years older than me and already a grown man of twenty. We loved Ruth! I had always dreamed of having an older sister.

Ruth especially wanted me to be at their wedding, and I, an eleven-year-old girl, couldn't be more delighted. Mom worked hard putting together a few floral arrangements and baking cakes. She wanted her son's wedding to be a little more "ideal" or "romantic" than her own wedding had been!

Many family members came for the big day in May 1936. I felt proud to be up there with them, in the dress Mom had made me. She had fixed my hair so beautifully I did not want even a fly to land on it and possibly ruin the work of art. (That may be slightly vain, but I did it for Herman and Ruth!) The couple said, "I do," and then gave each other a spectacularly simple kiss. They were Mr. and Mrs. Herman Dressler at last!

After marrying, they moved to Klamath Falls, Oregon, where Herman found a job working for a local meat business. We visited them shortly thereafter, and Dad inquired about work there as well. However, Mom stood firm in her conviction that—because there was no Church of GOD in town—they could not move to Klamath Falls. And so, they decided to move to Medford, a town seventy-nine miles from Herman and Ruth.

Dad happily found employment in Medford, and he moved before the rest of the family. Pastor Schmidt from Enterprise helped Mom and the rest of us move in September. Dad had taken his advice and trusted the Lord. One of the biggest "signs" of our move was the fact that our house sold for $300 cash! This was during the Depression, and no one ever heard of such a thing happening.

However, we all were sad to leave so many wonderful friends and family behind in Enterprise. In reality, it was the hardest move of our lives.

Before we arrived, Dad had already purchased a one-bedroom home in Medford. However, our family of four needed a home with more than one bedroom. Joe Hale, one of Mom's friends from Kentucky, helped Dad put in two additional rooms. While he and Dad worked to finish the house, we stayed in a motel. There were no five-star accommodations, simply a bed in a cabin. It was cramped for a while, but we made do.

The day finally came when we could move into our new home. Dad and Mom, Bob, and I would have our own bedrooms! Mom graciously served Joe a fine, home-cooked meal that first night in appreciation for all the work he had done.

Medford was a new town to get accustomed to. I had already lived in Northern Oregon (Portland) and Eastern Oregon (Enterprise). Now we were living in the Southern part of the state. I remember thinking how our state must be one of the biggest in the country! It seemed we could never escape its reach!

Dad's new boss in the meat business treated him very well. He felt respected among his fellow coworkers, and that was a blessing for our family. Of course, I knew all along Dad was one of the finest, hardest-working men in the entire meat industry!

As we had moved in September, we had only a short time before school started back again. Bob started ninth grade, and I, the seventh. One of Bob's favorite classes included woodshop. Dad encouraged him in this as he himself had already excelled in the art—having made many pieces of furniture, chairs, tables, and many other articles in his old woodshop. Bob loved to tinker with wood in our garage. The mess bothered Mom and me, but he seemed too busy to notice.

Anyway, he became quite proficient at working with wood and even made the neatest little bench to put near the fireplace.

While Bob messed around with wood, hammer, and nails, I was more interested in learning how to knit. I had seen ladies knitting in Enterprise, and it was an activity I really wanted to learn. My first few socks were not even worth trying on, but the process sure seemed fun! I felt very ladylike sitting at our kitchen table with needles and yarn, working carefully to craft what would be something I could wear.

Another activity I began included learning how to play the piano. My friend in Medford, Eva Taylor, thoroughly enjoyed playing. Sitting in a chair beside her piano, I would listen enthralled as she magically made her fingers fly across the keyboard. *How could anyone make their fingers that nimble?* I thought. I certainly wanted to give it a try. Mom and Dad talked it over with me, and they agreed for me to take lessons from Eva's teacher.

She explained all the technical elements of the piano to me, but slowly, I began to realize we were not on the same page. I wanted to play fast songs. My teacher wanted me to first master the basics, treating me like an eight-year-old instead of my real age, almost twelve. The process seemed too tedious; there were numerous things to keep straight. For instance, a piano is composed of eighty-eight keys; fifty-two of them are white, and thirty-six are black. The notes are A, B, C, D, E, F, and G. There are twelve different keys. I already felt lost! Simply give me fast songs like my friend, or I possessed no interest!

Needless to say, my piano career ended before it even began. I had even begun to dream about being a concert pianist! That dream obviously had to die fast. My parents could not be blamed. They had given me the opportunity. In this instance, Bob proved himself smarter than me. They offered him to take piano too, but he said they would be wasting their money.

Amazingly, my parents let me take steel guitar lessons afterward. Maybe this would be the instrument I really excelled at. Carefully moving the steel bar across the strings of the guitar produced a fascinating type of sound. My teacher made the mistake of playing an advanced piece of music on my first lesson—"to show you what you can become if you work hard at learning the steel guitar." He then handed the guitar to me to see what sounds I could produce. I made some very odd sounds with that guitar! He then smiled and said, "Let's get right to learning the basics. Once you have mastered these, I promise we can move on to more advanced music."

"How long will that take?" I silently mumbled. He spent the rest of the lesson teaching me things I was not interested in. When I arrived home, I went to my bedroom and had a serious mental conversation with myself. Did I enjoy hearing advanced piano and steel guitar songs? Yes, they were thrilling! Was the reality that it would take years of hard and dedicated work to learn how to play like that? Yes, again. Was I willing to stick out these first hard years of only learning and playing the basics? No. I decided right then and there that music would be something for me to enjoy hearing, not playing.

I humbly arose after my epiphany to apologize to Mom and Dad. No longer was I interested in taking steel guitar either. And no, I had no intention of trying out the violin either.

Bob excelled at singing. He and Dad enjoyed singing together, sometimes even in German. The two of them sang for church on occasion. A family friend, Bessie Davis, helped teach me the fundamentals of singing: how to breathe through your diaphragm, open your mouth wide, and pronounce the vowels.

As an almost twelve-year-old girl, I sang my first solo for our church congregation in Medford. Bessie had warned me I would feel the jitters walking onto the stage, but I thought if I could have a little positive self-talk in advance, I would not feel afraid. Was I ever wrong! I shook like an old beat-up automobile, sweating and walking past my smiling family, up the steps to the front of the stage. I don't even know what sounds came out of my mouth. The book may just as well have been upside down, for I could not even see it at all! Of course, the church graciously clapped after the song finally ended. However, I was too shaken to accept their applause that night!

*****

Our family learned quickly to love Medford and the good people who called it home. More attended the Church of GOD here than in Enterprise. Bob and I both had friends close to our ages, and our parents became close with their parents. Although Mom had desperately wanted to stay in Enterprise, she soon realized GOD had orchestrated this move.

As life unfolded for us in Medford, tragedy brewed in Eastern Oregon. The year 1936 would come to be known as one of the most difficult years ever for Grandpa and Grandma Hodge. Here's how.

Grandma had been completely blind for four years now. She had, through much difficulty and pain, learned to accept the fact that she would never be able to see her precious family again. Because of this, family took on a whole new meaning for her. She savored every sound, touch, and smell just so as to feel togetherness with them.

In February of that year, two of Mom's brothers, Steve and Joe, were herding sheep. While leading the flock through the hills of Eastern Oregon one day, they came upon a small stream. Thirst overcame them as they drank several handfuls of the cool water. They felt refreshed and continued their work with the animals.

Later, Steve began to feel overcome by dizzy spells. They did not come all at once, and he realized he could possibly just be tired. However, he became dizzier and dizzier and weaker and weaker. Joe had to help his ailing brother make the trek home.

He had typhoid fever—the same sickness as Grandma's first husband had died from in June of 1898. She had already lost him and was not about to see her son die from it as well.

Steve lay sick in bed with a high fever of one hundred and five degrees. The illness became so severe he lost his hair. Ellen came from LaGrande and Visa from Bend to take turns caring for their brother. Everyone, including Joe, watched him carefully day and night. They lovingly sat by his bedside—keeping fresh cloths on his forehead and praying he might recover. It was, indeed, a somber time. Steve had a wife, a child, and another little one on the way. Being pregnant and having to care for a small child, she was not able to care for her husband as she greatly desired. Ellen and Visa tried to calm her fears and reassure her that everything would turn out all right. They chose to hide the doctor's statement from her: "If he gets well, he is the sickest man I have ever seen recover."

Miraculously, Steve healed. Yet no sooner had he become well that Joe came down with typhoid. Joe, who had even helped his brother recover, now lay very ill in bed while the others cared for him in his time of need. After a few days, he died at the age of twenty-four.

Grandma Hodge could not accept the fact that she had lost both her husband and son to typhoid fever. Typhoid! She hated even the word. In silence, she sat in her chair toward the window, too devastated to eat or drink.

The sorrow faded, and she, with GOD's strength, knew life had to go on.

The next month, Grandpa and my uncle Albert spent a few days hauling sand and gravel to a construction site in Enterprise with their wagons. It was backbreaking work but paid well. After tediously loading and unloading heavy gravel, they left the pit outside of town and headed back to Enterprise. They each drove a wagon. To avoid a large rock, Albert made a sharp turn in the road, and having done so overturned the wagon. This trapped and killed him instantly. He was only twenty-one years old.

Grandpa immediately started blaming himself. How could he have let this happen? Maybe he should have ensured better safety procedures during the job. After a few minutes of thinking like this, he realized it produced only futility. His dear Albert was gone. And there was nothing he could do about it.

And yet another word entered the scene in 1936 for the Hodge family. Cancer. Lily, the second youngest child, was happily married to a fine man named Chuck. They had an eight-year-old son named Chuckie. The situation seemed peculiar: Why should Chuck and Chuckie both have such pain? After a checkup at the doctor's, the realization became apparent—they both had liver cancer.

Lily shed silent tears as she walked out of the doctor's office with her husband and son. Having one family member have cancer is hell enough. *How could they both have it? What is going on here?* she trembled in exasperation.

The aches and pains of watching her husband's and son's health slowly deteriorate caused her almost to despair. However, Chuck encouraged her through it. The pain on his wife's face was more than the pain of cancer. In their last few weeks together, the family needed to be closer than ever before—making the most of the time they had left. After just a short time of battling cancer, Chick and Chuckie passed away.

It was during the deepest pains of sorrow, the deepest hours of hell, when Grandpa and Grandma began attending the Nazarene Church in Enterprise. The two of them had each other and the Lord. There was much to still be grateful for. At church, they could pour out their hearts to GOD, and He gave them the strength and peace they needed to finish their course strong.

And life did go on. They still found ways to enjoy life and make it productive. Grandma learned how to crochet potholders and even spread rugs. She could do her own mending work, hem dishtowels, and sew dozens of quilt blocks. Grandpa helped her pick out the right colors and showed her which was the right side of the material.

They worked hard doing housework together and enjoyed canning fruit in the summer. Grandpa split firewood, cared for his few chickens out in the backyard, and gathered their eggs, and he also put in a fine garden. The two of them had a quiet, peaceful life.

Grandpa had struggled with alcohol in his younger years and had not always treated Grandma well. However, in their later life, he changed. Grandma became his top priority. He made sure she felt loved and cared for. At the dinner table, Grandpa always served her first, and no one ever sat in her special chair! He also ensured she did not bump into things in the house and always lovingly guided her by the hand when she was in unfamiliar territory. For all this, he never once considered praise for himself.

As an older stately man, he took an interest in the lives of those around him in Enterprise. Local children adored him and often came to his home to hear stories told. Some were quite the tall tales, but no one minded. Grandpa could turn any story into a high-flying adventure.

Yes, they lived a long, fruitful, and happy life together.

*****

MUSIC COMES IN SPRINGTIME

In Medford, Bob and I finished the school year strong. We learned a lot that year—both with school and extracurricular activities. Dad and Mom let us know how proud they were to have us as kids.

Cooking became a wonderful hobby of mine. Mom spent many hours in the kitchen with me, letting me make mistakes and learn from those mistakes. I enjoyed learning from Mom, and it was sure a pleasure to eat something I could claim to have made.

That summer, I would be in the kitchen lots. Mom found work sorting delicious Rogue River Valley pears, and I put together a lunch for her and her cousin Maryann. In addition, I made dinner. Sometimes it was a lot of work, but I enjoyed the freedom of choosing the meals.

Two new luxuries we enjoyed in Medford included an electric stove and a refrigerator. Meal preparation had been a much more tedious task for Mom before these new essentials.

Mom had ordered Bob and me to clean the house while she worked. Yet I admit, we did a lousy job. On more than one occasion, we flipped the rug over to avoid having to sweep them! Hopefully, Mom did not notice!

She generously shared half of her wages with Bob and me. It was the first time we had ever earned a wage, and she taught us the value of money. She reminded us not every penny we earned should be spent. Saving money could be just as fun as spending it.

As much as I enjoyed cooking, there may have been a few mishaps every once in a while. One day, I put the meat in the cooker pot on the electric stove to brown and forgot to turn it down. When I got home from school, the place was full of smoke, and the cooker pot was black and wrinkled from the heat. It's a wonder it didn't burn down the house! Gratefully, Mom was gracious with me.

Homelife took on a special meaning for Mom. She loved her family and wanted her home to be a special gathering place. We never locked the front door. However, one time, we had a visiting evangelist staying with us, and Dad, Mom, and he were in deep conversation. Then out of nowhere, a salesman walked right into our house trying to persuade them to buy his handmade butcher knives! Mom apologized to the evangelist for the interruption, and following the incident, she always locked the door whenever she was in the house. She loved people, she said, but could not just have anyone tromping through her house without her consent!

After having lived in Medford for more than a year, we received welcome news. Herman and Ruth had decided to move here from Klamath Falls! We welcomed them to town and introduced them to the many new friends we had made. Ruth especially seemed delighted to see me and pulled me aside one day soon after moving.

"Carolla, I have something I want to tell you," she said, beaming. "You are going to be an aunt! Yes, I am having a little girl."

An aunt? I could hardly believe it! I had been the baby of the family and always wanted a younger sibling—a baby—to hold in my arms and cuddle. Ruth and I hugged each other; my heart was racing with excitement.

Dad and Mom prayed for Herman as he faced one major problem in Medford—he could not find employment. These still were very hard times, and finding work was akin to finding a needle in a haystack. He decided to approach a butcher in town, offering to work for free to prove his worth. The owner of the butcher shop praised Dad for training Herman as he proved he, indeed, possessed a thorough knowledge at such a young age. He worked for free for only a short time as the owner soon wanted him to join the team permanently. How happy Herman felt to finally have a job again!

And before long, Herman, Ruth, and we all welcomed baby Nancy Darlene into the world. Mom and Dad had the hardest time believing they were old enough to be grandparents. Baby Nancy definitely looked like she belonged; I fell in love with her little hands and feet! Sometimes after school, I rode my bike over to Herman and Ruth's place to hold little Nancy and chat with Ruth. Rocking her back and forth, I sang little nursery rhymes. She opened her eyes wide as I talked softly to her. These were special times together, and I think Ruth really enjoyed the company.

Our family lived in the same town again. This especially brought joy to Dad and Mom. We had lived in Medford for two years now and felt at home.

At Dad's work, however, problems surfaced. Mr. Huber, his boss, was a very kind and respectable man and allowed Dad a certain amount of freedom at work. The sad reality came though when Mr. Huber's son became the new boss. This kid was a drunk. He should not have had authority over dad at all; his reasoning and judgment were impaired on an almost daily basis.

Dad greatly respected Mr. Huber but could not fathom how he would allow his son to take over as boss. Things at the company deteriorated quickly. No more could Dad simply do his work in peace and quiet. His new boss yelled at him and the rest constantly, with a beer bottle in hand.

As usual, when problems appeared in life, Dad talked the situation over with Mom at night.

"Nannie, I can't keep doing this. It is insane. Mr. Huber's son is destroying the company right before everyone's eyes. Yet no one can say anything. He has the power and authority to fire anyone on the spot."

"I am so sorry, Herman. It is so wrong for you to be treated like this after all you have done for that family. Is any other business hiring in town?"

"I have inquired at multiple businesses in the last few days, and no one is hiring. Besides, I am a butcher by trade. Working with meat, cutting sausages, and the like are what I was meant to be doing." He hesitated. "If it means moving, possibly back to Portland, to find another company to work for, are you willing to relocate again?"

Nannie sighed. "How many times, O Lord, must we pack up and leave?" she said aloud. "I have been feeling in my heart we were not meant to stay in Medford forever. To sit here and let Mr. Huber's son destroy everything is unthinkable. You need to have work, and if it means moving back to the big city, then let us be on our way."

Bob and I at first resisted the idea. We already felt well-established in our schools and could not bear to relocate again. Yet we were a family. Since Dad could not stay at the company for a very valid reason, then moving seemed essential.

Herman and Ruth, too, struggled with losing us. They had moved here only a short time ago to be nearer to us, and now we were moving away from them. By this point, Herman was well-established in his new job. He sympathized with Dad, however, and accepted the decision. Dad and Herman shook hands firmly, hugged, and then said goodbye. He kissed his new granddaughter and mama once more and then left before the rest of us to begin looking for work in Portland.

Mom, Bob, and I stayed in Medford for a short time while Mom finished working for the pear-packing plant. Once Mom had finished the job for good, we packed up the house and loaded our belongings in the car. The house sold quickly.

I said farewell to Herman, Ruth, and baby Nancy and to many other school and church friends as well. As the car rolled past town, a tear may have fallen down my face. Many wonderful memories had been made in this town.

The day we arrived in Portland was October 20, 1938. As my birthday fell in December, I was almost fourteen years old. A light mist fell as we left Medford. Mom drove, with Bob and me in the back—clinging to some of the larger items to ensure they stayed safe during the trip. We roared down the road but at a slow speed as the car was overburdened with stuff. Bob and I practically suffocated! We stopped for lunch in Eugene, and I could hardly walk; my legs and feet had fallen asleep. (Isn't that the worst!) However, of all my family members, I really enjoyed car trips and could not wait to begin driving myself.

I had forgotten just how large a city Portland had become! Traffic here was many times worse than in Southern Oregon. The whole city felt caught up in busyness—people racing to work and new buildings everywhere being built. Here, the sky was the limit.

Dad had been unable to find a job since coming to the city and had been doing odd repair jobs. We had a place to stay as Dad had since made a down payment on a home. It was located on Princeton Street in the Portsmouth district. He continued working wherever he could for a few months while Bob and I started school. We were a month late and had to work hard to catch up. Mom stayed home, repainting a few rooms, cleaning, making meals, and praying for everyone's safety and that Dad might soon find a steady job.

MUSIC COMES IN SPRINGTIME

Her prayers turned into a huge blessing. In the spring of 1939, Portland Provision Meat Company was hiring. They quickly noticed Dad's skills and hard work ethic and decided to choose him. The company had Dad make hams and bacon. He thoroughly enjoyed the work and had a stable job again. How much we enjoyed knowing he would be "done for the day" in the evenings. He came home sweaty and dirty, but we didn't mind at all.

Bob was a junior, and I a freshman at Roosevelt High School. Many more students crammed into the classrooms here than in Medford. I was nearly trampled to death on my first day down the south hall. One of my science books slipped out of my hand, and I went to grab it. Then who knows how many kids raced by, knocking me down flat on the dirty floor. Luckily, I knew one family, the Daniels, who had two girls attending this school. One of them noticed my dilemma and graciously helped me to my feet. I was a little shaken up when I entered science class that day but happy to have a friend!

Bob and I felt uncomfortable hanging with most of the kids from the school. However, most of our friendships developed with youths from our church on Eighth and Wasco Streets. Many fine young men and women attended the youth group there, so we never felt lonely.

One of our friends from church was the Timmons family. They lived on Thirtieth Street and wanted Dad to buy the vacant house next to theirs. Although it was comfortable living on Princeton Street, this home would be bigger and better. The man who owned the house next to the Timmons offered to sell it to Dad interest-free. We gladly accepted the offer and moved in.

As had held true in Enterprise and in Medford, church was at the center of our lives. We went to church every Sunday, and Dad usually attended prayer meetings on Wednesday nights. In addition, we enjoyed attending many other activities, such as youth group, to fellowship with the wonderful people there.

One of the things our church here in Portland had was a choir. Dad decided to join, and, I do not know how, but he convinced me to do it with him. After my horrifying experience singing in

Medford, I would never sing solos again. However, I could sing in a large choir just as long as I could sing quietly, and no one would be able to hear me. Plus, the songs we sang sounded simply astounding in the ornate church building. These songs could pierce any heart; I remember well feeling a sense of awe and wonder as our large choir sang sacred music.

Mom taught Sunday school in the tower room at church. She often stayed up late on Saturday nights, pouring over her Bible to effectively communicate biblical concepts to young children. She had a passion for teaching the simple things in the Bible. Love, forgiveness, and mercy were things any human can understand.

Dad also held the position of Sunday school superintendent and served on the board of trustees. He, and the rest of our family, stayed busy.

In 1939, some folks came over from the nearby German Church of GOD to join our congregation. We welcomed the Fritzler family, Herb and Art Smith, Emil Dietz, and others into our fellowship. However, we wondered, *Why have they left their church?* Mrs. Fritzler explained how she felt their old pastor, Brother Baseler, was too pro-German. As her son Ray would soon be drafted to serve in the US Army during the Second World War, she and her husband realized the futility of trying to stay in Brother Baseler's church.

I remember arriving at youth group one night shortly thereafter and finding several new young people had recently joined. *What a handsome fellow he is*, I secretly thought about one new young man. His name, I learned later that night, was Eddie Fritzler. I was fifteen, and he sixteen! *Maybe*, I just thought, *maybe*.

CHAPTER 8

The Kansas Clan

Jacob Fritzler and his wife, Mary, grew up in a small village in the Volga River Valley of Russia. They were Germans. A little history here is important. The queen of Russia, or czarina, in 1763 was Catherine the Great, a German princess herself. She gave appealing reasons for her people to settle in the Volga River Valley and nearby areas of Russia. These terms, explained by the American Historical Society of Germans from Russia, included the following:

> *Unqualified religious freedom.*
> *Freedom from taxation and licenses for 30 years to rural settlers.*
> *Government support with interest-free loans and repayments after 10 years.*
> *A guarantee of self-rule within the colonies.*
> *Permission to bring personal possessions with them duty-free.*
> *No military service for all settlers and their descendants.*
> *Free transport to areas of settlement.*

The offer enticed twenty-seven thousand immigrants to the Volga River Valley alone between 1763 and 1871. The difficulties, however, for the German people trying to adjust to the new ways of life in the undeveloped region were immense. Early farming techniques failed, and the area was plagued by marauders. Yet the Germans triumphed over these challenges and, over the years, came to develop the area into a modern region and lived at peace among themselves and their neighbors. However, in 1871, Czar Alexander II took away the highly valued rights as promised by Czarina Catherine the Great. Now the young German boys would be forced to fight in Russia's wars. Taxes would be paid. Self-governance would soon be banned.

Many Germans left Russia after the ruling of Czar Alexander II. Some emigrated to South America and others to Canada and the United States. A council was called among the German people in 1874 to scout out suitable land on which to dwell in America, notably in the states of Kansas, Nebraska, and Arkansas. The first of these states to be explored was Kansas, and hence, a sizable number of Volga River Germans settled in this area.

Now back to Jacob and Mary. Jacob Fritzler was born August 15, 1892; Mary Katherine Lorenz was born June 6, 1895. Both were born in the Volga River Valley, and both emigrated to Kansas.

Jacob, at the age of seven, came through Ellis Island in December of 1900 from Karamsch on the Oldenburg with his parents, Johan and Anna, and older sister Maria.

Mary's family came from a nearby area in Russia, yet the two families were not acquainted. She had three brothers and one sister and came through Ellis Island with her family also in the year 1900.

Now the two families were living in Kansas. For many of these settlers, it must have been hard to have left their beloved area in Russia. Yet America was also known as the place for opportunity and personal freedom. This, combined with the vast stretches of usable land in Kansas, was enough to be grateful for. Years passed. Jacob and Mary met, and before long, they became husband and wife. The two made a sweet couple.

Life in Kansas during the 1910s could be at times quite difficult and tedious. Crop failures could result in family devastation, meaning the loss of everything. All they had worked so hard for could be gone in the course of a bad harvest. Settlers became very tied to the land on which they stood. At the end of the day, bowing in prayer, they thanked GOD for one another, for their daily bread, and for the bountiful land beneath their feet. The land was their life; life was spent tending to and caring for it.

Jacob himself had witnessed both crop successes and failures. In Russia, he had, at a young age, seen the bountiful harvests his ancestors had worked so hard to ensure. Farming techniques were in their prime; the land yielded more than enough produce. At the end of a good harvest, his community would gather in a local barn for feasting—to partake of the bounty of the earth in celebration. He remembers seeing the joy and carefree spirit of his people as they sang and danced on those evenings. Life in Russia came with many sorrows and pains, but those were all forgotten at community get-togethers. His ancestors, who every minute toiled to make something of the land, would have rejoiced to see Jacob's day.

Yet in Kansas, he had also seen the joys and sorrows of farmers around him. One year, the community might be in great celebration over a wonderful harvest. And yet the next year, things might change drastically. Lives were ruined. Debts could not be paid. Ladies might spend time kneeling in church, tears in their eyes, as they brought their financial ruin before the Lord. Yes, entire communities could feel the heaviness and the disturbance brought about by crop failure. Whether a farmer or not, most people felt that heaviness. Now was not the time for celebration or frivolities. Instead, it was spent facing the hard realities of life. Some of the farmers might walk their beloved fields, heads down as the wind whipped past their faces. The earth, it may have seemed, mocked them after all the farmers had done. Yet this was no novelty for the farmers of Kansas. True loyalty meant giving the land another chance. Maybe next year, things might change. Next year, the land will yield such crops that we will forget the sorrows of yesteryear. Just maybe.

Living in such a reality brought soberness to many people. They could not simply control their own destiny. Every day, they learned to accept the circumstances thrust upon them. If they wanted to survive, an important lesson to learn was acceptance of the circumstances of life. In a sense, they had a clearer picture of life's realities than many people do today. The present was deemed more important than the past or future. Every moment was a gift. Every crop success was a blessing that could not have been earned by their own merit. Even in years of crop failure, they knew "this, too, will soon pass." This produced people who humbly lived their lives on the land, working it, and who hoped for the best at the end of the season. Years of hardship had tested them, but the sunshine could still shine over the horizon. Music could still come in springtime.

Jacob and Mary rejoiced when, on February 2, 1918, baby Raymond Jacob was born. How happy they were to be starting a family. All the aunts and uncles and grandpas and grandmas of little Raymond soon fell in love with this charming little boy.

Almost exactly two years later, Mary gave birth to a baby girl—Alvina Marie—on February 8, 1920. Raymond, even at such a tender young age, may not have seemed thrilled for another little one to "steal the show" which had been his exclusively. But Alvina charmed everyone! Jacob was glad to have a son he could teach how to be a man, and Mary was delighted to have a daughter to dress up and teach how to cook.

The two little ones brought great joy to their parents. However, Jacob struggled with life's other harsh realities. Sometimes to ease his mind, he drank. Prohibition had just gone into effect one month before Alvina was born. Jacob was a bootlegger. He hid his concoction in the local granary and sometimes would visit it after Mary and the children were in bed. At times, his conscience pierced him. *What are you doing bootlegging like this? You are in good health and have a wonderful wife and two adorable children. What more could you want?* Yet often in such times, he was overwhelmed with the hardships of life—broken relationships lost over his bad temper, financial difficulties, and the strain of simply trying to survive and "do life." The cool alcohol, in the dim of night, took him far away from his current troubles and heartaches. Yet even in the depths of his heart, he knew alcohol could not permanently solve his problems.

Clarence Frederick (Mike) was born on December 29, 1921—only a year and ten months after Alvina. These three kids consumed Mary's time—she clothed, fed, and cleaned for them day after day. Yet she was happy being a mother.

MUSIC COMES IN SPRINGTIME

They lived in the town of Bazine, Kansas, at this time, and their home was small yet met their needs. Constructed of stone, the house had a central room where the family cooked, ate, and lived. Two rooms bordered this on either side—one being Jacob and Mary's bedroom and the other for the children's use.

The home was not their own; they rented it. One of Jacob's most important criteria when looking for a place to rent was to ensure it had a storm cellar. This particular house had no storm cellar, and Jacob almost walked away from the landlord although he thought it a decent home at a good price. He made sure the landlord knew he would not be interested in the home unless he put in a storm cellar. The landlord, at first, was not amused, but as he saw Jacob walk away, he realized the wasted opportunity. Hence, he immediately told Jacob he would be willing to add a storm cellar in the front yard at no additional cost. Jacob was greatly pleased.

The structure could be drafty, especially in the winter time with so many cracks and holes for the wind to enter. All of the kids shared a bed and would snuggle real close when it especially got cold at nights. Yet it was a secure house, and both Jacob and Mary felt it a suitable place in which to raise a family.

Edwin Harold Fritzler was born on September 26, 1923, and the first baby to be born in the new house. Mary had since become used to home births, and this one was no different. A family friend came over to help while she lay travailing in pain. Jacob paced nervously on the floor outside their bedroom, fidgeting. Their friend would lay her hands on Mary, reassuring her that everything was all right and that the baby would be here soon—all sweet and healthy. After the final pains, Mary sighed in relief as she beheld her new baby boy. Little Edwin looked like he belonged!

Jacob and Mary now had four children of their own, and their family was as busy as ever. Later the next year, in 1924, Mary announced that they were to be adding an additional little one to the family household. Baby Victor was born on April 8, 1925.

Mary sighed as she beheld baby number five. Four boys and one girl now made up the Fritzler family! Hugging him closely, she felt something gnawing at her in her spirit. She could not pinpoint exactly what it was but only that she should hold him tight and love on him.

The rest of the kids shared a single bed; to conserve space, they slept crosswise. There may have been more than a few nights where Ray or Alvina scolded their younger siblings for having put their smelly feet up their noses! At least no one complained of being lonely in such small quarters! It was especially hard for the kids to get up to use the outhouse at night. One wrong move and they might wake another sibling or accidentally step on someone.

Ray remembers one night when he carefully tried to creep out of bed. He happened to be right in the middle and knew he would have to crawl over someone to get a steady footing. Very carefully, he crawled over Alvina and put one foot down on the floor. When he tried to get his other foot out safely on the ground, he accidentally slipped on some clothes lying near the bed and fell backward with a thud onto the rest of the kids! Screaming ensued immediately as they, including Alvina, thought some man had broken in and was attacking them! She screamed for their dad and Ray to help save them and pleaded to the "attacker" to not hurt them. Ray tried to explain, but in the midst of the cries of her siblings, she was confused. Their dad raced into the room and grabbed Ray by the shirt thinking him to be the attacker! Ray immediately exclaimed, "Father, it's me. Ray!"

He stopped. What was going on here! Where had that man gone?

"Father, I accidentally fell upon the rest of the children while trying to get out of bed to use the outhouse," he explained. "I slipped on these carelessly left-behind clothes and, I fear, affrighted them."

It took Alvina a few minutes to get over the episode. Their father placed her on his knee and tried to explain it was simply an accident, but she was shaken—believing Ray had been some terrible attacker who had broken in. Ray apologized to everyone and finally went to the outhouse. Alvina eventually forgave him and tried to go back to sleep. The next morning, their father talked about both the importance of making sure the bedside was kept neat and orderly and the importance of forgiveness. Discussing both sides of the incident was needed although some of the children may have needed to hear one over the other. Oh, the joys of tight spaces!

Jacob, Mary, and baby Victor had the other bedroom to themselves. It was not large or decorated but comfortable enough. Mary often awoke to feed Victor in the night. As she sat staring into the darkness, she still could not help but feel some inward feeling that concerned Victor. Again, she had an inward sense to simply hug him closely and enjoy his presence.

Alvina now was five years old and already acting like a little lady. She loved to dress Victor up and pretend to take care of him. Mary appreciated her daughter's and Ray's help as she often kept quite busy doing the laundry, cleaning, and cooking. What amused her was how sometimes during play, Ray would pretend to be the "father" and Alvina the "mother" while taking care of baby Victor! Edwin liked the little baby, too, and Alvina made sure he was not too rough!

The Christmas of 1925 found the bustling young family in high spirits. Mary busied herself by baking several delicious treats but had to constantly remind the kids to leave them alone until Christmas! How too often she found little fingerprints all over the food!

Jacob felt especially happy, too, this Christmas. Being German, he enjoyed sharing special Christmas traditions he had grown up with as a child with his children, such as the Christmas tree. Although he still visited the granary for a drink every once in a while, he had been starting to realize how blessed he was in life.

Finally, on Christmas Day, the children were allowed to eat their mother's tasty treats. For many years, the family could not afford to give each child a gift, and this year was no different. If they had any presents at all, they were either handmade clothing articles from their mother or a wooden toy from their father. The meaning of Christmas was not found in gifts but, rather, in enjoying one another's smiles and excitement around the glowing tree.

The year 1926 finally came, and the family huddled near the fireplace at night as this was a very cold winter. The freezing wind found its way into the house through little holes and cracks, and the children huddled together in bed, wrapping their blankets around them as closely as possible.

Soon, Clarence (Mike) came down with a cough and told their mother he ached inside. He lay on the children's bed during the day, and their mother came in every hour to check on him. Ray, too, came in and checked on his little brother and brought him small portions of soup their mother had prepared.

He soon felt better and was back to being a rambunctious young boy. However, no sooner had he recovered that baby Victor came down with pneumonia. Their mother became very concerned. Mike was able to recover speedily from his sickness, but having pneumonia as a baby could be very serious. What could she do to help her ailing child?

Victor's condition worsened. He soon developed violent and feverish coughs and had trouble breathing. His body was burning all over as he struggled for every breath. Their mother held her breath sometimes in a panic not knowing whether he would be able to draw another.

She and her husband were not really praying people. But she broke down in tears on her knees before GOD as she listened to her young son battling for his life. "O Lord, if you are out there, please heal my little baby boy." She gasped. "I have so little to offer you in return, but please heal him."

Jacob, in grief, went back to the place where he felt he could erase the cruel and harsh realities of life. As he sat, bottle in hand, he could not help but cry in despair. *What's the use?* he thought as he tossed the dismal bottle to the floor. *I can drink now and forget about the pain, but would I make it home in time to see him breathe his last breath?*

Ray and Alvina tried to comfort their mother, but she refused and wanted to spend time alone in her room. They left the room, tears streaming slowly down their faces as they went outside. They did not know what to do or how to pray, but they wanted to do more; they wanted to do everything in their power to make Victor well.

There are times when GOD answers our prayers the way we like them to be answered. And there are other times when we are left to quietly say, "Yes, Lord," and trust His judgment though it be far from our own desires. This was one of those times. Baby Victor died at nine months old on January 26, 1926.

The father and mother lovingly placed his body on their bed before being buried. As they waited until the next morning to bury him, they desired for him to have a proper place until then. They chose to sleep on the ground that night. In the morning, the kids were given one more chance to see Victor before their father dug a small grave near the home. They all watched as he lowered Victor, covered with a sweet cloth their mother had prepared, into the hole and covered it. They joined hands and said their goodbyes.

*****

The loss of Victor greatly shook the whole family. It was a great change to have no little baby in the home. Things may have seemed quieter, but inside, they longed for the cries and sounds of the little one.

Yet it was not long until Mary soon became pregnant again. She gave birth to another boy, Roy Lester, on November 18, 1926, at their home in Bazine. Some of the joys and fears again flooded Mary's heart and mind as she beheld her beautiful new baby boy. Never again would she take another moment with her baby for granted. To have a baby again in the house filled their hearts with joy.

Several months later, another great change came upon the Fritzler family. Jacob had a connection with a creamery in Garden City, Kansas, and they had offered him a good position there. This meant a roughly seventy-two-mile move as the crow flies for the family of seven.

It did not take too long for the family to pack their earthly belongings into the back of the truck. There may have been a few lost socks or other articles left in the house which no one knew where, but other than that, everything fit.

Jacob and Mary had a difficult time leaving Bazine as they had felt very comfortable in their stone-built home. Many memories had been made here, including the births of Edwin, Victor, and Roy. Yet

Jacob had high hopes for working at the creamery and believed it was in the best interest of his whole family to move.

The day finally came, and Jacob had to assign where everyone was to sit, stand, kneel, or try to cram in. Everyone was squished on all sides by clothes, tools, dishes, or furniture. Mike remembers having to hug his legs close to his chest to make room for everything.

"Children, I know this is tight, but I want you to be on your best behavior. No arguing or bickering is allowed on the way there. Now let's be off."

They said goodbye to the old house and drove, very slowly, over the bumpy, dusty roads to Garden City.

The friend of Jacob's, who had told him about the position at the creamery, welcomed the family as they arrived in town. It must have been a sight to have seen all seven of them squeezed between their earthly goods, looking exhausted and aching from their long trip. Mary made all the kids get out, stretch, and then go for a run down to the end of the road and back to get their blood flowing!

"Welcome, Jacob. I'm glad you all made it here safe and sound." He spoke while reaching out his hand.

He had been a true friend to the family. Not only had he connected Jacob with the job, but he had also helped arrange for a house in which the family was to stay.

"Follow me, and I'll show you the place," he said.

The kids, especially Edwin, hated to board the truck again, but it was not for long. A three-minute drive later, they arrived at their new home. Mary sighed a sigh of relief as, at once, she realized the new home would have ample space for their growing family.

"This wall could perhaps use a fresh coat of paint, but other than that, it will be a fine new home," she said.

This was a two-story home and had three bedrooms. There would be ample space for the children to live and breathe here. Alvina was the happiest of all the children thinking she would now be getting her own bedroom! Already she began planning it out. "My bed will go here, right against this wall. Then my dresser can go opposite on this end, and I'll place the rug here."

MUSIC COMES IN SPRINGTIME

Yet the boys also loved their new spacious bedroom; they named it the "big room." Ray, Mike, and Eddie planned out who would get which wall and divided up the space accordingly. No more sharing beds! They could finally sleep without being poked in every direction by little hands and toes!

A few yards from the house stood a crudely built shed. The inside was rusty; a few shelves and work benches lay about, and the ground lay littered with chicken poop. Jacob went to work cleaning up the shed and arranging his tools on the benches and shelves.

Meanwhile, Mary adored her new kitchen. "A place for everything and everything in its place," was her motto. She carefully unwrapped her special dishes, which had belonged to her mother in Russia, and placed them again in the cabinet they had brought from Bazine. Heirloom items took on great importance to Mary. She swept the floors of the new home, unwrapped the most treasured of items, and hurriedly prepared a supper.

"Ray," their mother called from upstairs, "go out and try to find Mr. Garner, please. Tell him he is welcome to come tomorrow night for supper."

Nine-year-old Ray scurried down the stairs and headed out the door to find the honored guest. Their mother felt he should receive some sort of tangible thank you for all the kindness he had shown the family. Two streets down, Ray found him, and he gladly accepted the invitation.

That night, the family sat around the table thoroughly exhausted yet excited to be in a new town and a new home. After a small supper, the kids headed to bed and dozed off for a long sleep as Jacob and Mary cleaned the home, rearranged things, and talked long into the night.

The next day, Mr. Garner appeared at the door right at 6:00 p.m. for supper. He had dressed quite nicely, in his suit and fedora, and his face shone just the same. Alvina took his coat and hat, and Jacob welcomed his friend to their new home.

"Come in and welcome. We are glad you were able to join us tonight." Jacob spoke warmly.

"It's a pleasure," Mr. Garner asserted. "I see you all have busied yourselves in making this your new home, sweet home."

"Yes." Mary spoke. "There's a lot of cleaning and unpacking to do with a large family, but we do love the new place. Thanks ever so much for helping to make the home available for us."

Mary served roast chicken, green beans, and bread for supper that night. The children beforehand had been all told to be on their best behavior and to listen to the adults' conversation. As Jacob was to start his new job at the creamery the following day, he had a few questions for Mr. Garner, who also worked there.

"It is a rather small creamery. I personally know the owners, who are honest and people of integrity. You will fit in quite nicely," he said.

For dessert, Mary served a fine German chocolate cake. "Mary, your meal was one of the best I have had in a long time. Thank you for your hospitality," he said.

Jacob spoke. "We highly appreciate you. Thank you for connecting me with the job and for helping our family find a new home."

The children, who by now were very fond of Mr. Garner, all waved goodbye. "To say it in our native tongue, '*Auf Wiedersehen!*'," he said.

*****

The Fritzler family found themselves enjoying their new life in Garden City. Jacob soon became well-established working at the creamery, Mary enjoyed the space afforded them by their new home, and the children made new friends among the locals. Mr. Garner continued to be a family friend, and he was one of the children's favorites to have over at the house.

Mary gave birth to her seventh and final child, Elwin Wesley (Al), on July 13, 1929. This was her first and only child to be born in a hospital! As Mary had spent very little time in a hospital, she was nervous and apprehensive about the doctors and their instruments. As she lay in the hospital bed, she could not help but feel uncomfortable about her surroundings as she had previously been used to the comfort of being home. Regardless of the novelty of the situation, she was thankful for the convenience of giving birth at a hospital. The children had to wait longer than normal to see the baby now, but they waited with intense anticipation. Jacob had to hush them as they rushed into the room to see their mother and the baby. There were more than enough arms willing to be the first ones to hold Al!

Again, Mary appreciated all the help her older children gave in taking care of the new baby. With each additional blessing, she had more laundry to do and more mouths to feed!

It was summertime in Kansas, in 1929, and most children went barefoot outdoors. The plains provided ample space for them to play and roam about. On those long hot days, the children passed the time by playing "ring-around-the-rosy," racing one another, or swimming in the Arkansas River.

Eddie especially loved the water as he couldn't stand the heat and sweat. He, his siblings, and a few other palls from town went several times a week to the little swimming hole on the river. They would be gone for hours at a time, swimming, splashing, and escaping the heat.

One day, Eddie and his brothers and sister were on their way home from the swimming hole. As they were about to race up the porch steps to the house, Eddie slipped and fell on a milk bottle that had been lying about. How he screamed! Fountains of blood were oozing out of his wrist. Their mother immediately appeared from the kitchen and ran to grab a towel to wrap around his wrist.

"Mama, Mama, help!" he asked tearfully.

Their mother's brows showed she was deeply concerned. While her son writhed in pain, she shouted to Alvina to go and fetch her father at work. Jacob and Mary then rushed him to the doctor.

"Can you explain to me exactly what happened?" the doctor asked Mary as he began putting Eddie on anesthesia.

"All I know is one minute I heard several footsteps racing up the porch steps and the next screaming. Eddie fell and cut his wrist on a milk bottle," Mary said. "Oh, Doc, is he going to be all right?"

"Don't you worry about that. The cut is very deep, I see, but he will recover in time," the doctor reassured. "Before long"—he chuckled—"your boy will be up and running like dynamite like he used to be. By the way, I see he has not had his tonsils removed. Would you like me to remove them now so you don't have to worry about the hassle of coming in later for them?"

Jacob and Mary agreed, almost hesitantly though. Having his tonsils removed was far from their worried minds, but at least, it would save them a trip!

Upon arriving home, Eddie lay down in his bed to rest and let his wrist heal. Mary came alongside him and spoke softly. "How are you feeling, Eddie?" She kissed him on the forehead.

"I'm feeling okay," he replied.

"Do you know what the doctor did while you were asleep? Not only did he take care of your wrist, but he also removed your tonsils."

"My tonsils! They're gone?" He was mortified.

Mary laughed; she explained what tonsils were anyways to her young boy. "No, Eddie, it's nothing to be worried about. Many people have their tonsils removed. It just means one less trip to the doctor!"

Eddie beamed. If it meant he didn't have to return to the doctor's, it was worth it!

The doctor was right. After a little while, Eddie returned to his old self—being as rambunctious as ever.

Most of the time, the family was healthy. However, whenever someone felt ill, Mary always had a few "sure cures" up her sleeves. These were remedies that had been passed down from generation to generation. Growing up in Russia, her mother had used these same techniques when she was a little girl. Mary believed firmly in following the old rules and ways of life. As the good-old remedies had worked for her, she would use them, when necessary, for her own children.

If they had a stomach ache, she put a candle on the navel, lit it, and put a jar over the candle. When the oxygen in the jar was consumed by the candle, a vacuum caused the stomach to go into the jar. The patient was to stay still until the vacuum relaxed. One of her favorite medicines was Z-M-O oil, which was an ointment used to cure most anything. When a baby had colic, she took the right arm and the left leg and pulled them together and then did the same with the opposite arm and leg. She believed in all these sure cures.

Although her family remained in good health, and she was grateful for this, that didn't stop the number of bruises and bumps her boys received over the years! With five boys, wrestling was inevitable. And the boys usually could not be stopped until their father ordered it to be so!

Growing up in the 1920s may have meant either a pristine and orderly or rough and tumble childhood, depending on the family. The Fritzlers may have been a unique combination of both. The strictness and attention to detail and orderliness came from Jacob and Mary's German background. Things were done properly. The family meal was set apart as a special thing. It was to be eaten at exactly 6:00 p.m. Jacob expected his children to have washed hands and combed hair. When guests, such as Mr. Garner, ate with the family, the children were to remain silent and listen to the adults' conversation. First names were never to be used; adults were to be respected and honored. In a sense, the family rules might appear strict, yet in a large family, things could become quite chaotic without them.

At the same time, Jacob knew boys were boys and needed to let their energy out at times. The outdoors were the place for such happenings, not the kitchen floor. There was plenty of space to roam, run, wrestle, and tackle out of doors. And so, the outdoors were the place where most children of the last century spent a great portion of their time.

In our modern day, the writings of John Muir capture much of the spirit to return back to nature. He wrote, "The mountains are calling, and I must go." "In every walk with nature, one receives far more than he seeks," was another of his famous quotes. Children of the last century seemed to understand this inseparable relationship between man and nature. Though important things like history and mathematics were learned through books and reading, other things, being equally important, were gained out in nature. For many, it was at the swimming hole or on the dirt playing marbles where the intersection of theory and real life took place.

These boys and girls may not have necessarily intentionally thought about it, but being outdoors helped to shape their character. Life lessons were never far away. *Don't mess with Johnny's girl, or you'll get what's what! Billy may not be the coolest kid, but you'd better treat him fairly (otherwise, his older brother will take care of you!) Don't stick your nose where it doesn't belong! You'd better listen to Sally's intuition; she is usually right!*

Were there social media? No. Did the day pass in sitting and lounging? No. As a matter of fact, these kids could hardly keep their britches in the seats sometimes. They learned to be well-mannered and polite in the presence of adults and in the pews of the church. At times, they may have also had to dress up in what some thought were the most uncomfortable things to wear in the world. Yet at the end of the day, it was in the great outdoors where they longed to be. To just go swimming, play ball, or run around allowed their adventurous side a chance to show itself.

To be sure, there were troubles and hardships each child may have faced at one point or another in the home or at school. Let's not leave out reality. Yet let's not forget about the sweet old days of childhood either. These were the days when the sun shone bright, birds sang, and kids dashed freely across the open landscape.

*****

October 29, 1929. The day that began a new era in American history. Prices of stocks dropping in New York City may have seemed irrelevant to many, but the Depression affected all. The roaring twenties culminated in a tense and difficult time for the American people. Survival was now important. At the forefront of every mother's mind was how she was to feed her children the next meal. Gaiety became replaced by the sober realities of life. Somewhere over the rainbow was a pot of gold, yet how elusive such a dream could be! The breadwinner's wages often only brought in enough for a meager meal. Waste was not optional now. Everything had to be saved. And if it didn't work, it had to be fixed. If the clothes wore out, take that material and make it into new ones. Shoes in the winter might have been made out of anything the family had on hand.

Tears may have been shed amidst the pain, but life had to go on. And plus, life was not all entirely gloomy. The newly invented radio brought a source of entertainment for many. Political leaders, including President Roosevelt, could use this platform to try to quiet the fears of the American people. Poverty abounded, banks shut their doors, and soup lines went on and on. This was the era of "hard times." Yet one of the most valuable treasures one could have was hope. Hope meant that, truly, regardless of today's hardships, tomorrow will be better.

That first Christmas following the crash of the stock market was a special one for many. Time spent remembering the important things in life proved invaluable to the depressed and worried. Far away, two thousand years ago, a baby had come to bring them life. What they needed now was that life—for life to be breathed back into the cold reality.

The Fritzlers, again this Christmas, could not afford to indulge their six children with expensive gifts. The joys and peace and hope of Christmas had to be found outside of wrapped goods. With a little creativity, any child could again experience the awes and wonders of the season.

In preparation for this Christmas, Mary spent hours sitting in front of the fireplace after her children had gone off to bed. She wanted to make a pair of dolls for Alvina. Though it took her a considerable amount of time, as she lovingly formed the dolls in her hands, she thought of the excitement in Alvina's eyes when she opened this gift. Alvina had grown up with several brothers; she was the only girl in the family. She was used to rough-and-tumble play. However, their mother wanted her daughter to grow up with girly things too—including dolls!

Meanwhile, Jacob spent much time in his workshop around Christmas as well. One of his projects this year included building a cork gun for his boys. As work at the creamery took up most of his day, he only had time to work on the cork gun in the evenings and Sundays. Usually, the boys were welcomed into their father's shop to watch and learn from him but never around Christmas time! He closed the doors, lit a kerosene lamp, and went to work. Nights in

Kansas can become bitterly cold, and sometimes, he had to pause to warm up his hands. Having nimble fingers became very important when trying to perfect the toy gun.

As can be expected, the children knew their father and mother were up to something; they just weren't sure what exactly. They might not have had sugar plums dancing in their heads, but they dreamed of their mother's cakes and puddings and of their father lighting the Christmas tree.

While the older children were on break from school, they enjoyed the time out of doors. Snow was common for the folks of Garden City and came as a delight to the children. Whenever someone shouted, "It's snowing!" that became the magical cue for the kids in town. Everyone hurried to don a cap, scarf, boots, or whatever they had to enjoy every minute of the beautiful white powdery snow.

Almost everyone's favorite activity was an all-out snow war. The children gathered and then divided into two teams. They then went to their "forts" to form as many snowballs as possible in a few minutes. After having built up a considerable arsenal, it was time for war! Someone shouted, "Charge," and all the boys and girls emerged from their forts with bundles of snowballs. Everyone ran about shouting as they threw their tightly packed snowballs at their opponents. Eleven-year-old Ray especially enjoyed this game as he benefited from having good aim. Alvina preferred other games, but she went along and played too. Almost none of the children wore gloves, and after a little while, they would call a "truce" out of necessity—they were too cold!

A snowball war often showed who liked who in the group. If a boy liked a girl on the opposite team, he would especially throw snowballs at anyone else he thought liked her. The same held true for the girls! Often, simply through the game, boy-girl relationships became obvious. Sometimes, however, a boy might like a girl but not the other way around, or vice versa. Alvina soon learned of a boy who had an interest in her, but she could not stand him. As a result, he actually became her primary target in the snowball war!

No one really became seriously hurt in the course of the game. There was an unspoken rule among the kids that, to participate, everyone had to be tough. Crying showed that one was not mature

MUSIC COMES IN SPRINGTIME

enough to play. Of course, a few times, anger flared up for the poor kid who had a snowball land dead center in the face or went down his shirt. Now that was the worst! Fights occurred only every now and then, and it usually resulted from someone's stubborn pride. For the most part, the kids liked one another and enjoyed the camaraderie. A kid might suddenly start shouting in anger, only to forget about it five minutes later and go on as if nothing had happened! At least grudges really didn't exist!

After snowball wars, the next best thing had to be ice skating on the Arkansas River. One had to be careful, however, if the river was frozen enough to actually skate on. Not every person in town could afford to have skates, but those who did enjoyed the exercise afforded them by gliding across the smooth ice in the wintertime. There was something about skating along the crystal ice that made it a very peaceful, whimsical, and popular sport. Whoever didn't own skates could still go down to the river and try to glide across the frozen water in their shoes. Sometimes, the kids held ice skating races across the river. Usually, the more advanced skaters congregated in one area and the amateurs in another. Everyone dreamed of being able to skate like the pros.

One day that winter, the Frtizler children and their friends passed the time skating as usual. Everyone was in high spirits as Christmas Eve lay only one week away. While rapidly racing across the river, Mike stopped in his tracks as he heard a cry for help. Nine-year-old Tommy had accidentally ended up in the wrong area, slipped, and found the ice too thin! He fell with a thud, and an arm and one of his legs were stuck as the ice had, to his horror, cracked open!

Mike immediately changed course and shouted to the rest of the gang, "Guys, Tommy is in trouble." They rushed over to his aid and tried to pull him out of the deathly freezing water, but to no avail! His leg was stuck, and the current beneath was too strong. Ray carefully tried again and successfully pulled Tommy's arm out of the water. Tommy was breathing heavily and shivering, trying to be tough, but it was evident he had to be pulled out immediately, or it could be serious. His leg was in a dangerous position. Yet getting him out required caution or more ice would crack open, and they would all be in danger. Ray took the lead.

"Form a chain behind me. Let's see if we can carefully yank him out." Tommy was shaking all over and begged the gang to hurry. His eyes widened as he heard the gentle creak of more ice around him. After three gentle heaves, his leg finally came out of the freezing ice. But, in panic, he realized he had no control over his leg! Ray ever gently pulled him across the ice, being mindful that at any moment it could crack wide open. The boys eventually made it to safety, and just then, the rest of the gang clapped and cheered while they collapsed on the more stable section of the river. They were safe!

Ray shivered as he and the rest of his siblings made their way home that day. What an adventure they had to tell their mother! Their faces shone bright purple, and their hands felt deathly cold. Their mother's eyes widened big as she beheld her freezing, stiff children trying to open the door and enter in. "For land's sake! You all are as frozen as the river. Come in immediately and warm yourselves by the fireplace."

This they did heartily. No one could speak; they were just too cold. The ice melted into a little puddle by the hearth as they sat rubbing their hands, arms, and legs. Their mother lovingly took care of their boots and coats and lay them out to dry. Later, she came and sat down by the fire. "Are you all right? You are certainly no strangers to the cold, but this time, you look particularly freezing." Their mother seemed slightly worried.

Ray spoke. "Mother, Tommy fell through the ice. Mike heard his scream first and hollered for us to come and help him."

Mother gasped and put her hand over her mouth. "Oh, dear God! Is he all right? Did you get him out?"

"We did, Mother. We did," Ray reassured her. "The whole gang pitched in to help get him unstuck. He was in pretty bad shape. He couldn't move his leg. I've never seen a leg so frozen. But we got him to safety, and Frederick offered to help him home."

"Oh! I am so glad to hear that he is safe. What you boys and girl did in helping your friend in need was a very honorable and good thing. I am very proud of you all and am sure your father will be too. Why don't you go change your clothes and get ready for supper? Father should be home shortly."

Jacob heard from Mary the brave actions of his children around the dinner table, and he was pleased to hear of their selfless actions. "You children do need to be very careful when out on the river," he said. "But today's event was purely an accident, and I am glad that everyone is safe."

The children, especially Ray, slept well that night. Doing the right thing and helping a friend in need felt good! And Christmas Eve was now one day closer!

*****

The week passed quickly in Christmas preparations. Mary spent a good portion of her day in the kitchen preparing delicious foods and treats. For the big Christmas Eve meal, she prepared a roast, potato dumplings, and red cabbage—a very traditional German supper. *Stollen*, a delicious German fruitcake, would be their main dessert. Additionally, she decided to try making a sort of gingerbread cookie, called *lebkuchen*, complete with icing. She had never made this before but knew of many relatives who had this special treat every Christmas. For Mary, the anticipation of trying this cookie was equal to the children's desire to open their gifts!

Jacob decorated the tree beautifully—being careful to place the garlands and lights in an aesthetically pleasing manner. The thrill of Christmas returned to the children once again upon seeing the tree.

Christmas Eve came, and Mary set the dinner table, complete with candles. The children dressed properly, washed their hands and faces, and combed their hair for the occasion. "*Frohe Weihnachten!*" (Merry Christmas!) Jacob said as they dished up the delicious roast, potato dumplings, and red cabbage. The feeling in the air was merry and bright!

"Now I hope these taste well." Mary spoke as she brought out the gingerbread cookies. This is my first time making these."

"I'm sure they will taste exceptionally fine," Jacob reassured her. "And if not, you're fired from being our cook!"

"Ha! Have fun trying to find a replacement for this many people," she retorted with much pleasure.

The *lebkuchen*, indeed, was very much enjoyed by the entire family, in addition to their traditional *Stollen*. Mary had been careful not to overbake them and smiled in delight as she bit into the warm cinnamon-spiced cookie. After filling their stomachs to the brim, they made their way over to the Christmas tree for the long-awaited gifts.

Jacob and Mary had had the most difficult time keeping the children away from the enticing packages lying beneath the tree. Finally, they threatened to confiscate the gifts if any child were to, in any way, touch or try to pry into them! So the Fritzler children had gotten together and made a "pact" that no one was to touch the tree or anything beneath out of fear of losing their gifts. Ray and Alvina especially threatened the younger children with the loss of gifts if any dared to mess with those packages!

But tonight was Christmas Eve, the long-awaited night, and it was time to find out what those oddly shaped packages contained. Jacob handed an especially long and skinny package to Eddie and Mike. Alvina received a smaller package but could tell by the shape that it held two items!

After the presents had all been passed around, the children—eager with great anticipation—were finally allowed to rip open the packages. Alvina carefully untied the string around her gift and tore off the paper. Inside lay two little homemade dolls! Mary sat with a sweet subtle smile as she beheld her daughter enjoying what had taken her hours and hours to create.

"Oh, Mother! These are beautiful. I shall enjoy very much, indeed, playing with them. Oh! Look at the beautiful calico dresses and the laced shoes for her feet. How long did it take you, Mother, to make these?"

"Seeing you enjoy the dolls makes every minute spent creating them worth it," their mother simply replied.

Jacob had allowed Eddie to open a joint present for the brothers—the one long and skinny present.

"Is it a new baseball bat?" he asked.

"I won't tell you now!" his father replied. "Open it up and let's see."

Eddie voraciously tore the packaging and inside found a handcrafted cork gun!

"Whoa! Wait till the gang sees this!" The boys beamed with delight.

After all the gifts had been opened, the house came alive with noise! These new toys had to be tried out! Jacob and Mary felt exhausted, and upon hearing the clock strike ten, bedtime was ordered. The children, full of boundless energy, too much sugar, and excitement over their new toys, raced up the stairs with their arms full and almost broke an important picture on the wall.

"Oh, good heavens! Careful of the picture!" their mother shouted.

"Merry Christmas, my love." Jacob came and put his arm around her.

"What a life!" she declared with half a smile. "Merry Christmas."

*****

Eddie and Mike's friends adored the cork gun. This became the trendiest new toy the boys owned! Anything in the world suddenly became a worthy target—old bottles, a nearby tree, even the neighbor's cat.

Of the Fritzler family, the two most inseparable, mischievous pair had to be Mike and Eddie. The two of them were only about twenty-two months apart and had each other's back. This new cork gun may have only added to their existing mischievousness.

Mike and Eddie knew they were not really supposed to use the cork gun in the house; it was an outside toy only. But they had this idea, you see, to try to knock over an elaborate stack of books, papers, and other articles piled high on a table in the living room. Glancing out one eye to make sure their mother, who was in the kitchen, was not paying attention, Mike readied the cork gun. He and Eddie seemed delighted to see the books and papers go flying in every direction. After carefully steadying the gun, he pulled the trigger! Crash! At the last second, the gun had been aimed in a slightly different direction, and the lamp chimney had gone flying, crashed, and broken into pieces!

"Oh, dear! What will we do?" Eddie asked his older brother, worried sick.

"Run! Before Mother gets here!" Mike answered.

"What just happened in there," their mother raised her voice from the kitchen. "I thought I heard something break!"

Entering the room, she noticed two things: the door swiftly shutting in front of her and her lamp chimney shattered.

"My lamp!" she exclaimed. "Boys, you get back here this instant!"

She ran to the door, raced down the street, much to neighbor Mrs. Parker's amusement, eventually found the boys, and dragged them back to the house, one in each hand. She was furious.

"How dare you leave the house and not come and immediately tell me of the broken lamp chimney!" she reproved. "Go to your room. Father will talk with you when he returns home."

The boys waited in anguish. Hearing the old warning "when father comes home" brought a chill down their spines. Their father came home too early, it seemed to them, that night.

Upon hearing about a sibling-related issue, Jacob's mind usually traveled first to Mike and Eddie. Today's events came as no surprise. He questioned them in his bedroom, as usual, that night.

"Mike, Eddie," he said in his booming, powerful voice, "I'm tired of hearing about these incidents regarding the two of you. In the first place, you know the cork gun was an outside-only toy. Secondly, and perhaps more importantly, you ran like cowards from your mistake instead of facing up to it. Why did you not go and immediately tell your mother?"

Mike and Eddie were red-hot in the face, ashamed of running away.

"Boys, it will cost a few dimes to replace the lamp chimney. If you had come and told your mother in the first place, I would have paid for it myself. But since you didn't, I'm going to let you pay for it."

MUSIC COMES IN SPRINGTIME

"Yes, Father," they both said. They knew the proposition was only fair.

"The lesson I personally want you to learn is this: When an incident or accident happens, whether intentional or otherwise, I want you to come to either your mother or me and tell us and apologize. Do you understand?"

Mike and Eddie both nodded in agreement. After they had paid for a new lamp chimney, the whole episode dropped. However, something would happen a month later that would test whether they followed their father's advice or not.

Alvina thoroughly enjoyed her new dolls. Although she spent most of her free time playing with her brothers and friends in town, playing with the dolls made her feel more ladylike and "grown-up" as she cared for and loved them. She even hosted a little "tea party" for Susan and Lucy, as she called them.

However, she was not the only one intrigued by the dolls. The boys had never grown up with stuffed animals or dolls, and having a "Lucy" and a "Susan" in the house were novel concepts. One day, as Alvina accompanied her mother to the grocery store, Mike and Eddie got into a big argument over the dolls. What they were arguing over did not really matter, but they were fighting anyway. Somehow, in the midst of their commotion, both dolls broke! At this, both boys panicked! What would Alvina say? Oh, they had better expect the biggest whipping in their lives for this! But wait, what had their father said only one month earlier? "Tell the truth immediately even if it hurts." Little eight-year-old Mike and six-and-a-half-year-old Eddie knew what they had to do.

Mary and Alvina returned carrying a bundle of groceries, and as their mother and sister put them away in bowels and cupboards, the boys approached timidly. Their mother could tell by the look in their faces that something had gone haywire.

"Mother," Mike said, "we have something to say to you and Alvina."

"What is that?" their mother asked.

"Well… Eddie and I accidentally broke both of Alvina's new dolls."

"You're joking, right?" Alvina was horrified. "My dolls! Lucy and Susan, oh…how could you!" She was devastated.

The boys felt sick to their stomachs. Their father was not pleased with their actions but did thank them for coming clean and telling the truth first and not waiting until someone else had discovered the truth.

"Boys, you will have to pay restitution for your actions. You will need to make it right with Alvina," their father said sternly.

"What should we do?" they asked.

"Your mother says she thinks she can fix the dolls but is not sure. However, it will take your mother time to do this, which is something she has little of already. I want you to pay your mother to fix the dolls."

"Pay her?" they exclaimed.

"Yes, pay her," he said again sternly. "I expect you to compensate her for the loss of her time spent fixing the dolls. Your piggy banks have already suffered from the last incident a month ago. You need to learn to pay when you damage someone else's property. And one more thing, I expect you to go right now to Alvina's room and apologize for your actions."

Alvina sat crying, still very upset over what they had done. She almost refused to forgive them but ended up doing so, knowing it was the right thing.

Mike and Eddie's piggybanks suffered quite a blow that year, but they learned a few invaluable lessons that would stick with them for life.

*****

The year was now 1930, and the family would have to pull closer together now more than ever before. A new decade had dawned before them. Little could they have ever imagined the changes coming in this new decade. Who could have predicted the immense joys and deep sorrows to be had in the coming years? Who would have predicted that their fairly comfortable, slow-paced life might at any time be altered? The Great Depression had brought about change so quickly that some people sat mesmerized by the sheer novelty of everything around them. Would the Fritzler family come through, or would they be torn apart like so many others in America during such hectic times?

CHAPTER 9

Changing Horizons

A little gathering of believers at a local Garden City Church met on Wednesday nights to pray. Amid the dimly lit stained glass window and kneeling on rough ground, the group prayed for things important to them—their country, President Hoover, those greatly affected during these hard times, and the unsaved in their community. One such family to be prayed over, mentioned by a young man in the congregation, was the Fritzlers. He prayed earnestly on their behalf, asking God to touch their hearts, to please show Himself to this family. The man was Mr. Garner, one of their dear friends. He knew all too well the struggles of Jacob with alcohol. Although a "decent" family, he desperately hoped and prayed that one day they might see the truth and the light.

Mr. Garner and Jacob both worked together at the creamery in town. Often during the long work days, Mr. Garner talked about the hope and the amazing peace he had found in Christ. He asked Jacob, "Where do you find peace, Jacob? What satisfies your soul?"

This question probed deep into the heart of Jacob. Quite frankly, there was really only one thing in this world that brought him temporary peace.

"Alcohol, yes, alcohol is the only peace I have in this world, my friend."

"But, Jacob, alcohol will never be the real answer to your problems. At most, it will help you to forget your present troubles. But the joy and peace found in Christ are for life."

"You try raising a family with six children," Jacob raised his voice slightly, "and then come and talk to me about 'peace.' I live in the real world, my friend. You are not married nor have children. Alcohol is what helps me balance everything in life."

Even while Jacob spoke, however, the stress lines were evident on his face. Life had many blessings, but trying to balance work and life while being a father and husband was more than he could bear at times.

Mr. Garner was very careful not to overstep his bounds. He had an invaluable relationship with the family and intended to keep it that way. The children especially liked his "surprise" visits to the house. Sometimes in the evenings, he would come over and stay for an hour or two, chat with Jacob and Mary, and play games with the children. Sometimes he would tell them entrancing stories by the fireplace.

"Once upon a time, in a very faraway land, there lived a..." The children loved his stories!

"Tell us a story about princes and princesses," Alvina would plead.

"No, we want to hear about knights and castles and battles," the boys would protest.

They sat close to the fire and listened intently to the young man tell tales of adventure. During the intense battle scenes, he raised his voice, while at other times, he spoke in soft whispers. Sometimes he used wild hand gestures and made the children laugh. Jacob and Mary watched from the other room.

"I'm glad we have Mr. Garner in our lives." Mary spoke. "The children love and really look up to him. He is a man of character and a good influence on them."

"I couldn't agree more, Mary," he said.

After telling many grand tales, Mr. Garner headed back to his quiet house. He thoroughly enjoyed and appreciated the camaraderie and friendship with his "adopted" family. A silent prayer was offered on his knees beside his bed, thanking the Lord for life and asking Him to show himself to the Fritzler family.

At the prayer meeting the next evening, someone announced that a weeklong revival meeting was to be held next month, and the whole church was invited to participate in the event. This revival meeting would take considerable preparation. Unsaved friends and neighbors needed to be invited, fervent prayer for their salvation offered, and much food prepared. Those gathered at the prayer meeting eagerly pitched in to help.

Meanwhile, Jacob sat alone in his "bootlegging" workshop. The day had not gone too well. His boss had yelled at him over a minor error, and when he got home from the excruciatingly long day, the house was not in order, one of his pet peeves. He sat down in the dark, on the dirty floor, and sighed, opening his bottle. He drank one huge gulp, sat the bottle down, and then wiped his face. "Oh, I shouldn't have much more, but—" *gulp*. That's how it often went. He got drunk one drink, one gulp at a time.

Oddly enough, the place where he hid his "secret" operation was not more than a block from church! "Wha…what is that I hear, music?" Yes, the music came from the old church building. Those gathered for the prayer meeting that evening had opened up the hymn books. One of the ladies had hopped on the piano, and they were singing "Amazing Grace."

Never noticed that before, he thought. *Hiccup!* "They sound beau…beautiful."

The singing continued: "*I once was lost, but now I am found, was blind but now I see.*"

Jacob had tears streaming down his eyes. *Am I lost?* he thought. *Because certainly, I don't feel "found." What does it all mean?*

At work the next day, Jacob spent time pondering this question. His boss noticed his more "thoughtful" work and his contemplative attitude that day and apologized for his outburst of anger the day prior.

Mr. Garner noticed a more serious and quiet Jacob too. He came over to his friend and asked, "Jake, are you feeling all right today? Is there something wrong?"

"Oh…everything is fine. I would rather not discuss it." He beat around the bush.

"Well, can I suggest a remedy? There is going to be a revival meeting happening here this next month. I am going. Would you and your family care to join me? You would be most welcome."

"I'll think about it and let you know," Jacob said.

He talked the proposition over with Mary after the children had gone to bed.

"Oh, Jacob, why not go? What do we have to lose?"

"Mary, we are not Christians like these people."

"'These' people? Mr. Garner is our friend, and he invited us to this revival meeting, whatever that really means."

"It's some gathering of Christians. I just don't want to hear about hell and all that garbage anymore. We would all feel very uncomfortable there." At that moment, he felt a sudden urge that he should take his family to the meeting. "Mary, you are right," he said panting. "I have been going back and forth in my mind about the whole thing. Darling, we are lost."

"What do you mean by 'lost'?"

"I'll tell you about it later," he said. "For now, let's just plan on going. Who knows, maybe nothing will happen."

The next few weeks seemed to pass very quickly, and Jacob and Mary both felt nervous and apprehensive. Yet some small urge within Jacob told him he needed to do this. The children didn't seem to mind going, but they also had no idea what it was they were going to. They were excited about the event because most of their friends attended church.

Mr. Garner met them at the doorsteps of their home on the first night of the revival meeting. As usual, he was all dressed up for the event. His face shone as he hopped in the truck with the rest of the family to head to the church building.

No one really talked much in the truck on the way—Jacob and Mary still very much nervous about attending the service. But Mr. Garner tried to make small talk about anything and everything to calm their fears.

When they arrived at the church, the Fritzler family could not believe how many people were crowded into the building! The service was supposed to start at seven o'clock, and it was only six forty-five now. Few seats were available, and Mary and the children sat down while Jacob and Mr. Garner stood near a wall. Before long, the service commenced, and everyone rose to their feet for the opening prayer and a hymn.

Mary rose with her children, feeling awkward. None of them knew these songs! Why, there was Mrs. Schmidt, sitting right in front of them! What would she think now that "the Fritzlers" were finally coming to church! These thoughts troubled her mind, but then she finally started thinking about the words of the songs. One of these songs included "Amazing Grace." As she sang the line, "I once was lost, but now I am found, was blind but now I see," her thoughts returned to her earlier conversation with Jacob. Is this what he was referring to? Was her family, even though they loved one another, "lost"?

She sat down in the pew in a more solemn manner. Maybe they were here at the church tonight for a reason. Just then, the traveling evangelist who led the weeklong revival meeting approached the pulpit. He prayed a prayer specifically asking GOD to touch the hearts and lives of those who needed to hear the message that evening. Following the prayer, he opened his old black leather Bible and began preaching about the amazing grace of GOD.

Jacob stood in the back and couldn't help but feel something moving inside him when the evangelist mentioned that GOD's gracious gift to humanity was free. "The wages of sin is death," the evangelist said, "but the gift of GOD is eternal life through Jesus Christ our Lord." He spoke on how "GOD so loved the world that He gave His only begotten Son that whosoever believeth on Him should not perish but have everlasting life." The evangelist passionately spoke. "Believe in Him, repent of your sins, and put your faith solely in the One who loved you so much He died for you."

Had the time finally come? Mr. Garner had on many occasions spoken to them about putting their faith in Jesus. But back then, nothing seemed to ever stir in their hearts. They just gave him a blank stare. Yet now, the words of the evangelist, mostly coming straight from the Bible, pierced their hearts. Mary did not even have to glance back at Jacob. As if on cue, the two of them at the same time headed down the long aisle toward the altars at the front of the church. Tears streamed down both of their eyes.

Who cares what anyone thinks, Mary thought as she wiped her tears, and they walked past many of their friends and neighbors. They both knelt side by side at the crudely built altar, and the evangelist soon came over and prayed with them. That night, Jacob and Mary accepted Jesus as their personal Lord and Savior.

Following the service, many, many remained in the sanctuary praying and confessing their sins before the Lord. It was a solemn time in the dimly lit church building. Jacob and Mary headed to the back and rejoined their family. Jacob gave Mr. Garner a big hug and thanked him for always being there for the family and for praying for them. Mr. Garner shed a few tears.

Upon arriving back at the house, the children asked what had happened to them. Ray and Alvina, young as they were, had noticed something different about their mother and father. They had both had some sort of emotional experience at the church that night, it seemed.

Jacob and Mary told the children they had decided to follow Jesus. "Although not all of you may understand exactly what that means, we pray that you will in the coming years." Their father made an announcement that excited them all. "From now on," he said, "our family will be in church every Sunday."

The changes that had occurred happened incredibly fast, it seemed, to Jacob and Mary. Yet much prayer had been offered on their behalf. Tonight's happenings were not random chance but rather a divine grace. Mr. Garner praised the Lord that evening as he drifted off to sleep.

Between friends and neighbors, the news soon spread that Jacob and Mary had now decided to follow Jesus and that they were attending church every Sunday. However, one of the first changes that Jacob made spread like wildfire around town. After he had become a Christian, Jacob decided to destroy every bottle of alcohol and completely disassemble his "bootlegging" operation.

CHANGING HORIZONS

It was one night, just after the weeklong revival meeting, that Jacob went back to the place he knew all too well. Except this time, he came with a smile on his face. He gathered up all his hidden bottles, those cruel devils, and took care of them once and for all.

"Get away from me you, devil!" He vehemently spoke, hurling and smashing them to the ground. The spilled liquid ran away from him.

"Never again," he promised, "will I ever touch this again." And truly, that was the end of that.

*****

Following Jesus was the best decision of Jacob and Mary's lives. By attending church together with their family every Sunday, they grew in their relationship with one another. Jacob made it a priority to stop his bad temper, and Mary chose to deal with her children in grace and love, not in anger. Spankings and punishments were common in the Fritzler household. But now, there was a reason behind them. It wasn't simply a spanking from Jacob's belt anymore because now it included the fact that the child had sinned and needed to get right with GOD and with the other sibling who had been wronged.

This was the biggest change that occurred in their lives. However, much more change would soon appear just over the horizon.

Jacob finally decided to end his career working at the creamery. Though Mr. Garner wanted him to stay, Jacob greatly desired to open his own small business. He found a great niche opportunity. Before long, he had developed a business of delivering fuel in drums to local farmers for their tractors. This provided a much-needed service to the farmers in the area, and Jacob felt glad to meet this need.

As much of his time now was spent on the road, he often missed the camaraderie he had been a part of back at the creamery. However, now he had more time to think and to pray. Sometimes he passed the time in his old truck along the dusty roads singing some of the hymns he had learned at church. At other times, he might allow one of his children to ride along with him to keep him company. All the boys fought long and hard to see who would get to ride with their father next!

There was one time, in particular, that Eddie will never forget. His turn to ride with his father had finally come, and boy, was he excited. After the long, hot, and dusty ride to a local farmer's house, he became very thirsty. While Jacob unloaded fuel for the farmer, Eddie went up to their house to fetch some water. He soon found the pitcher pump out back. This pump, however, was very old, and after a moment, Eddie soon found himself being electrocuted. The painful shock sent him into a serious panic; he thought he was going to die. He screamed for help. His father came running up the hill and immediately knew what was wrong. "Dear GOD," he said in horror as he raced over to his son and yanked him away from the electrocuting pump. In doing so, though Eddie was not aware, he had risked being electrocuted as well. The boy was so terrified he could not speak. They rode on to the next farmer's house in silence. How thankful they both were for GOD's protection! That incident could have turned out much worse.

Happily, though, such traumatic events occurred very infrequently in Jacob's new enterprise. In reality, his new business was thriving. He had developed a considerable number of clients in the local area who trusted and respected his honest business. The large family, indeed, welcomed the increasing income. It seemed there was no end to the buying of food!

The family greatly appreciated this new change, and Jacob rejoiced over this blessing. However, no sooner had this blessing taken root than something dreadful began on a much larger scale—the Dust Bowl.

There had been a severe drought in the 1930s in Kansas and neighboring states. The precious water so needed for crops was nowhere to be found. Farmers who had plowed up the natural bunch grass to grow wheat found at first a productive crop. However, when the drought came, the wind blew as well and swept the ground away. Overplowing of the soil had released tons of topsoil into the open air. The wind carried this dust in thick clouds over miles of land. Before their very eyes, the people so endeared to the land watched as it slowly withered away into a barren sea. Farms were utterly destroyed. Jobs were lost. Farmers who had lived on the same plot of land for generations were forced to relocate and start again. The tragedy of it all took its toll on the people of the Midwest.

In 1933, Franklin Delano Roosevelt took office and, two years later, created the WPA (Works Progress Administration) with the goal of helping the unemployed in America. These men would work on meaningful civic projects, such as bridges or amphitheaters. The WPA in Kansas approached Jacob and offered to pay him for the use of his truck in transporting goods and supplies to their work camps. However, Jacob was hesitant to allow someone he didn't know to use his truck. Instead, he offered to drive it to transport the supplies free of charge.

Driving in the midst of the swirling dust was very difficult. However, he was glad he could be of help to his fellow man. Jacob transported supplies to various projects around the state of Kansas. Some of these projects included new bridges, schools, civic centers, and cabins. He arrived at these makeshift camps, unloaded the supplies, sometimes had a quick bite of food, and then drove back to carry more supplies.

He often observed the men at work on these projects. The young men came from various walks of life. Some of them had been the sons of farmers who now desperately needed a job. Others had been unemployed for longer periods and were now grateful to have employment. These boys worked voraciously hard and set their minds to the task at hand. Often, the workday could last over twelve hours. For those who had lost everything, be it from the depression at hand or the Dust Bowl, these work camps provided a place where young men could work and then send a large portion of their paycheck back home for their families' use. It provided them with a sense of self-worth as they sweated and toiled building bridges, lodges, stadiums, and other buildings for the use and benefit of the public.

Ray was now a young man of seventeen, and he went to work for the WPA. He was sent to help with the building of a schoolhouse— the project not being too far from home although he did stay in the makeshift camps they had erected. His job could be backbreaking; he had to shovel rock all day so they could put in a steady foundation.

MUSIC COMES IN SPRINGTIME

How he missed the home-cooked meals of his mother! But it brought him a sense of self-worth and confidence that he could be out working with the rest of the young men and send home a paycheck to help his family. Simply having a job in that day and age in the Midwest, whether pleasant or not, was enough to be grateful for.

The dust affected everything. People's livelihoods had to be altered, and transportation in some places became very difficult. Mary remembered how, when the dust was blowing, one could not even see the sun. She sat inside her home and gazed out into the dark dusty road before her.

This dust will ruin everything, she thought. *I pray to GOD for all those farmers—our own friends. What challenges they must be facing right now?*

Indeed, local farmers found their crops in ruin. Many had lived on the land for generations and had become accustomed to years of crop failure. However, who knew when this dust bowl might end! The beautiful golden plains of wheat had been replaced by heaps of dust and flying debris.

Jacob's business delivering fuel to these local farmers soon died before his very eyes. The farmers could not pay him for the use of the fuel. One day, Jacob drove, as usual, to one of his regular customers. Upon arriving there, the farmer came over to the truck, his eyes heavy-laden. He looked up, and Jacob beheld his sorrow-filled face; he almost started crying.

"Jacob," he said, "I can't pay you for the fuel. You have been more than generous and even extended credit to me before, but this time, I just can't. We have nothing we can offer you in return. Our children are having to go to bed hungry because we can't provide decent food for them to eat! My grandfather would have hated to see this day! To think that we will have to be leaving Kansas—Kansas! This little plot of earth has been our lives. I'm so sorry, Jacob. I wish there was something I could do."

Jacob exited the truck and hugged the farmer. "Oh, Sam," he comforted. "You will get through this. We all will. Only GOD knows when it will end. But with His help, we can make it through."

CHANGING HORIZONS

He got back into his truck and drove on to the farm of another of his regular customers. He sighed. How could such tragedy have come so suddenly? Deep in his heart, he knew many of his other customers, some of whom he had even extended credit to, would not be able to pay. He settled in his heart, right then and there, to drop their charges. It stung his heart. The business had been such a success. But to see the rampant poverty and the starving children! No, he willingly resisted the urge to put money—what an elusive thing to chase!—first. At the very least, he and his family still had a roof over their heads and enough food to last for a while.

At another farm Jacob visited, the farmer took Jacob into one of his barns to the pigpen. "Jacob, would you please buy these pigs? I can't afford to buy them grain for food, and without it, they will soon die. I can't care for them anymore. It would be a big misfortune, indeed, to let them go to waste. They will be prime food soon."

Jacob had gone to deliver fuel and collect payments, as was his usual job. He hadn't intended on buying a whole load of weaner pigs! However, as the farmer said, it would be a pity to let them go to waste. Jacob carefully took out a few bills out of his pocket and handed them to the farmer. "Here, I will give you $5 for them."

Now the challenge would be loading them up in the back of the truck! Jacob didn't really want to be chasing pigs around a muddy pen for the rest of the day! Pigs can become a little ornery when someone tries to pick them up and put them somewhere they don't want to be. But the farmer was used to hog raising, and he called his children to come and help load the pigs into Jacob's truck. The whole thing took only a few minutes, and before long, Jacob roared down the dusty lane with a load of screaming little pigs.

What will Mary and the children think? he thought. *Well, at least we will have a good supply of meat. The children need something to do anyway.*

Mary's first reaction was to put her hand over her mouth and open her eyes big and wide. "Wait!" She stopped. There must have been some valid reason for these pigs. The children soon fell in love with their new little critters. Alvina thought they looked really cute! And Mike and Eddie started chasing them around the yard.

MUSIC COMES IN SPRINGTIME

"Think about all the meat we will soon have, dear," Jacob shouted to Mary as he and the children unloaded the animals.

"Yes." She sighed. She didn't really love animals—especially dirty, disgusting pigs! But at least they would make a good pork roast and bacon someday! "I'm sure these things will be a great delight—to my stomach, of course, in a little while."

Meals these days were meager but eaten with gratitude. The dust was so bad that Mary had to turn the plates upside down to keep them clean before supper. It seemed one could feel the dust everywhere, on the outside and inside. Everyone had a nice layer of dust to wipe off before going to bed at night. As Mary strived hard to keep her home clean, neat, and orderly, the dust was a new enemy to be fought! Only, she could not keep up with cleaning everything all the time and had to suspend some of the usual cleaning duties. The "clean feel" she so longed for would only last a minute before the dust came again!

One of the things that brought Jacob hope was the upcoming German Church of GOD camp meeting, to be held in York, Nebraska. In fact, he felt even more excited when Eddie was chosen to sing a song for one of the evening services. The leaders of the camp meeting wanted special music to be performed by members of various congregations from around the Midwest. One of the churches to supply this live music was the Fritzlers' own local German Church of GOD. As the pastor had heard Eddie sing before, he knew it would be a blessing to let the youth sing with his beautiful voice to the gathering of believers.

The family, plus Mr. Garner, all piled into the truck and headed from Garden City, Kansas, to York, Nebraska. Ray had been allowed to join them, much to Mary's joy. Along the way, they saw many deserted farms, hills of dirt, and devastated communities. The sight brought about a feeling of sadness. What a time for a camp meeting! Hopefully, this gathering would be an encouragement for local believers. They had had much sorrow over the past year; it was now time for gladness and joy.

Amidst the quaint camp meeting grounds, Jacob and Mary had the opportunity to meet many believers who had also been affected by the Dust Bowl. Story after story revealed many of the same happenings. Yet the people they met still had hope for tomorrow and knew everything would turn out all right. Though these believers had endured much, their faces now shown with joy at the ability to be gathering for a week of fellowship and powerful teaching.

As usual, a large white tent had been erected on the old camp meeting grounds. Folks gathered from all over the Midwest to attend the weeklong gathering. A few of them stayed in dormitories on the grounds while many pitched a tent wherever they could find a spot. The Fritzler family, of course, chose the latter option and set up camp near one end of the grounds. Their tent was rather old, but at least, it fit everyone. Mr. Garner owned a small tent, and he set his up right next to theirs.

After setting up the burly tent, the dinner bell rang. Lines as long as California formed to enjoy the home-cooked food prepared by the ladies. Friendly servers dished up their plates, and then the family sat wherever they could find a free space.

At times, the Fritzler children could be shy, especially in large crowds where they did not know many people. However, they soon made friends with many of the other children. They scarfed down their plate of chicken and potatoes and raced to play tag with the other children.

At eventide, another bell rang; this one declared that it was time for the service to begin. Kids scurried about here and there trying to find their parents as everyone entered the great white tent.

"To begin our service this evening"—one man spoke as everyone settled in their seats—"I just want to thank you all for being here tonight. You have traveled far and wide and made it a top priority to attend our annual camp meeting. I trust you are all full from the delicious meal. Thank you, ladies. Behind me is our wonderful choir, and they will be singing a few specials for us this evening. But before we begin, I would like to open with a word of prayer.

"Dear Lord, thank You for this gathering of believers. We trust You will speak to us in the coming week. Refresh our hearts, Lord Jesus. These are difficult times, what with economic turmoil and the never-ending dust storms. But thank You that we can rest in full confidence that You are sovereign over it all. Lord, we give this evening to You. Use it to challenge us and to bring glory and honor to Your holy name. We pray in Jesus's name, amen."

The choir behind the man began singing a beautiful song about the joy found in the Lord. Next, everyone in the tent rose to their feet and sang congregational favorites, such as "I Ought to Love My Savior" and "A Mighty Fortress Is Our God." The songs were all sung in German, and such a large gathering produced a magnificent sound. Oh, how they sang! For many, the music had become one of the most important and special parts of the camp meeting.

Following a late night of powerful preaching, Eddie began to feel jittery inside. He was to sing a special for that night's service. Mary sat in the tent and listened as Eddie practiced the song.

"Eddie," she said as she wrapped her arms around him, "you will sing just fine. Your voice is very pleasant and, I'm sure, will touch many hearts this evening."

The evening service finally came, and it was announced that a young Eddie Fritzler from Garden City, Kansas, would be singing a special for the folks that evening. Eddie, around twelve at the time, took a deep breath and then headed up to the podium. He was dressed in his best Sunday suit. The bright lights blinded his eyes for a moment as he gazed out onto the large crowd. Because he was too short to reach the RCA mic, he had to stand on a box to sing! There he stood, his eyes shining, as he sang in his sweet German voice.

Everyone sat intently and watched as the young boy sang with passion. After the song ended, the whole building came to life with cheers and applause. Jacob and Mary were proud of their son; he had conquered his fears and had been a blessing to a people who, in the midst of the Dust Bowl and the Depression, needed a blessing.

*****

Jacob, Mary, and the whole family came home from that camp meeting feeling inspired and refreshed. What a relief it had been to spend a week at the camp meeting; it was like spending a week in heaven.

Now back at home, Jacob reevaluated his business. With much sadness, he realized the business would have to end. None of the farmers needed gasoline right now; his services were no longer important as they used to be.

Days passed, and the family's money supply became very disconcerting. It's not that Jacob feared working; on the contrary, none could be found. No one posted a "help wanted" ad in the newspaper anymore.

Mary had internalized the thought, and so had Jacob. Neither of them, however, said anything. Both realized the necessity of leaving Kansas. It cringed Mary's heart to think of leaving Kansas. Although technically a native of Russia, almost all of life's memories had taken place in Kansas. She knew moving could take its toll on their family. A new environment could either make or break them. How comfortable they already were in Garden City! But alas, the dust had created an almost unrecognizable barren landscape.

Finally, Jacob felt the need to talk it over with Mary. He announced a huge consequence if the children were to leave their rooms that night; he had no desire for them to hear their private discussion. After saying goodnight to both the boys' and Alvina's rooms, he headed downstairs to talk with his wife.

"Mary," he said as he sat in his old worn chair by the fireplace, "we cannot stay here any longer. The farmers—the whole town—are suffering. I have scoured every street in town and can find no work to do. In just a blink of an eye, our town went from thriving to survival mode."

"Oh, Jacob," she said wearily. "Although everything within me wishes it were not so, I realize the truth of what you are saying. Our family has had wonderful memories here, but that season of life has ended. Where? I mean… I don't even know where to move outside of Kansas."

"We are both from Russia, but really, we are both from Kansas," Jacob concurred.

"It is important to me, Jacob, that if we leave Kansas, we have connections. Mr. Garner was there for us when we moved here. It's hard to believe how many years ago that was now."

"Mary, your two brothers moved a few years ago to the town of Ferndale in Washington. Would you be willing to move there?"

"That thought crossed my mind. Last I heard, they seem to be thriving out West. It's just I can't believe how far away that is from here."

"Sometimes the hardest decisions in life lead to the greatest of blessings. If we try to hold on to our beloved Kansas, we will not make it, Mary. No, we have to be willing to make the necessary change. Washington is by no means close. It would be a challenging move. But I have heard of the opportunities in the West. The land is still very much untapped, unlike if we were to move to the East. Even now, I have read in the paper how scores of families are leaving the Midwest and starting afresh in places like California, Oregon, and Washington. Why, a few of our very own friends are up and leaving Garden City! Jesh Parsins told me last week that he planned on taking his family in his old truck to California, along Route 66. He said he would love to return home someday, but right now, that 'somewhere over the rainbow' lies in California."

"Really? I had no idea the Parsins were leaving. That Route 66 you mentioned sounds very familiar."

"Mary, it's almost iconic. Most people heading West on Route 66 are from the Midwest—natives like us—who are escaping the Dust Bowl and the dismal realities of these hard times to find new opportunities out West."

"So is it settled? Are we moving out West?" Mary asked.

"The time has come. I have been praying lately about this. Mary, we are moving to Washington."

*****

As can be expected, the children responded with various emotions at the thought of leaving Kansas and moving to Washington. What would the other boys and girls be like out there? Would the land look the same? None of them had ever seen the ocean before, and the thought of living not too far from the Pacific put them into a world of frenzy.

But then, there was the other side too. As much as they wanted to, they could not take their friends with them. The old swimming hole, the yard out back, and even the streets they knew all too well would have to be left behind. While the younger ones thought about these special places, the older children pondered how hard it would be to leave the people they had come to know and love. What about Mr. Garner?

Not long after making the final decision, they had him over for supper and told him the news. He himself still worked for the creamery, although his salary had been significantly cut, and had been considering moving someday as well. The news affected him; he was practically part of the family. However, he greatly respected their decision. In a sense, he "let them go" but would forever love and have a place for them in his heart.

In preparation for the massive undertaking, Jacob sold the truck and purchased a 1932 Chevy and a four-wheel trailer. All of their earthly belongings went into that little amount of space. The hardest thing to pack was Alvina's piano! Jacob did, at first, consider leaving it behind, but Alvina cried at the thought of losing it. Lovingly, he lifted it into the trailer and made sure to secure it properly. They secured a canvas top over the trailer.

Moving day came, but first, Jacob had something he needed to settle. He walked into a field, the wind and dust blowing about, carrying a worn book. The book contained all of the outstanding bills the local farmers owed him. He knew the contents of that book and that a great amount of money should have been put in his pocket to feed his family. But he didn't care. With a solemn face, he tore the book into shreds. Digging a deep hole, he then buried the pieces and so left, resolved to completely forgive and forget all debts owed him. He had been given a great gift—forgiveness—from the Lord. What his fellow man could not repay him, he resolved to relinquish all claims to. (Years later, some of the farmers were able to pay him back, but not all.)

The Chevy engine turned on and began to roar—it was time for a long road trip. Friends gathered around the Fritzler home, and many sad goodbyes and farewells were said and hugs and handshakes given. A glorious life they had known in Kansas was soon to become a sweet memory.

Jacob, Mary, and Alvina all rode in the front seat while the five boys squished in the back row. An ammunition box was placed in the back. Roy was forced to sit on top of the very uncomfortable box while Al put his feet inside. The family dog rode on the running board in a cage. What a tangled ride! Mary told everyone to sit as still as a mouse for the first few hours as everyone had so little breathing room. Although the car was relatively new, Mary wasn't sure how it could possibly hold them all. However, she couldn't imagine leaving anything else behind!

After a word of prayer for safety, down the dusty roads of Kansas went the family of eight—headed west toward Washington. All that could be heard for a while down the road was the sound of the car engine, the dust blowing out the window, and the dog's heavy breathing! *What an adventure*, the younger children thought! Eddie sat and tried to pet the dog. His legs already ached as so much lay piled all around him, but he strained to look out the window. How crazy, it seemed to them, when they finally left the dust. They left it all behind. The flatness, which they had known their whole lives, gave way to hills and mountains!

The family would stop for dinner and supper, parking wherever they could—be that in some town along the way or even on the roadside. How everyone felt glad to be out of the car! Stretching and running laps around the car were deemed essential by Mary. At some roadside areas, Jacob would make a fire, and they would cook their supper over the fire. The children thought this reminded them of back in the olden days when people went across by covered wagons! Occasionally, another truck might come along with a clunk down the road. Most everyone they met along the way had the same goal: to make it to the West for a new life. The journey for many was not comfortable or pleasant yet still deemed a necessity.

How tall the mountains stood! The car crept slowly along the steep roads and back down them once more. In those days, traveling—even by car—over the mountains could be dangerous. Especially with an ultra-heavy trailer, one wrong move, and they could end up at the bottom of a precipice.

To pass the time, the children enjoyed singing. On many of these songs, Jacob and Mary joined right in, and they had a jolly good time of it too. Jacob had a map open on the dashboard, and he assumed that when they made it to the Columbia River, the road would finally straighten because they would have crossed the mountains. But what a surprise when the road never straightened! There was never a bend in the road in Kansas, but here, it was a different story.

The old Columbia River Gorge Scenic Highway twisted and turned; he was shocked! Yet at the same time, as they drove slowly on the gorge overlooking the Columbia River, he could not help but wonder at the beauty of the scene. *Truly, the sight of the Columbia River is one of the most beautiful I have ever seen before*, he thought.

Because of the crooked road, the family stopped for the night when they made it to Hood River, Oregon. They had no money for a hotel, so they pitched a tent next to their car and trailer like they had done every night since leaving Kansas. Jacob and Mary lay there, listening to the rustling wind that night. What a journey it had been; they both felt exhausted. They had so little money, and what they did have needed to be conserved for essentials like food and gasoline. Jacob had no job lined up when they made it to Ferndale. The whole move seemed insurmountable. "This is the life, hey, Jacob." Mary looked over at him as she wiped her forehead. He smiled back. They didn't take thought for the morrow; sufficient for the day were all the troubles at hand.

As so many others had, they finally made it to the West. The unparalleled beauty of the gorge and river below gave way to the bustling city of Portland. The children sat with eyes open wide. They were no longer in Kansas!

Sunday was the following day, and Jacob wanted to take the family to a German Church of God he knew of on Thirteenth and Skidmore Streets. As they had attended the German Church of God back in Kansas and the camp meeting in Nebraska, they had already had the chance to meet the pastor of this church as well as a few members of the congregation.

After one more night sleeping under the stars, the Fritzler family, dressed as best they could after such a long trip, headed up to the church building. As they neared, Jacob felt both a feeling of sadness and hope. What were they to do when they made it to Ferndale? Would there be work there? What if all the talk of the "golden opportunities" out West had all just been exaggerated half-truths? He had a family to support! These thoughts plagued him as he tried to smile and shake the man's hand as they entered for the morning service.

Some of the members of the congregation, after a moment, recognized the family and graciously welcomed them to their church service. Mary's heart felt warm and glad as she took her seat that morning; she felt blessed to have people encouraging them as they made this difficult move.

Several hymns were sung, in German, and following these was a rousing sermon. There was nothing flashy or big about this church. They simply desired to follow Jesus in this journey called life. It touched Jacob's and Mary's hearts.

After the sermon, a man came up to Jacob and introduced himself. "Good morning. I am Martin Brockman, and I don't believe I've had the pleasure of meeting you before?"

"Nice to meet you, Martin. I'm Jacob Fritzler, and this is my wife, Mary, and our six children. We are from Kansas and on our way up to Ferndale, Washington."

"What a beautiful family you have! My, that is quite the move! It surely must have been for some good reason. Have you found employment in Ferndale?"

"Actually, no, not as of yet. We moved because of the dust storms occurring in the Midwest. My wife has family up in Ferndale, and so we chose to relocate there."

"Jacob, I know I only just met you, but I believe I can provide you with another option if you are interested. You see, I work for Director's Furniture Store here in Portland, and they are currently seeking to hire. I am good friends with the owner and could vouch for your character. I am sure he would hire you."

Jacob felt stunned. He hadn't anticipated the possibility of finding work in Portland. Then again, he considered. *Could this be a gift from GOD? Is it His will that we stay here in Portland?* he thought.

"I understand, Jacob, that it might take some thinking over," said Martin. "Unless you folks have any other plans, would you care to join my wife and me for supper? We can talk things over, and then you can decide from there."

As they drove to the Brockman's home, Jacob and Mary sat quietly considering the proposition. Actually, their plan had been to finish the last leg of their journey that day right after church and make it to Ferndale before dark. However, Mr. Brockman had assured them he could find employment for Jacob at the furniture store. Maybe they wouldn't be living in Washington after all! As much as Mary loved her family up north, she knew reality. This job could have been a sign from GOD.

Martin and his wife welcomed the family into their small, but beautiful home. Around a simple supper of sandwiches, potato salad, and fruit, the Brockmans told of their life story and how they had come to Portland many years ago. Later on in the course of the meal, he began explaining his relationship with the owner of the Director's Furniture Store and how he enjoyed the steady job. "You might not become rich working there, but it is a decent job and has honest pay. The city of Portland has been growing like weeds lately. Business is booming, and Mr. Director is seeking to expand."

After the meal had ended, Jacob asked, "Martin, could we leave the children here with you and your wife for a moment? I would like to go for a short walk with Mary and just think it over."

"Take as much time as you need," Martin reassured.

The two stepped outside and walked far down the street. For a while, neither of them spoke; they simply enjoyed the fresh air and the sound of birds singing. Finally, Jacob spoke. "I don't know about you, Mary, but I believe this job might be a gift from GOD. I think we are supposed to stay here in Portland."

"I think you're right," she said. "Who could have guessed? The city is large and will take some getting used to, but the folks at the church are very friendly and welcoming. In some ways, Mr. Brockman reminds me of Mr. Garner." She smiled.

"Are you ready to go back and tell them and the children?" Jacob asked.

MUSIC COMES IN SPRINGTIME

"Let's do this!" she exclaimed.

The two prayed as they walked back to the Brockman home. What an adventure life had been! And who knew what life might look like here in Portland! They didn't know what the future held, but they knew He was holding the future.

*****

Before they could realize what was happening, the family found themselves becoming settled in the large bustling city. Not long after meeting Martin Brockman, Jacob was introduced to Mr. Director, the owner of the furniture store. Mr. Director (what an ironic name!) himself did not believe in the Christian religion; however, he deemed it important to find people of high moral character to work for him.

After a short conversation about Jacob's prior work experience and his personal values, Mr. Director hired him to deliver furniture to customers. After a firm handshake and a promise to report to him bright and early the following morning, Jacob headed out the door. How happy he felt to have a job! The salary they had negotiated would not be large, yet it was sufficient enough. What a change in work! He had spent years working with milk at the creamery, then transporting fuel to farmers, and finally transporting furniture from an upscale part of Portland!

Like Mr. Garner had treated them back in Garden City, Mr. Brockman took it upon himself to help the family settle in. He knew of a few homes for sale in the neighborhood, and after only about a week in the city, the Fritzlers moved into one of these.

Their new home stood just down the road from the church on Thirteenth and Skidmore, and Mary was thankful for the convenience of being close to church. The house needed some work on the inside, such as a fresh coat of paint and new windows, and Jacob, Mary, and the older children cleaned and repaired as they had time.

At first, Mary seemed overwhelmed with all the new changes that had taken place so suddenly—the move, Jacob's job, and the new home. However, the family stood in a circle, on their first night, and prayed a prayer of blessing and protection over their home and all who entered in. This greatly helped to calm her fears and gave a sense of peace in her heart.

Jacob settled in quickly at his new job, and Mr. Director took a keen interest in Jacob—helping him greatly. Jacob already had experience working in the service industry, and he proved himself highly capable of working with customers.

To supplement their income, Mary and some of the children picked cucumbers in the fields outside of Portland. During the summer, many children picked berries and vegetables in the fertile Willamette Valley. It was commonplace at this time and gave children something to do during the long hot summers. They could save a little money to give to their parents or for some exciting new item in the *Sears* catalog.

Picking cucumbers all day could be backbreaking work. At least as part of the deal, they could take several of these fresh healthy vegetables home! Interestingly enough, Mary and Mike made thirty cents an hour while Eddie and Roy worked for only fifteen cents an hour. This especially bothered Eddie! Why should his older brother of less than two years make twice as much as him! As they and dozens of other mothers and children picked away in the fields all day, Alvina stayed home to clean the house and care for Al.

The family all put in long hours during that summer. Time in the evening took on a special meaning as everyone came back together and shared the day's happenings. Perhaps Jacob had a difficult time making it on time because of traffic! (Something they had not experienced before back in Kansas). Maybe Mary had met some other believers out in the fields, and the two struck up a nice conversation. Or Alvina almost panicked when Al went outside and thought it hilarious to hide behind their neighbor's house for her to go find him! Whatever had transpired during the day—whether good, bad, funny, or sad—they shared around the dinner table. Alvina took it upon herself to prepare the meals because her mother often had little time to do so now. Everyone felt a sense of family responsibility and wanted to contribute in whatever way they could.

Little time remained, after work and chores, to live a busy social life; however, church stood at the center of it all. Though the family had few connections in the area, these welcomed them into the community with arms opened wide.

One time, shortly after moving into their new home, a church member and neighbor a few houses down welcomed them with a fresh batch of chocolate chip cookies. She came in, delivered the delicious baked goods, and genuinely wanted to know if there was anything she could do to help Mary. The latter almost started crying at the warm, hospitable act, and this was the start of a sweet friendship.

Jacob especially appreciated the new church family. He worked long hours for the furniture store and had a considerable commute as well. Sometimes he came home in the evenings, had a quick bite of food, and then walked down the street to the church—tired and with sweat visible on his brows. He had a lot on his plate, but the prayer meetings helped to quiet his soul and gave him much-needed refreshment. Feeling worn, he lay himself on the altar and silently asked the Lord for strength and his daily bread. Knowing he was not alone and that other men in the church went through the same struggles and battles encouraged him greatly.

The older children especially enjoyed making new friends at the German church. There were a considerable number of youths who attended the church, and these formed their own social circle. One of their favorite activities to do together included playing baseball. On Saturday evenings, the gang came together and loved to play ball! Some were better players than others, that is for sure, but they all had a great time together. Like any teenager, they laughed at the little things, enjoyed the game for what it was worth, and just enjoyed hanging out with one another.

The bustling summer soon ushered in the season of rustling leaves and cool breezes. How beautiful a fall, with rich hues, could be in the Pacific Northwest! The Fritzler family marveled at the green and reddish-brown colors of the Douglas fir and western red cedar intermingled with that of the golden maple and oak leaves.

With the changing of weather and scenery also came a change to the children's schedule. Now it was time to say goodbye to the picking in the fields and hello to learning in the classrooms. Alvina and Ray attended Jefferson High School while the younger children went to Vernon Elementary. Although they had lived in Portland now for several months, the large schools and classrooms astounded them. What they pictured as "school"—a one-room building in a small town—turned out to be quite different from the large settings here.

School could not have been more boring for Eddie at times as he sat there in a tightly packed classroom with little leg or breathing room. While the teacher lectured on "things of importance," such as proper grammar, he gazed out the window at the rain coming down in torrents. How he wished summer could be extended just a little bit! Oh, to be back in the sunshine, out of doors, in the fields earning money! But then, he heard a sharp sound coming from the front of the room. "Are you paying attention, Edwin Fritzler?" That was it. His short mental vacation ended, and he was back in the world of books and learning! Such went the first semester for Eddie.

That is until his father found out about his report cards! Jacob and Mary were well aware of what days the children would present their report cards to them for close analysis. Eddie dreaded these as he hated to make his father disappointed. Jacob did not hide his facial expressions: smiling and raising his eyebrows probably meant the child had earned an A or B grade; however, a puzzled look with brows drawn down meant a C or D.

"Eddie, I see your report card and have no need to mention what it states. You are well aware of its contents. What do you have to say for yourself? If any problem existed in school in the last semester, why did you not come and talk to me or Mother for help?"

"Well, I understood most of the material—"

"Then just you explain this grade to me, young man!"

Eddie fumbled for an answer. What was he supposed to say? School was the most boring, miserable thing known to man. How could grown-ups torture children like this? Of course, he would be whipped for giving such an answer.

"Eddie, I have the strangest notion to believe you are daydreaming in class and not paying attention to your teacher. What is the point of school if you are not going to take it seriously? Besides that, you are under my roof and will do as I say, and for now, your job is to go to school, to learn, and to earn good grades. Do you understand me clearly?"

"Yes, sir."

To Jacob's delight, Eddie, indeed, improved over the next semester, and his later report card brought him joy. Deep in Eddie's heart, he wanted to please his parents and make them proud of him. Although overcoming the problem of daydreaming seemed like a ginormous hurdle, he strived to pay attention when in the classroom; daydreaming had to be saved for another time!

For all the younger children, Sunday school had to be considered the favorite place to learn new things. At the German church, the importance of teaching the younger ones biblical concepts was highly stressed and deemed necessary. Time in Sunday school was spent learning about stories in the Bible—such as Moses and the Ten Commandments, Noah and the flood, or Jesus healing the sick. The children also learned scripture verses during the week and would recite them back to the teacher in Sunday school. Although this was a German church, most of the other children recited the passages in English. However, much to the Fritzler children's delight, they earned extra credit for learning their scriptures in German instead of English!

As had eventually happened after moving to Garden City, the family grew into a new routine and way of life in Portland. To Jacob, having a job during the Depression years was always something to thank the Lord for. Actually, the family rejoiced in how GOD had brought them safely thus far. Time unfolded fast before their very eyes, and scarcely could they believe the year 1939 had just dawned. How fast things in the world changed around them! Cars became faster and more reliable, and the magic of television stunned people of all ages.

Twelve years earlier, in 1927, Charles Lindbergh crossed the Atlantic in his aircraft, the *Spirit of St. Louis*. Excitement ran wild as people envisioned a future where air travel would be possible! Technological changes and innovations which improved people's lives came out seemingly every day. However, even in a world where breathtaking discoveries and technologies awed the public, a more subtle yet deadly reality slowly began to emerge across the Atlantic. We know this as World War II.

The struggle Jacob and Mary faced was real. Should they stay at the German Church of GOD, or should they leave? How they loved the congregation. These people became very dear and close friends. Yet at the same time, their beloved pastor, Brother Baseler, appeared to be almost siding with the Germans. By blood, the folks at the church were German; however, their loyalties lay in their country, America.

As difficult as it felt for Mary, her oldest son, Ray, would soon be drafted to serve in the US Army, and many other boys would follow the same path. Now was not the time to side with the people her boys were going to fight against, regardless of their German lineage. Through much prayer and thoughtful consideration, Jacob and Mary, along with their children, and friends Adele Guiner, Emil Dietz, and Herb and Art Smith finally decided to leave the German church. Instead, they began attending the other Church of GOD in Portland—the one on Eighth and Wasco Streets.

Here, at youth group one evening, sixteen-year-old Eddie Fritzler met fifteen-year-old me. As previously mentioned, I noticed this new fine young man. But to bring it full circle, Eddie noticed me too!

CHAPTER 10

The Innocence of Youth

"Hi, I'm Eddie. What's your name?" Eddie mustered up the courage.

"I'm Carolla. It's nice to meet you, Eddie," I said with a smile.

After a moment of silence, I asked, "So tell me. How many brothers and sisters are in your family?"

"There are six of us kids—five boys and one girl. How about you?"

"I have two older brothers. Who are, um, your friends over there?"

"Oh, Carolla, I want to introduce you to some of my friends from the German church. This is Herb and his brother, Art Smith, and this guy here is Emil Dietz."

"Pleased to meet you all. It's good to have you here at our church."

They responded very cordially, and after our brief introduction, we took our seats. One of our youth group's favorite activities included singing, and our first number that night was "A Mighty Fortress Is Our God." Now I'm not one to pry, but I think I saw my friend casting glances over at Eddie. I tried to frown back at her, but she didn't pay any attention to me! Well, I know where her heart lies!

The Sunday following that first night at youth group, Eddie introduced me to his mother and father and the rest of his family. They seemed like really nice folks, and Mom Fritzler invited me to come over for supper that evening. I soon learned that Eddie, his brothers and sister, and several of their friends played baseball after church on Sundays, and Mom Fritzler invited everyone over for supper afterward.

Although this sounded fun, I hesitated. This could be a little awkward; I barely knew the family. Besides, baseball was never really my fancy. But knowing myself all too well, this could also be an opportunity to get to know the Fritzler family better! Eddie noticed my hesitation at the invitation, and he asked, "Oh, please, Carolla, join us. We'd love to have you."

Really? I thought. *Well, if he wants me to go that bad, I guess I should!*

They played baseball over at the tennis courts for most of the afternoon.

"Batter up!" Everyone stood ready in their positions. Art manned first base. Emil took second. Someone else took third. Eddie looked fierce; he was up to bat. He clenched his teeth, set his eyes firmly on the ball, swung, and then *whack!*

I couldn't believe it; I jumped up and down. "He's going for a home run!" I screamed.

The person standing next to me kind of looked over at me funny. Oh, well, I didn't care!

While the sun shone on a lazy Sunday afternoon, I enjoyed leaning up against the fence and watching them play ball. They asked if I wanted to play, but I said I'd rather watch this time. However, my athletic brother Bob jumped in there and played very well.

As the day came to a close, everyone packed up their gear and headed in their cars over to Mom and Pop Fritzler's house, not too far away. Bob and I headed there as well, and Mom Fritzler looked especially excited to see me. All the kids loved her; she knew how to cook! What a spread she served everyone again with a sweet smile. We all piled our plates full and headed out to the porch. Everyone was talking and laughing in between bites. In a way, that evening, I felt like I belonged there. The Fritzlers welcomed me graciously to their home; I felt very loved and accepted.

MUSIC COMES IN SPRINGTIME

Back at Roosevelt High School, sometimes my thoughts drifted back to Sunday afternoons. How quick my teacher could be in spotting when someone was not paying attention! One time, a girl who sat next to me had to recite a poem, and following the rather long oration, the teacher asked if I would give my thoughts as to the nature of the poem. "Oh, I thought it sounded beautiful!"

"Beautiful?" my teacher asked half-outraged. The poem, she informed me, dealt with the subject of death. Whoops! I learned my lesson to never comment on anything unless I actually listened in the first place.

I came home feeling slightly bad about myself. How could I have been so rude? Father and Mother would be displeased to hear about my lack of respect for other people. I vowed then and there to become a better listener.

The next thing I knew, the telephone rang. It was Eddie! "Hi, Carolla. I just wanted to invite you over to our house on Saturday for a taffy pull. I hope you can make it!"

"Yeah, it sounds fun. I believe I can make it."

"Great. I'll pick you up around six o'clock then. See ya!"

The phone call ended. I had succeeded in listening first and talking second, but then I realized something: "I haven't even asked for Father or Mother's permission yet!"

Father and Mother listened while I tried to explain the situation. I had expected them to be irritated, but Father spoke kindly. "We forgive you, Carolla, for not coming to us first before accepting the invitation. I know that is what you meant to do. Besides, the Fritzlers seem like decent, respectable people. You may go have a good time. But remember who you are and behave like the respectable young lady you are, understand?"

"Yes, Father." I respected my parents and their decisions even when sometimes I didn't understand their intentions.

Mother helped me dress for the event and fixed my hair, and before long, I heard a car horn in the driveway. Apparently, Eddie's brother, Mike, had driven him and started honking before the car had stopped. Eddie about broke his neck dashing up our steps so I wouldn't think it was him doing the honking! Of course, I knew he wouldn't do a thing like that.

The Fritzlers and some of their friends from the German church gathered in the kitchen. I had never been to a "taffy pull" party before. Mom Fritzler busied herself by making ready pots and pans and giving each person an apron and napkins. Molasses boiled in the pans. Our hands had to be buttered, and then we pulled the sugary taffy over and over to aerate it. Following the messy ordeal, we all had our fair share. The hot gooey taffy simply melted in my mouth! What a mess we made in the kitchen! But how worth it!

Following the taffy pull, it was cleanup time. I helped wash some dishes while Ray mopped the kitchen floor. It impressed me how diligently and thoroughly he mopped that floor.

Next for the evening's events came more singing. Everyone gathered around Alvina's piano, which I was told came all the way with them from Kansas.

"What should we sing tonight?" asked Eddie.

Emil replied, "What about 'God Bless America'?"

"Let's. That's a great song," I replied.

God bless America, land that I love
Stand beside her and guide her
Through the night with the light from above
From the mountains to the prairies
To the oceans white with foam
God bless America, my home sweet home

What a patriotic song! How it thrills the soul! And how beautiful it sounded to hear all our youthful voices singing together. After a stirring "God Bless America," we opened the Fritzler's old worn Church of God hymnal to sing timeless favorites. One of my own personal favorites included "A Child of God." Of course, we couldn't just sing one or two verses of those hymns; we had to sing them all. Our group could become passionate while singing those rousing, stirring lyrics.

MUSIC COMES IN SPRINGTIME

Alvina sat at the piano with all of us crowded around in the dim light trying to see the words. It's funny how one normally remembers the chorus of a song but then actually needs to look and see the words for the verses! Mom and Pop Fritzler came into the living room and joined in on a few of the hymns. Eddie enjoyed waving his hands, pretending to be our choir director!

Following the hymns, we sang a few of the popular new songs. It was 1940, a new decade, and some of our new favorites included "This Land Is Your Land" and "You Are My Sunshine." These lighthearted lyrics were sung with a smile: "This land was made for you and me," and "please don't take my sunshine away." "You Are My Sunshine" spoke to me.

Even during challenging times, how comforting it is to have others in life. Life's burdens, indeed, become much easier when we share the load. Whether through a loss, a financial struggle, or a personal hardship, we truly need one another. I can't imagine trying to go through life alone. Having family to lean on and friends, new and old, to share a laugh with is such a blessing. How I would need to remember this important fact in the coming years, for what could be brewing across the horizon? Who knew the struggles, the hardships, and the tears to come? No prediction could have accurately estimated what lay ahead for our country—our people.

*****

With a pencil in hand, I sat at our dining room table trying to think when, who could be singing loudly but my wonderful brother Bob? Practically agitated and unable to concentrate, I went into my bedroom and sprawled myself across the bed. I had been given an assignment to write a report on Christopher Columbus's sailing to America in 1492. A few library books lay at my side as I pondered not only the actual, physical happenings but also the historical significance of Columbus's expeditions.

Yes, Columbus and his crew sailed across the Atlantic Ocean in the *Niña*, the *Pinta*, and the *Santa Maria*. However, what is the significance to be drawn here? Explorers such as Columbus paved the way for the eventual colonization of the Americas. The once sparsely developed land soon boasted sprawling cities, such as Boston and Philadelphia. Columbus's bold explorations inspired others. Lewis and Clark trekked to the other side of the continent, allowing the idea of "manifest destiny" to finally unfold.

From such explorations and discoveries, I can now sit and ponder these things in the modern city of Portland, Oregon, in a state greatly affected by the ideas championed by Columbus himself! How amazing it is to find oneself wrapped up in history! The actions and ideologies of those who have gone before us greatly affect our lives today in 1940.

I went to church feeling tired the next day after having stayed up too late working on my report. However, Dad required us kids to sit as straight as a ruler in church! I guess he had good intentions; there is something about sitting up straight which made me pay more attention anyway.

Following the service, and after a quick yawn, I glanced up and noticed Eddie walking excitedly toward me.

"Hi, Carolla! Guess what? I just got my driver's license this past week! My dad's gonna let me drive the Chevy. Would you like to get a milkshake with me sometime this next week?"

Would I? I thought. *Wow, I feel old. I can't believe he's asking me!* "I would very much enjoy to go with you, Eddie, but I need to ask my folks' permission first."

"No problem. Why don't you call me after supper tonight to let me know. See ya!"

And as quick as he had come, he vanished off to go play ball with the gang.

After arriving back at the house, I asked Dad and Mom about going, and they approved. Honestly, I felt a little apprehensive about his driving skills. Yet I knew Eddie had become quite the responsible young man. He worked at Director's Furniture Store, where his dad also worked, sweeping and dusting the furniture. My dad could testify that he possessed a strong work ethic and could vouch for his character.

MUSIC COMES IN SPRINGTIME

A few days later, at six-forty-five sharp, he arrived at our doorsteps. After filling up with exactly two gallons of gas, we headed in his parents' 1932 Chevrolet over to Broadway at about Nineteenth Street.

Streetlights, neon signs, and theater lights shone brilliantly on Broadway Street. Eddie pulled up right across from the drugstore with the ice-cream parlor and came over to the other side to open the door for me. The cars with their honking horns came quickly past us as we hurriedly crossed the street on that misty night.

He opened the door, and we headed into the drugstore. The owner was a friend of a friend of the Fritzler family, and one of the workers recognized Eddie. The drugstore had a checkerboard floor, a counter that ran down the middle, and swiveling seats in front. A man stood at the counter scooping ice cream and putting delicious hot fudge on top.

"Hi, Eddie! Who is the friend with you?" the kind man with a mustache asked.

"Jerry, this is my friend Carolla."

"Nice to meet you, Carolla! What will you two have today?"

"Two chocolate milkshakes, please!" he said while excitedly handing over twenty cents.

A minute later, he came back. "Here you, two, go! Now you just sit down and enjoy yourselves!"

We sipped down the milkshakes for a while and listened to a little Count Basie coming from the lit-up jukebox on the other side of the counter. I, as a fifteen-year-old, felt so grown-up.

Our conversation seemed sporadic. One moment we talked about Eddie's work at the furniture store, and the next, it drifted to what someone said at school. War in Europe had erupted recently, and kids at school imagined the ensuing chaos and the possibility of our country going over there. Though war is a terrible thing, it certainly sparks some thought-provoking conversations. After a short amount of time, one can easily become wrapped up in the spirit of it all.

But we were just two young teenagers enjoying some milkshakes in downtown Portland. After a while, he drove me home. I was tired;

it had been a long day. Yet at the same time, I felt energized after having enjoyed our time together.

I think Eddie enjoyed spending time with me, too, because after that little "date," he seemed to have all sorts of ideas as to where we should go next! There was always some sort of school play or church event going on, and he seemed delighted to become my personal chauffeur. His dad asked him all the time if he had enough money to go out with me. Eddie did not make much working at the furniture store; however, he saved money by refusing to ride the bus. Almost always, he walked from Jefferson High School to downtown SW Second and Yamhill Streets, which was a distance of three miles. The bus fare cost only five cents! But I guess if you do the math and walk four days a week, that saves enough money to buy two milkshakes!

A few months later, he picked me up, as usual, in their 1932 Chevrolet, and we headed to church for a potluck as well as a singing and prayer time on a Saturday night. After going through the lines (so many options!), I sat down by Eddie at a table with the rest of my family and his. His sister, Alvina, had a big smile on her face. After everyone had sat down with their heaping plates of food, and the prayer had been given, Emil stood up and gave an announcement.

"Can I have your attention for just a moment? Alvina and I have an announcement. We're engaged!"

Oh, my goodness! I couldn't believe it. Alvina had become a close friend after our two families had become acquainted. I felt so happy for her. She sat there beaming and showed us the ring. It shone brilliantly! (I wondered how much it had cost.)

The wedding date was only two months away, and as they needed another bridesmaid, they chose me. Everyone at the wedding was German, so it helped that I had a little German in my blood as well!

Being a bridesmaid really excited me. The day of the wedding finally arrived, and the ceremony took place at the First Church of God. How the sun shone brilliantly through the stained glass window! And the flowers lit up as Emil and Alvina said, "I do."

Underneath a beautiful cherry tree at the Dietz family farm, the reception took place. The occasion was exceptionally fine. Strolling along the grass in my bridesmaid dress, I could not help but be excited for my own wedding someday.

Tables were arranged around the beautiful cherry tree, and Al Dietz and Eddie were the servers. Though we only drank water, one of our friends made a toast to Emil and Alvina.

"Ladies and gentlemen, I propose a toast—a toast to this newly-wed couple and to their happy and joyous future together. May they follow the Lord first and foremost in all things and never forget the true meaning of love."

"Hear, hear," we all chimed in, lifting our glasses in agreement.

"Can I fill your water glass, Carolla?" It was Eddie.

"Why, thank you, kind sir!"

All of our church family celebrated their marriage together and prayed for them as they entered this new exciting season of life. Of course, Mom Fritzler may have shed a tear at the service as her "baby girl" was now leaving the house. But she and Pop Fritzler both wholeheartedly supported the marriage. Ours was a tight community, and we knew it was meant to be!

*****

Marriage is a wonderful thing; it brings people together. War is something terrible; it tears apart families and separates loved ones. Things continued to worsen across the Atlantic Ocean. More and more, kids and adults talked about the war and what America's response might possibly be.

We could see pictures of the fighting in Europe. One could not help but see the despair almost everywhere. Innocent people shot. Beautiful ancient cities destroyed. I saw photos of the soldiers themselves. How many of them must have been scared to death. The unspeakable horrors they found themselves in are not worth repeating. That mankind could create wars on this scale broke the hearts of many.

A little bird chirped softly as I hopped in the car to head to church in 1941. I could not believe it, but that day, I turned seventeen. Dad and Mom sang "Happy Birthday to You" to me as we drove along. I felt very old!

We took our seats and listened intently as our pastor discussed the difference between the mercy and the grace of GOD. I had never thought about that before. Of course, I knew that GOD had shown both mercy and grace to me by allowing me to become one of his dear children. Yet what about when I sang about America and how "GOD *shed His grace on thee*"?

Our pastor explained how GOD truly has blessed this country, and His overarching grace is evident in the last two hundred years since we became a nation. Our forefathers recognized the need to humbly bow before GOD in submission, recognizing their utter dependence on Him for their daily bread. Because of this, GOD blessed their efforts, and these men went on to make documents such as the Constitution and to create an entire country and system based on sound, biblical principles.

Now of course, we need to remember our Founding Fathers were not perfect. Not everything that has happened over the last two hundred years has been romantic or ideal. Yet no other country on earth in modern times has ever been as blessed as our nation. We know we make mistakes; it is even easier to point out the mistakes of our leaders. But our country is special. Our country actually has ideals and strives to live according to high standards and principles. GOD really has shed His grace on our country. This fact should humble every American and allow him to humbly kneel at the cross while at the same time stand tall and lift his head high. From sea to shining sea, we are one nation under GOD, indivisible, with liberty and justice for all.

I went out of the sanctuary feeling inspired and encouraged. Despite the problems of the modern world, I recognized the blessings and the hand of GOD above and before us. Speaking of blessings, I was part flattered and part embarrassed, but all my friends came up to me and sang "Happy Birthday to You!" At least I felt loved and couldn't believe they had all remembered this was my actual birthday until coming to find out Mom had told them!

We walked down the steps of the church into the cold December air laughing. Then I suddenly saw a boy of about fourteen in a cap

MUSIC COMES IN SPRINGTIME

running past the church, shouting, "The Japs bombed Pearl Harbor! The Japs bombed Pearl Harbor!" For a moment in time, Dad and Mom froze, and my hair stood on end. I didn't even know where Pearl Harbor was located. I only knew it must be somewhere in the United States.

Through radio broadcasts and our newspaper, *The Oregonian*, I soon came to understand that Pearl Harbor was located on the island of Oahu in Hawaii. To me, it still seemed so far away, but then I had the realization that this was much closer than the war going on in Europe. Though Hawaii may not have been a part of the contiguous forty-eight states, it was America! This was our land!

Dad, Mom, and I sat in the living room by the fireplace in the evening to discuss the attack. Though Dad was a native of Germany, he took pride in becoming a United States citizen; he had worked very hard to obtain his citizenship. Dad truly loved our nation and wanted to make a lasting impact. He worked hard every day at work and raised a family of freedom-loving Americans.

"It is just so hard to see this attack on our country," Mom said.

"You know what this means, dear, don't you? I can easily see us becoming actively involved in the war in Europe now. Our boys are going to be on the frontlines."

"This is so wrong! Why? This is not our war to be fought! But now that Japan has attacked us—"

"Nannie, so little in this world could be considered 'fair.' War is a disgusting, messy business. Last September, a new piece of legislation, the Selective Training and Service Act of 1940, passed in Washington. We will be saying goodbye to many of the young men here in Portland. Some will return, and others will die on the battlefield."

"Dad, do you think our country is in great danger?" I asked.

"I could not tell you, Carolla. This attack on Pearl Harbor comes as a shock to the American people. I do not believe we, as a country, are prepared for such an event. Just look at the devastating photos in *The Oregonian*. Many of our important naval ships now lie sunk in the harbor. The smoke, the loss of life, the destruction—it is hard to even look at the photos."

THE INNOCENCE OF YOUTH

Our country immediately went to a halt. The very next day, President Roosevelt told the nation, "Yesterday, December 7, 1941—a date which will live in infamy—the United States of America was suddenly and deliberately attacked by the naval and air forces of the Empire of Japan." It was on that same day, December 8, 1941, when we declared war on Japan. And no sooner had we declared war on Japan than Germany declared war on us.

The idea of war had sounded so far off in Europe. Now through the attack on Pearl Harbor, the war reached America. Suddenly, our entire nation became caught up in the war effort. No sooner had we entered the war than it became very personal. Dad was right. One by one, and then dozens by dozens, our boys left Portland. This included close friends. Ray Fritzler became one of the first to be drafted into the Army.

Ray had formerly worked at the meat market where my dad worked, and after he left, Eddie took the job. He felt very proud working there as it seemed to him an upgrade from sweeping and dusting at a furniture store. Like my dad, Eddie soon came to prove himself in the meat business. He may have been one of the youngest men who worked there, but he was also one of the most honest and hardworking.

Eddie loved his family. The Fritzlers, by no means, were wealthy individuals, and each of their children wanted to contribute to the best of their abilities. To stay afloat, it took the sum of each person in their family. Through everyone's efforts, including the children's, they purchased a house on Thirteenth Street. They may not have had much in terms of this world's good, but they knew how to spoil their friends rotten. Their church family and friends were of more value than anything one could buy with money.

One of the ways Eddie could contribute through his new job included purchasing all of the meat for the family through his wages. He soon became the "family expert" on all things meat! His mom still cooked the meals, but he loved to chime in on the best way to cook or cut any particular meat dish.

Eddie and I enjoyed heading over to a place called Spada's and picking raspberries. (They are one of my favorite berries!) We would drive over to the farm before Eddie began work at the meat market, grab a few buckets, and simply go through the berry field picking for a few hours. Often, it was early morning, and one could not help but simply smile and enjoy the fresh air and the birds singing gently. We talked as we walked and picked, carefully, as many as we could in the given amount of time. The berries picked were not for our consumption, but the owners allowed us to enjoy some fresh raspberries here and there. I remembered picking huckleberries with my mom back in Eastern Oregon. She usually watched her siblings during the berry-picking season as a young girl but loved picking berries with me; it was just another way in which to bond.

Well, Eddie and I enjoyed our time bonding and talking as well. I seemed to have no end of conversations whereas Eddie took his time and thought more about things and what his response to them might include. I respected him for that.

One time, we both started joking about something. I was in front of Eddie picking voraciously, and we both could not stop laughing about what someone said on the radio.

"This guy said something really funny on the radio yesterday," said Eddie. "I think he must have been talking about the overall business scene in Portland. Well, anyway, one of the commentators mentioned how business was booming like bees in springtime. Then the other host asked, 'So you liken business to bees? Then the city must really be all caught up in the *buzz*!'"

Why that was so funny, I don't know—maybe it was the way Eddie portrayed it. But I quickly forgot about looking ahead of me, stepped in a hole, and flung out all of my handpicked raspberries in the process! They went everywhere and quickly splattered (raspberries are very soft) all over the place. I was laughing so hard but at the same time slightly disappointed! Eddie offered to help me pick my share of the berries during the remainder of our time. Oh, we had some good times!

We used the money earned from picking raspberries (which amounted to about $1) to attend youth camp. Our church and other churches of GOD in the state participated in youth camps held at a campsite in the woods. I attended a few of these, and camp for me was always one of the highlights of summer. Living in the busy city of Portland, I enjoyed getting away from the hustle and bustle of it all to return back to nature. I myself had always enjoyed the outdoors and loved hearing the stories my parents told me of their childhood and early adulthood on the other side of the Cascade mountains.

The day finally arrived for our youth group to all pile on top of one another in the hot, crowded vans to head a few hours south toward Central Oregon. I was especially excited as Mom had volunteered to be the camp cook. My legs became stiff quickly as they had little room amidst the handbags and suitcases and dozens of other legs in the vans, but there was always someone to talk to. I also enjoyed simply staring out the window and watching the buildings and the lights, and the hurried people give way to small-town service stations and cafés.

The camp lay on a large plot of land covered with towering ponderosa pines. A hill sloped upward to the west while much of the camp lay flat. A great big American flag stood stately in front of the log-built hall, which had a large deck. To the east, and a short walk away, lay a small chapel. The setting, indeed, felt idyllic for an amazing week spent in nature, with friends, and for learning more about Jesus.

I loved the campsite! Around the dining hall, in a circular fashion, lay areas to pitch our tents. This was our first order of business after arriving. I never knew exactly how to set up a tent properly but always relied on a friend to show me which pieces went where! That night, everyone met for dinner in the beautiful dining hall. A good old-fashioned meatloaf and potatoes supper awaited us.

"Welcome, folks, again to camp this year! We are so pleased to have each and every one of you here. The camp would be incomplete without you. I am your camp director, Mr. Wesley. Now a few ground rules to go over. Mr. Wesley then discussed the ground rules to the campers.

"We are all going to have an amazing week. Remember who you are and don't act too crazy. Now in just a moment, I will bless the food, and we can kick off camp together."

MUSIC COMES IN SPRINGTIME

After a long day and a heartfelt prayer, I could eat an elephant; I was starving! My hands and fork tried to cram as much food in my mouth as possible while talking at the same time. And then I remembered my manners! Whoops! I felt embarrassed and that Mr. Wesley would not approve of my unladylike behavior.

Eddie greeted me the next morning. "Hey, Carolla! How did you sleep last night? I was so tired [he ran his fingers through his curly hair] I slept like a hibernating bear."

"Oh, hey, Eddie! Last night's rest was fine. I discovered that one of my new friends is an avid snorer, much to my dismay."

"That's too bad." He laughed. "Well, I hear the bell ringing. We had better head over to the flagpole."

On a quiet crisp morning, there is nothing quite like one hundred young people saying the pledge of allegiance. Following a short prayer for the day, we each grabbed a plate of pancakes and eggs. One of my favorite activities of the day included hiking to a nearby waterfall.

We had so many youths in our group this year that the hike had to be split into two groups—one group in the morning and the other in the afternoon. Roy, Eddie, and I all ended up in the morning group. The hike twisted and turned as we made our way up a mountain. It reminded me of what it must have been like for the early frontiersmen, without our modern highways! Though they may have been able to enjoy the peace and quiet of the woods while traveling (if not on the alert for Indians or others), they had to endure rough trails, which became thick with mud when it rained. Whereas we have our modern road signs and mile markers to tell us where things are located, they had to rely on past experience, crude markings on trees, a compass, or simply intuition. But back to the trail! It was simply grand on this particular July morning. And the waterfall again invoked my awe. I had seen it before, but the novelty had never worn off.

"Carolla! Come over here and feel the mist!" Eddie shouted as he opened his arms toward the waterfall.

"I'm coming," I replied while trying to carefully crawl over the wet moss-covered rocks. What a mist, indeed! How it felt so good as the day had become hotter. I could simply have stood in that one spot all day.

But alas, the time had come to head back. And a good thing, too, as the hike had been long, and we still had all the way to head back. But I, in a poetic sort of thought, imagined this hike to be not unlike life—there may be mountains to climb, but after facing them, comes the rewarding downhill leg of the journey. Oh, well, I dreamed and thought a lot while hiking!

Throughout the week, we had several games, including tug-of-war and a sort of capture the flag. The boys' tug-of-war was definitely more interesting and intense than the girls' version! And guess who won more points for their team than any other player for capture the flag? Eddie! I didn't realize he could run like that. He could sprint past you and back before you had the chance to even try.

Mom made all the meals in the camp, so I could trust the cooking! One of my favorite suppers included her apple dumplings. It was fun to stop by the kitchen after some activity to say hi and chat for a minute. Back home, she only cooked for a few people, but not here! It intrigued me to see cooking on that large of a scale. The large mixing bowls looked like they could have been used by giants themselves! Although Eddie became homesick after only a few days, I still had my mom and her cooking there with me.

On a few of the days, we had designated times for swimming. I enjoyed swimming but not always in large crowds; that made me nervous.

"I'll race you, Carolla!" Eddie said as he darted off making a splash.

"No, thanks! You swim like a fish, and I swim like, well, a starfish!"

And then out of the corner of my eye, while bobbing between above and below water, I noticed Eddie arguing with a few of the other boys a ways downstream. I couldn't make out what they were arguing about, but later, he told me. Apparently, a bunch of the boys thought it would be fun to pretend they were drowning and frantically ask the girls for help. Of course, they only wanted to scare the girls and try to get them to swim out farther; most were as scared as myself. But Eddie stepped in and told them no, saying it would be wrong to do so. After some bickering and "come on now!," they listened to Eddie. I was thankful and proud of him!

Time spent around the campfire at night was always a delight. While the embers glowed and sparks flew, a rip-roaring fiddle was got out and played too! (Whoa! That rhymed!)

> *Old Joe Clark, he had a house;*
> *Fifteen stories high*
> *And every story in that house*
> *Was filled with chicken pie*
> *Fare thee well, Old Joe Clark*
> *Fare thee well, I'm bound*
> *Fare thee well, Old Joe Clark*
> *Goodbye Betsy Brown*
> *I went down to Old Joe's house*
> *He invited me to supper*
> *I stumped my toe on the table leg*
> *And stuck my nose in the butter*
> *Fare thee well, Old Joe Clark*
> *Fare thee well, I'm bound*
> *Fare thee well, Old Joe Clark*
> *Goodbye Betsy Brown*

"Old Joe Clark" was still ringing in my ears as I headed back to the tent late that night. And then my friends and I stayed up even later telling stories—from romances and fantasy to travel and adventure.

Before closing our summer camp story, I want to mention that even with all the fun and laughs, the most special thing to me included the time spent in the little old prayer chapel. The chapel was a short walk from the main dining hall, and we all headed there following suppers.

To start the evening, the song leader opened with a few fun camp songs—you know, the ones we all know and love. And then later, leading from the piano in the room, he would guide us in singing special songs such as "Amazing Grace" and "This Is My Father's World." Songs like these always take on a new meaning when one is far away from home, out in nature, in a small chapel, and facing a wooden cross yet aware of the situations facing the world.

I felt peace in my heart—a peace I had not felt in a long time. As the guest speaker that week spoke on loving your enemies and forgiveness, I knew this applied to me. After kneeling in front of the cross, in the dimly lit chapel, surrounded by other people my age who were kneeling and confessing their sins, I felt at peace with God. I felt at peace with other people. And I felt strengthened to return home and live the life God had called me to live following that sweet week at camp.

*****

As much fun as I had at camp, it felt good to sleep in my own bed and in my own home again. Dad welcomed me (and shortly thereafter, Mom) back to Portland.

"Welcome home, my little girl!" Dad enjoyed referring to me still as his "little girl."

"Hi, Daddy! I missed you! It's good to be home."

Those hot and dry summer days were full of all sorts of other fun and excitement. Of course, work was important, and I continued to pick berries to earn money, volunteer at church, and help Mom around the house. Yet if time remained, I enjoyed other activities, such as reading out on our front porch or spending time with friends.

After church on Sundays, we enjoyed getting a group together and cruising around for a nice Sunday afternoon drive in Art Smith's old Ford. Eddie, Gene Brockman, Art, his new bride Pearl, and I were the usual crowd. (Art and Pearl Smith had their wedding only five days after the attack on Pearl Harbor. Eddie and I were both in it; at twenty-one, his brother Mike was the oldest at the wedding!)

Of course, back then, none of our cars came with seatbelts, and so we all piled in after having met at Art's house. Some days, we went driving around the city, checking on the progress of the many new buildings in the downtown area.

"It's crazy to me," Art noted, "how Portland has developed so fast. I grew up here, and a lot of these buildings around us didn't even exist back when I was a kid. All these old fields, farms, and tracts of land are fast being developed."

I personally enjoyed the architecture of the older buildings. "Look at the ornate detail on this old hotel!" I pointed to one as we drove through the city. "The towering spires hover simply majestically. And look at the carvings underneath every windowsill!"

"Wow, Carolla! You have a way with words," remarked Eddie.

"I just like to describe the world around me," I replied.

After checking in on the progress of our fair city, we enjoyed getting away from the busier sections. Sometimes, on a blazing hot day, we went cruising down the old Columbia River Highway, with its ornate stone bridges and railings. The water below us sparkled as we drove along through the gorge, enjoying the shade provided by the overhanging oak trees. Our little group enjoyed especially finding areas along the highway we had not explored before. So many waterfalls and viewpoints lay hidden "just around the corner." As if we had not seen enough, our hunger to see more kept us going. It was times like these when, instead of the radio, we had our own singing voices to keep us amused!

"Driving along this old highway brings back a lot of memories for me," Eddie reminisced. "I remember we were packed tight in the truck but trying to all look out the window at the river below. After coming from dusty Kansas, we could not believe how beautiful and green Oregon appeared. We sort of fought for whoever could obtain the best view!"

One time, we all were practically being roasted alive by the heat and decided to stop for an ice-cream cone at a little shop not far from the highway. Most of us finished our treats before heading back into Art's "oven" (as Eddie called it), except for me. I enjoyed taking my time when eating food—especially dessert.

Anyways, Art reluctantly allowed me to enter his car with my ice-cream cone, but he made me promise to take a bunch of extra napkins and use extreme caution. Well, the day was hot, and we headed back on the road, and I tried to lick the cone faster than it melted. A second later, we must have hit a bump because all I remember is that my sweaty hands lost control of the cone, and it went flying and hit the floor down toward Art's feet who was driving. You know that feeling where you are mad at someone but also mad at yourself because you probably caused that other person to make a mistake? (Like Art driving too fast and hitting the bump too hard!) Well, let's just say that was Art for the next minute. After some awkward silence and me whispering about a hundred times "I'm so sorry!" he finally came to forgive me, in a humorous way. What days on those old country roads!

CHAPTER 11

Love and War Together, Part I

Time passed, and the seasons changed. Eddie proudly graduated from Jefferson High School and, following his short time at the meat market, took a job at a shipyard. The war effort, as we all observed, began to ramp up quickly. "Help wanted" ads and posters sprung up all over the city for work in the great shipyards of the Pacific Northwest. These ads went something like, "Serve your country and those on the frontlines by doing your part" or "Join in the fight! Help build the great ships!"

Before long, I started to notice a change in Eddie, a change which saddened me. He ran around with Herb Smith, Howard Davis, and his brother Mike, which was fine. But Sunday after Sunday, he began making excuses for why he had to miss church. They seemed valid at first, but then I realized how his heart must have strayed from GOD. We were never really dating, but he stopped calling me, stopped taking me on dates, and stopped hanging out with our group. One Sunday morning, I questioned Art whether he knew what Eddie had been up to lately.

"Carolla," he said apprehensively, "I recently learned from my brother that Eddie got engaged to a girl from high school, named Nellie."

My heart just about jumped in my throat. "Oh, really! Well, I'm happy for him." I tried to sound happy for Eddie and show that

I supported him. But as soon as we arrived home, I dashed for my bedroom, and the tears started rolling.

What happened to him? How could he have changed almost overnight? Is this the real Eddie all along, or has he simply been running around with some people he shouldn't? These thoughts plagued me. I needed an answer. Our family had not known the Fritzlers for very long, yet we had come to greatly respect and trust them. Eddie and I had become fast friends. There was nothing serious between us, but we knew we could trust each other and had each other's backs. If my friend, who appeared to have been thriving, suddenly started going down the wrong path fast, I wanted to march right in and help. *I wonder who this Nellie is? What business does she have just waltzing right into his life? She's got a lot of nerve—*. No, I couldn't let my mind go there. After crying and feeling helpless, the only thing I knew I could do at this point was pray.

Not long after, more news came from the Fritzler house and elsewhere. Almost all of the boys had been drafted or signed up to keep from being drafted. Inwardly, I knew this day was bound to come. I just didn't realize it would arrive so soon. Mike volunteered for the Navy, Eddie joined the Coast Guard, and like Ray, Emil Dietz and Art Smith found themselves drafted into the Army. (The other Fritzler boys could not join as Al was too young and Roy had a congenital heart problem.) Bud Timmons became a paratrooper, and my brother, Bob, went into the Navy.

Our family missed Bob greatly, and I can only imagine how hard it must have been for Mom and Pop Fritzler to have had almost all their boys in the service at once. Life quickly seemed duller and more monotonous now that so many of my friends had gone off to war. Even though Eddie's choices broke my heart, I resolved to pray for him and the other boys daily. They needed our prayers. This was not the time to simply lay back and talk about the good old days as kids. We were now grown up. The people I cared about would soon be facing a world of hatred, death, and hardships. They were leaving their comfortable homes, families, friends, and communities in Portland to enter into a world and reality they had never known before. It is a tragedy they had to experience the horrors of war. But yet, I was thankful for that and indebted for their love and devotion. Patriotism and loving one's country took on a new meaning for me.

Back on the home front, not much occurred; those three years were pretty lean. I graduated from high school, and while it was just the three of us at home now, Mom made a special cake for us to celebrate. I loved them both dearly and appreciated all the support and encouragement given to me over the last several years in school.

Like so many kids, I needed them when school was rough and challenging. Like so few kids, my parents actually *were there* for me. The night of my commencement, we sat at home around our dining room table, ate cake, chatted, laughed, and talked about old, school memories as a kid. We continued to pray for Bob and asked the Lord to protect his body, mind, and spirit. We did the same for all the other young men in our church and community. My formal education days had come to a close, but I still took place in the great classroom of life itself. One of the "daily lessons" at that time included how to pray fervently.

During the war, gas rationing occurred. Everyone was issued an "A" ration card with an allowance for a very minimal amount of gasoline. Those who needed more for commuting needs were issued a "B" ration card. I remember hearing Dad come home one day praising Jesus because he had received the "B" ration card. Dad had always been very resourceful, and he became even more so now. For instance, when our tires got bald, Dad fired up an electric tool that cut new grooves in the tires and gave them more traction. He always got excited.

"Let's give these tires a little more juice!" he exclaimed.

Following my graduation, I immediately began searching for employment. My friend Pluma worked at the National Biscuit Company downtown packing crackers. She had been there for a while, had connections, and helped me get a job. Because of the gas rations, I decided to take the street car. The job description didn't seem very flattering. I would spend my days turning down the lids of the boxes and putting them in a machine that wrapped them in wax paper. Repeat. All day. It sort of became monotonous after the first fifteen minutes!

On my very first day there, the boss walked past me and said, "You can go now." I, at first, thought he was sending me home, or perhaps I had been fired already because it was only eleven in the morning.

What could I have possibly done wrong? I thought. *How could one make any major mistakes in this type of work?* Soon, however, I realized he meant I could head to the break room for ten minutes. Whew! A lady at the break room table named Barbara told me, "He didn't mean that you were fired. The boss needs as much help as he can get." I imagined myself being stuck there forever! Those six weeks were the longest of my entire life!

Thankfully, that door came to a close as another opened. At church one Sunday morning, I struck up a conversation with Woody Wilson, who worked for A. H. Barbour and Sons; they were paint contractors.

"So, Carolla, I know you graduated just recently, and congratulations! What are you up to these days?" he asked.

"Currently, I work for the National Biscuit Company in downtown," I replied.

"That's wonderful. Are you happy with what you are doing there?"

"Well, it's fine. It may not be the most flattering job, but I am striving to learn contentment."

"So you may be saying you're interested in finding employment elsewhere?"

"Well, probably. I mean, yes."

"You know I work as a paint contractor, and most of our jobs these days take place at the shipyards. With the war in full swing, the demand for naval ships is very high. The military is needing more and more. It seems the current capacity cannot keep up with demand. Anyway, if you are interested, there are jobs open at the Vancouver Shipyards."

"Woody, that sounds very interesting. Let me pray about the job and contact you in the next day or so."

It didn't take long for me to recognize this job was meant to be. Grateful for my time at NBC but ready to learn something new,

MUSIC COMES IN SPRINGTIME

I began working for the Vancouver Shipyards. One of the first tasks Woody helped teach me how to perform included running the nine-key adding machine, as well as how to do payroll. These fascinated me. I always had a strange sort of fascination with numbers and loved to keep things organized. I watched people in the office who were amazingly proficient at the nine-key adding machine, and I wanted to be just as fast. Whereas I had a small space in which to stand and perform my work at NBC, now I had a desk of my own, with pencils and paper! The people in the office treated me very well.

On some evenings after work, I would walk outdoors and simply observe, amidst the thousand and one lights, the great hustle and activity happening in the shipyards. The size of these ginormous ships simply took one's breath away. Each of these ships required an immense amount of manpower. Hundreds of people would be busy all about the ship, on various levels, performing their specialty tasks.

Watching the skeleton slowly but surely turn into a powerful naval ship is an unforgettable experience. I had the privilege of talking with a few of the painters, welders, and crane operators, and they all recognized that, regardless of the task, it took the sum of everyone to build a ship. Everyone was needed—to build a ship and contribute to the war.

I really appreciated something about what they said. They showed up at the shipyards seven days a week and then finally had a day off to perform their duty. Their own names and work may be forgotten in history. Yet it never was about making a name for themselves. The jobs they performed individually may not have been the easiest, nor did they come with fancy titles and recognition. But they simply desired to contribute in their own amazing way—even if that meant remaining nameless and faceless in history.

Together, they accomplished great things. Together, they created amazing works of art. The great victories of the war can be traced indirectly back to these men and women. Without them, our brave soldiers would not have had the necessary means to win. The same holds true for the airline industry and dozens of other industries. In the midst of war and chaos, I learned to simply stand in awe and show appreciation for those who gave their very all. May I never forget the soldiers across the sea nor the dedicated patriots at home!

*****

I felt it a privilege to be working and to be a part of the war effort. The worst part of the job, however, involved the commute necessary to get there. I had to take the Killingsworth bus, transfer to the Vancouver bus, and then walk up to Tenth Street in Vancouver. At least the last leg of the journey allowed me some much-needed exercise! Imagine my joy when they decided to relocate the operation much closer to home! This allowed me to take the Alberta Streetcar straight to the office, and I could come home on lunch breaks to fix something to eat.

My friend Woody eventually found employment in the administration building at the Swan Island Shipyards working for the engineering department. Ironically, we happened to be chatting on Sunday at church when he mentioned his new position, and he said I should come and get a job there. In a familiar fashion, I followed his advice!

I continued to work in the administration building at the Swan Island Shipyards until the end of the war. Just as in the Vancouver Shipyards, I had a desk and worked the nine-key adding machine and occasionally helped with payroll. They hired me at a starting wage of sixty-three cents an hour. I remember feeling excited about that wage as it was a few cents higher than my previous job! Woody ended up being drafted into the Army, and I missed him greatly. Time continued to pass as the war progressed further and further.

*****

Missing Eddie was something that happened on a daily basis for me. Thinking about him brought back so many memories from the last few years. Although we were not as close as we had once been, he said goodbye to me before he departed for the Coast Guard. I could simply tell he was not the same person. Apparently, he had broken up with Nellie and called off the engagement. I wondered what must have been going through his mind as he packed his bags and, for the first time in his life, left his family behind. He had always had a special relationship with his parents and siblings. It broke my heart watching him say goodbye to them and especially kiss his mother. In my spirit, I felt the urge to pray for him as he had stopped going to church. Joining the Coast Guard would either make or break him, I knew. He had to, at this point in his life, choose what route he would take. This would be a crux for him.

Thinking about him, my brother, and our other friends and the challenges they faced at that very moment sometimes made me feel lonesome and sad. Why this war ever had to start, I didn't know! What brought me peace during that time especially included prayer, writing, and music. Our church prayed fervently for all the young men who had left Portland, and I tried to make as many prayer meetings as possible.

Dad had always been a prayer warrior, but even now, I watched him pray as I had never seen him before. Sometimes, I would feel chills up and down my spine as I heard him praying fervently for God's protection and mercy over them. On some days, the rain poured mercilessly out of doors as we kneeled in silence. The only sounds came from the thundering downpour outside. We had all seen the movie reels and the images of battles in Europe and in the Pacific, and it rented our hearts. But it was on those evenings when I especially felt the peace of God. That feeling, I knew, could have come from God alone.

Another activity I enjoyed outside of work included writing. I kept a few journals to record my thoughts and also composed poems. There was never a shortage of things to write about! My thoughts, dreams, and hopes all found their way there, as well as my concerns and prayers. Writing helped to orient my life aright. The act of writing in my own little leather journal calmed my spirit. It helped me make sense of life and the world around me. Sometimes what I wrote made me laugh out loud, and other times, it made me cry and think deeply and critically. Yet I believe writing also helped me remain grateful in life and to see the beauty in things and in the people around me. I loved "working" with words and could spend hours outside underneath a tree trying to find the right words to fit in my poems. That was another thing I enjoyed, spending time outside, especially for the sake of finding inspiration for my writing.

On some occasions, I crafted nonsensical love stories or poems about abstract concepts such as love, joy, and peace. One time, on my day off, I headed over to Mount Tabor Park in Portland to have some time simply to walk the grand gardens, smell the roses, and sit down and write. Portland is famous for its beautiful roses and has been dubbed the "Rose City."

On that particularly fine day, I found a secluded bench near a section containing bright red and yellow roses. As I sat down, a few bees alighted on the flowers, and I watched in eager anticipation as they buzzed about doing their job. A butterfly danced overhead and then vanished into some nearby fir trees. The sunshine warmed my back as I opened my journal and began to write. I could not help but smile. *What a wonderful world we live in!* I thought. *And yet, why do wars rage?* I struggled and grappled with the concept and began writing furiously fast all the thoughts I could get down on paper. The joy, peace, and beauty of the moment seemed to stand in sharp contrast with reality for so many millions of people across the Atlantic and the Pacific. And yet, a thought came to me.

Only yesterday, Mom told me something that had happened to her years before I was born. Their firstborn child had been stillborn. How both my parents had endured so much in their early years! They both went through such challenging times. And yet, before Herman Jr. was born, Dad had told Mom something she would never forget. "Music comes in springtime," he said. My mom said she almost started crying after what he had said because it made sense. "I realized," Mom said, "that following a hard winter of life, so to speak, the sun would soon shine—music would come in springtime."

Music comes in springtime, I thought. It hit me, and I slowly started crying. Life right now felt so hard, and so many people were hurting and suffering and dying. I had seen and heard of the bloodshed, the starvation, and the rampant destruction of life all over the world. And yet, just as surely as I sat near some beautiful rose bushes

MUSIC COMES IN SPRINGTIME

basking in the sun, I knew music would come in springtime. This war would not last forever, nor would any war or challenges faced under the sun because every challenge and war has an expiration date. Right will always win in the end. Hope springs eternal. Music comes in springtime!

That day, I experienced an epiphany. I left feeling joyous and triumphant! How I wanted others to feel the same and long for that "music" which would most assuredly come.

We still had a choir at church on Sunday mornings, and singing those songs always encouraged me. As a young child, I took music for granted. It seemed to be something that was always there. Yet the older I became, the more I came to appreciate music. In the evenings, when I wasn't listening to war news, I enjoyed the classical music station. How I always wanted to play the violin! The instrument, with its dark wooden hue, seemed to beckon me to play it.

Of all the varied sounds in an orchestra, that of a violin seemed to me the sweetest. One can almost hear a distinctive voice in a violin, unlike other instruments. It mimics the human voice most clearly. But whether Vivaldi on the radio or a sweet chorus in church, music always had the ability to stir my imagination and bring peace to my soul. I truly believe music is one of GOD's greatest gifts to humanity. We have only to listen, and we will find this gift.

Standing between the rough pews in church, singing about "What a Friend We Have in Jesus," the thought of my earthly friend, Eddie, popped into my mind. *I wonder what he must be doing at this very moment*, I thought. Regardless of how hard I tried to focus on the hymns that morning, I simply could not stop thinking about him and his circumstances.

"Good morning, Carolla!" Mom Fritzler greeted me after the service.

"Good morning! How was this last week for you?"

"It went just fine, thank you. I wanted to let you know about something, Carolla. Eddie is planning on coming home on leave in October!"

"Really! Oh, that's wonderful news. I am so glad to hear it."

"Jacob and I just found out this past Friday. I will admit to you, Carolla. Fear for him has been something that I have struggled with ever since the day he left. For some reason, I just couldn't let go of him, and it really was an internal battle. But now that he is coming home for a visit, it really calms my spirit. I am so grateful. GOD is good!"

"Amen," I replied.

Wow! It had been three years since I had last seen Eddie. I was so excited for him to finally come home! That day in October finally arrived, and he came back looking much older and more mature than I had remembered. (I had forgotten how handsome he was!) His twenty-first birthday had been in September. He arrived on a Saturday afternoon, and we said hello to each other for the first time in three years on a bright and cheery Sunday morning. I sat patiently in my pew looking all around for him when suddenly he came rushing down the side aisle.

"Hey, Carolla! It's so good to see you again! I missed you so much." Dressed in his Coast Guard uniform, he excitedly gave me a side hug.

I closed my eyes for just a moment and fought back tears. "Oh, Eddie! I missed you equally! So much has happened in the last three years since we saw each other. But tell me, I want to hear all about your adventures."

That's just about when the call came for the morning service to commence! But before he left to go back to his family, he asked if he could take a walk with me around the block after service.

"Of course! I would greatly enjoy catching up with you!"

Just a few months before, I had sat in the same spot missing Eddie greatly, and now, here he was back with us!

For one reason or another, the sermon seemed to last a little longer on that particular day! Sure I may have nodded in agreement with the message. Yet need I confess what really occupied my mind?

We talked and walked around the block several times. Eddie wanted to know all about what I had been up to.

"I started working for the National Biscuit Company in downtown right after graduation at the start of the war," I said. "There were great people who worked there, but may I confess that my job was monotonous and got old quick? You remember Woody Wilson? He had connections to the shipyards and helped me get a job running the nine-key adding machine and doing payroll. I started out in Vancouver but switched over to the Swan Island shipyards a while ago. Other than work, my life remains pretty much unchanged from a few years ago, such as church life, except for the rations and the finding out about news from the frontlines."

"That's wonderful! I'm happy to hear you are at the shipyards at Swan Island. Thank you for what you do for the war effort. I am so glad to hear you and your family are doing well. I missed you all so greatly. Often, when I felt lonely, I remembered all the fun times we had—only a few years ago. Remember all those days laughing so hard we could hardly pick raspberries? Or what about drives with the gang on Sunday afternoons like these." His eyes brightened as he gazed off into the distance going down memory lane.

"I know! Those times were so fun. Do you remember camp? I so hope things can go back to normal someday, and we can relive those memories and make even more!"

We walked on in silence for a while, just enjoying each other's company, and then I asked, "Eddie, what has life looked like for you these past three years? Tell me about your time."

"Well, my job in the Coast Guard included working in the radio room. This past year, I was aboard a ship known as *USS Hunter Liggett*. It's massive! There are hundreds of rooms, including dozens of tight living quarters, a spacious eating hall, storage areas, and massive weaponry. The bunks are laughable; we each have a few square feet—just enough to barely breathe in. Privacy is virtually unheard of. The meals are decent. They feed us well. It's just not Mom's cooking.

"During the day, I sat in our high-tech radio room with a headset on, through the crackling waves listening for neighboring ships' messages, sending messages, and doing other tasks. It took me a while to learn the functions of all the various switches and buttons, but after having done it for a few years, it became almost automatic. Nonetheless, my team and I still needed to remain alert at all times. Who knew when an important life-altering message might come in.

Radio operators are the link between the ship and help in the case of an emergency."

"That's amazing," I replied. "Were you doing this work recently? I thought I heard from your mom that you currently are stationed in Atlantic City, New Jersey."

"Yes, that's right. I worked aboard *Hunter Liggett* for my first two years. Since this last year, I have been stationed in Atlantic City. Let me explain. Our ship sailed all over the Pacific Ocean and made many an encounter with the enemy on islands such as Guadalcanal and Bougainville, a part of Papua, New Guinea. We transported much supplies, as well as fresh, able-bodied men to these desolate, challenging areas. Another of our jobs included taking the wounded to friendly islands where they would receive treatment. After faithfully performing its service for a few years, the ship suffered some damage.

"In December, it docked in San Francisco for repairs. Then, this past April, it was relocated to San Diego and has been converted into an amphibious training ship. My hope is to, one day, rejoin the ship and some of my buddies and to be a part of this training program for other fellow soldiers."

My mind raced with what adventures Eddie must have endured, the places he had been, and the people he had come in contact with. To me, it was evident Eddie had been subtly changed over these past few years. He had grown up living a simple life in both Kansas and Oregon. He had grown up protected in the church and had always had family there to guide him, as well as close Christian friends. Now, his world had since expanded—whether for better or for worse, I could not tell. He seemed to now possess an acute awareness of the realities and challenges of life, a solemnity I had not seen in him formerly.

I could not necessarily accurately detect whether his heart had grown closer to GOD or further away. Sure, he had gone off with a Bible in his bag, but that did not automatically mean he was reading it. All I knew is that so many people back home were praying for him daily. Though I partially saw in him a look of solemnity, yet again, I also saw my friend as what I remembered him from before. Here again was the same old Eddie—kind, smiling, laughing, and innocent looking.

Unbeknownst to me, his father had pulled him aside shortly after arriving home and said, "Eddie, I know you might like her. Don't fool around with her, though, unless you're serious."

With that piece of advice in mind, Eddie continued to spend a lot of time with me over the next two weeks of his "vacation" from the war. On one of the Sundays, our church had a lovely potluck-style picnic at a nearby park. The wind blew in a cool breeze on that day as we sat on rough-hewn picnic tables underneath the soaring Douglas fir and grand oak trees. The leaves shone in their opulent radiant colors on the trees, and some had since fallen to the ground to be enjoyed by children. What potlucks we had in those days!

No one left feeling anything less than stuffed! Our church always enjoyed these special times together. It seemed every lady in the church had their own "special something" that they usually brought on these occasions. Someone might bring the beloved tender fried chicken. Or there were mashed potatoes and gravy, rolls and homemade raspberry jam, or freshly baked strawberry rhubarb pies. Oh, the choices!

Eddie and I sat together with our heaping plates and tried to stuff all this deliciousness in our mouths while trying to talk at the same time. And then I would eye one of the elderly ladies in the church giving me a quick glance with the words, "Where are your manners?" blazing through them. Whoops! Slow down, Carolla, there's plenty of time!

Once during these two weeks, we drove in his parents' car east of Portland to our beloved get-away-from-the-city area—the Columbia River Gorge. En route, we stopped along the banks of the rushing Sandy River and had a rock-skipping contest. At one point, he was winning, and there was something inside me that wanted to win this contest. I avidly searched the ground for that perfectly sized rock, found one, then stood close to the river's edge. In all my excitement, I never realized some of the moss-covered rocks I stood on near the river's edge were quite slippery.

"Carolla, careful!" Eddie shouted. "Those rocks are slippery."

LOVE AND WAR TOGETHER, PART I

He was just in time. As my arms swung forward to throw the rock, I suddenly lost balance. "Whoa!" I screamed as my hands and arms went *plunge!* into the raging water while my feet stood shaking on dry ground. Water splashed into my face and nicely fixed hair! As I stood up and flung the wet hair back out of my face, I could not help but see a smirk on Eddie's.

"Do you need a hand?" he asked as he pulled me away from the water's edge. The whole incident was so embarrassing yet funny too!

But anyway, I dried off, and we eventually made it onto the old Columbia River Highway just cruising along. Eddie wanted to take me up to the Vista House at the top of Crown Point. We made it to the top, and what a magnificent view awaited us! It is no wonder Samuel Lancaster, who supervised the building of this octagonal splendor, desired it being used as an "isle of safety to all the visitors who wish to look on that matchless scene." He wanted his German "Art Nouveau" observatory, completed in 1918, to inspire travelers.

The promontory site ensured "the view up and down the Columbia could be viewed in silent communion with the infinite." For truly, one cannot quite describe the view in all accuracy without having experienced it himself. One looks to the right and beholds a widening shining river and sloping hills rising on both sides, full of trees. This scene goes on and on, until finally at the edge of the painting, the hills and the great big blue sky unite. At eventide, when Eddie and I leaned against a stone wall with ornate lampposts at varying intervals, the red-orange sunset transformed the landscape into a scene of shining gold. No amount of priceless treasures in Aladdin's secret cave could compare to this. And besides, I gazed on at the scene not alone but with a dear friend.

We decided to stay longer than we had thought, just to take it all in. I ran past the sandstone house to the car to grab my basket containing sandwiches, cookies, and milk for supper. The chocolate chip cookies had been freshly baked before our drive, and Eddie thought he could still feel their warmth in his mouth as the temperature slowly began to change. I bit slowly into my cookie and closed my eyes after tasting the soft chocolatey gooey treat. *You know,* I thought inwardly, *I really missed him. The times we had together are what I treasure. I really hope his heart has softened...like it used to be.*

Eddie then spoke. "Carolla," he almost choked up, "I really, really missed you while I was away. Out there on a ship, one can easily become lonely and forget what the purpose of life is anyway. I know I hurt you by going with someone else and avoiding you before I went off to the war. Please forgive me for that. I now realize what a treasure it is just to have a true friend. One who will not stab you in the back when you do something wrong. One who genuinely cares, loves, and prays for me, quite frankly, when I need it the most. My pop was right. He said, 'People, especially true friends, are what make life, life.' 'Eddie,' he says, 'friendships are an investment. They require time, effort, and love. But at the end of the day, be grateful you've got them because you couldn't live without 'em.'"

"That's really profound," I said with half a tear in my eye.

"And Carolla, you are that friend to me. You have never once stabbed me in the back or done anything hurtful or said anything unkind. There aren't many people in this world who are like you. Thanks for being a friend to me."

Now I almost started bawling! There was something I was going to say, but I forgot it. So I simply said, "Thank you, Eddie. Thank you. You're a good friend, too! And I really, really missed you!"

We stood there both gazing as the landscape around us slowly changed and faded away. As long as I live, I will never forget that day.

As could be expected, those two weeks with Eddie flew by very quickly. He felt a responsibility to the American people and knew my love and prayers kept him going. Our parting was not very long. He simply gave me a hug and, with a sigh, said, "I'll be back, darling."

As the Fritzler car sped down the lane, I waved goodbye to Eddie. *He'll come back*, I knew while fighting back the tears. (The song may not have yet been written, but this was definitely one of those Regina Spektor's "The Call" moments).

*****

LOVE AND WAR TOGETHER, PART I

To Eddie's delight, the Coast Guard transferred him to San Diego, California. His old ship, *USS Hunter Liggett,* had recently been converted into a training ship, and just as Eddie hoped, he again rejoined his fellow comrades.

Formerly, I had not communicated with Eddie directly. He had sent telegrams to his parents, and they conveyed a lot of what he said to me. Yet at the same time, there is only so much that can be sent in a telegram. After arriving in San Diego, he began writing me letters, calling long distance occasionally on the phone, and sending me my own telegrams. After a long day at work at the shipyards, I always looked forward to checking the mail.

Some days, Eddie seemed lonely, and on others, he wrote to me about the beauty and amazing weather of Southern California. He especially loved the swaying palm trees over the wide sandy beaches. Growing up in Kansas, he never took trips to the beach. But now, I could tell through his writings that he especially loved the beauty of the Pacific Ocean. There must have been something about its peace and tranquility that mesmerized him. Being so far from home, I am glad he found comfort in GOD's creation.

After carefully reading his letters, I would fold them gently back into their envelopes and place them in a special old wooden box I kept underneath my bed. I treasured each one of them.

He often wrote asking me to tell him about what I was experiencing and even my own thoughts on the war. To be honest, sometimes I had trouble writing about what was new in my life. I continued working at the shipyards and spending time at church and with church family and in prayer. But I could also write telling him about what GOD had recently been teaching me, whether it be revealed through scripture or through private prayer. Learning to forgive one's enemies seemed especially pertinent. So much hatred and bitterness, mixed with a little patriotism, seemed to circulate in Portland. I found it difficult not to partake in conversations at work having to do with the Japs or with the Germans. I needed GOD's grace and strength just as much as the next person to not harbor hatred in my own heart toward them.

MUSIC COMES IN SPRINGTIME

I remember one evening following a nice meal heading over to the piano in our living room to sit down and play a tune. I loved our old ornate piano, with its dark carved wood paneling. By no means was I a virtuoso, not even close, but sometimes, I liked to pluck out a hymn or something I heard on the radio. Secretly, I hoped that one day, my children would come to play the piano splendidly. Classical music always brought such joy to my soul. But all that is another story.

This evening, I began playing the tune of "I Surrender All." While the piano produced its soft tones, a thought hit me, and it hit me hard. The world housed more countries than simply my own beloved America. I suddenly and dreadfully thought of all the devastation occurring across the Atlantic and across the Pacific and how common citizens in those countries suffered greatly. These were common citizens, living ordinary lives like me. They were not the ones in charge, making the rules, or ruling the world. Yet living in their innocent and simple lives, they became engulfed in the chaos and struggle of humanity. I stopped playing for a minute and just bowed my head and had a moment of silence. A moment of silence and prayer for all the innocent people hurting and suffering as a result of the war. May GOD heal their broken hearts and lives!

In December of 1944, on the third anniversary of the attack on Pearl Harbor, I turned twenty years old. It sounded amazing I had already lived on this earth for two decades and was just beginning my third! I think Mom cried a little as she carried my birthday cake into the dining room from the kitchen. She couldn't stop mentioning how all her little babies were in their twenties!

"Nannie, you've mentioned it enough. I know she's no longer a teenager. Let's face it. Our daughter is a full-grown woman!" Dad said.

"I just can't face it! She is and will always be our little girl. She is not only the youngest but also my only daughter."

Well, at least I feel special!

On April 12, 1945, I sat at my desk running the nine-key adding machine working on the company payroll. Performing this job was one of my favorites, but it was very time-consuming. The shipyards were huge operations—practically minicities in their own rights—and a lot of people needed to be paid. While working with dollar figures, I, along with several of my coworkers, listened to the radio playing in the corner of the room.

"We interrupt our daily broadcast to bring this urgent news report," the crackling voice said. "As some Americans may have been aware, the health of our beloved president had been in decline over the last several months. The war has taken its toll. Earlier today, President Franklin Delano Roosevelt passed away at the age of sixty-three in the state of Georgia. For what he has done for our country, may all be truly grateful. May we honor his legacy by having a moment of silence."

It seemed as if our entire floor froze in the blink of an eye. Our president dead! What a terrible blow for our country! I truly respected and honored our president. Following this tragic message, everyone in the office became very quiet and solemn. We all stopped whatever we were doing, came together, and had a moment of silence. A few of us shed tears. In 1945, America greatly respected and looked up to its leaders. President Roosevelt may have worked and lived on the other side of the continent, but we, in Oregon, supported him.

Following the announcement, funeral music was played for several days. I saw a picture in *The Oregonian* of a man playing the accordion in tears over the death of our president. Most of America could resonate with that photo and with that feeling.

I felt weary of war and hearing about death. It seemed one could not escape the daily news. Little of it contained any novelty anyways—simply a never-ending episode of tragedy sprinkled with a dose of victory. During this time, I found a lot of peace and comfort in writing to Eddie. He wrote me three hundred letters in total, and yes, I responded to every single one, happily.

CHAPTER 12

Love and War Together, Part II

I am a man of twenty-one years old. In the Coast Guard. Away from home, thought Eddie. *They don't really know who I am, what I'm doing, or who I'm hanging out with down here in San Diego.*

This troubled Eddie, walking on a dock one day about to board *USS Hunter Liggett*. Memories of the past few years flooded into his memory. How vividly he could recall the innumerable hours spent in the crowded radio rooms as the powerful ship cruised along in the Pacific Ocean. He sat with a headset, listening intently for calls or messages from nearby ships and ready at a moment's notice to convey information to them. Sometimes, it was "all hands on deck" down in the radio room. The situation felt intense and required mental stamina and a good amount of technical know-how to quickly and accurately receive and transmit information. But most of the time, the crew sat on standby or only performed routine operations. To pass the time, they talked, joked, sang, and even played cards sometimes when no one was around.

"So when is the next sentence or phrase gonna come through? I don't know about you, but I'm getting cramps. What are we even doing down here anyway? I'd like to just set up a dummy of myself sometime and go back to bed," fellow radio operator Ronny vented in anger.

"I love you my man, but you're always complaining," said Robert, sitting nearby.

"Oh, and you have anything better to do with your time? You're such a joke, Robert. I'm so tired of your holier-than-thou attitude and ways. You think a few prayers are gonna change everything."

"I know things aren't perfect—life isn't perfect. But we can still choose to face whatever challenges and hardships endured with joy and gladness rather than wallow in anger and bitterness."

"How poetic and romantic!" Robert mocked. "I love how you don't live in the real world! You're not really in the midst of a war, are you? Your mind has drifted off to fluffy clouds and harps!"

"Hey, Ronny! Settle down! Robert's right. Having a bad attitude isn't gonna make things any better or make time go faster either. We have been given a duty. Now let's get it done. No arguments or complaints," Eddie interjected.

These conversations happened, well, every now and then. Robert, Ronny, and Eddie shared the same shift down in the radio room together, so they spent a lot of time talking. Mostly, they got along well and enjoyed one another's company. But every now and then, a bubble might burst.

Robert maintained peace and order. As a Christian, the youngest son of a minister from Texas, he felt it his duty to set a good example and encourage those around him. Before leaving Texas, his father had given him a special Bible that had belonged to Robert's grandfather. He treasured the book more than anything onboard the ship, and it uplifted him during challenging times. He firmly believed the Bible to be his own "weapon." For truly, just as a physical war raged around them, the wars went much deeper internally.

Daily reading of his old torn Bible became a habit for him every morning, in addition to time spent in prayer. Many things occupied his list—his mama, father, sister, and girl back home in Waco, Texas. His older brother, Jonathan, who was serving in the Air Force. He prayed for his officers and the captain. He even prayed for the enemy. Oh, and he prayed for Ronny and Eddie.

Ronny had a little bit different outlook on life. An adopted child from Seattle, Washington, he experienced the gravity of what it means to be rejected by one's own parents. He spent so much time by himself—gazing out onto the waters of Puget Sound on lonely nights, thinking about his real parents. What did they look like? What kind of lives did they live? Did they care about him even just remotely?

But after years of disappointment, bitterness engulfed him. As America declared war on Japan and eventually went full force into the conflict in the Atlantic and the Pacific, Ronny found an opportunity to get out of Seattle and try something new. He wanted to live the adventure—no matter what the cost. It would be a chance to see the world and prove his real self—the identity he so desperately wanted to shine.

It wasn't his dream to spend all day in the radio room. But as he had a knack for technology, his superiors thought it prudent to place him in this position. Sulking, he took it. He didn't really have a choice. At least it was better than being back home.

He thought Eddie was all right but couldn't really stand Robert. Not that Robert had done anything wrong, to be honest. It just bugged Ronny to see Robert happy all the time. Ronny wished they could change shoes in life.

As for Eddie, you know his backstory. He came from a solid Christian home in Oregon. As a charismatic, likable youth, it was not hard to be friends with Eddie. One thing that made him stand out among other people on the ship included his caring attitude and spirit. But Eddie had compromised his faith to "fit in." This bothered his conscience for a long time. He lacked the conviction found in Robert. Eddie found it too easy to compromise on the little things, feeling bad about it later. He felt empty in his heart.

Yes, he had a Bible in his bag, but that didn't mean he read it all the time. A prayer or two may have been offered in bed after a rough day, but he didn't feel like he really knew GOD. The hole in his heart seemed to be getting bigger and bigger. Knowing that Carolla and his family prayed for him daily may have been one of the only consolations he felt. He half-realized that their prayers were what helped him make it through each day.

"You know, the captain is so proud to see his gallant ship now used as a training base," Eddie noted to a few old friends. Guess who he rejoined in San Diego? It was old Ronny and Robert! And just as rowdy and talkative as ever.

"Yeah, I'm proud to be stationed here. Our old ship served us well," remarked Robert.

"I just like the California weather. Give me my palm trees and sunshine, p-lease! I'm glad to be out of rain city Seattle," said Ronny in typical Ronny fashion.

"That was, sort of humorous, Ronny." Eddie laughed. "I'm with you about leaving the rain back home in the Northwest."

"You know, it's funny you mention that. In Texas, we're grateful for the rain because we get hardly any of it. The rain feels refreshing and brings life to our plot of earth. Of course, one keeps things in perspective. I hear y'all get a lot up in Portland and Seattle?" asked Robert.

"Drenched, Robert, drenched! Trust me. Summer besides, we are a sponge—just soaking it all in, you know?"

"Is that…good?"

"If you're a fern living in the Hoh Rainforest, yes. If you're a Seattlite, chances are, no," he replied with a little sass.

To be honest, Eddie enjoyed hanging around Ronny and Robert. They provided him companionship while stationed in the warm sunny city.

But one day, he walked the docks just by himself. A seagull cried and flew overhead, and then another one followed. The sun shone so brightly it made the sea and the docks nearly invisible. The sound of the waves stilled his mind as he went along at a leisurely pace. He had a few minutes to spare and then needed to board the ship. A moment of reflection followed. The day before, in the bunk room, Robert had asked him if he wanted prayer for anything in specific. At first, he seemed surprised. But then, he put his arm on Robert's shoulder and broke down.

"Man, I'm not doing good," he cried. "I don't know, sometimes I feel like a Christian, but most days, I feel lost and empty."

"Eddie, listen to me." Robert looked him square in the eyes. "Jesus saves."

It took him a second to process the power of that statement, and then another came shortly thereafter.

"Jesus loves you," he said emphatically. "Jesus died for you, and He wants your heart, Eddie. Nothing else in this world matters.

"Eddie, you can spend the rest of your life trying to be a good person, whatever that looks like. But it'll never, ever be enough to fill the void in your heart. You have only to call upon the name of Jesus, and He will save you."

Tears filled Robert's eyes as he spoke that last statement. So did they in Eddie's as well.

"Robert," he stammered slowly, "Robert I want to know the truth, but I feel so ashamed for the things I've done and the things I've thought. I want to fill the hole in my heart! But I'm scared to go before a holy GOD. I don't think I'm ready yet."

"I'll be praying for you, Eddie. I know now what to pray for. I have decided to follow Jesus and won't turn back. I pray the same for you. Only believe."

"What?" Eddie asked.

"Believe," he said softly again.

Believe. It rang through his head; it rang through his heart as he slowly walked the docks. A mysterious solemnity rang through his soul.

What if, what if I actually do believe? he thought. *Am I ready?*

Days later, he found himself caught up in a discussion with Robert and Ronny at the mess hall. Robert had just knelt his head to say a prayer over his meal as Ronny, Eddie, and a bunch of other fellows looked on.

"Hey, preacher boy! You blessin' our food too?" they taunted.

So normally, Ronny would have gone along and taunted him too. But for whatever reason, he yelled at them.

"Mind your own business for once in your lives!" he retorted.

"So, Eddie, are you coming with me tomorrow?" Robert asked.

Eddie felt a little embarrassed being asked this right here, right now. "Umm—"

"What's all this?" Ronny asked with a big bite of potatoes in his mouth. "Where you going?"

"I invited Eddie to go to church with me tomorrow."

Ronny almost spit his food out, started coughing, and tried to hide the smirk on his face at the same time (it was quite the sight). "Uh, don't you think that's a little pushy, ol' Robby? I mean, you're not really gonna go, Eddie, are you?"

"Well, yes, as a matter of fact. Yes, I'm going to church tomorrow with Robert."

It was one of those deer-in-the-headlight moments for Ronny. "Oh, well in that case, uh."

"Do you want to join us, Ronny? You're invited!" Robert interjected.

"Well, no, I mean, I probably should write a letter to an old friend tomorrow, I mean—"

"Since when do you write letters? Is that a new hobby?"

"Well, I mean, I know it's the right thing to do and all."

Robert and Eddie exchanged glances, and they both had a smirk on their faces.

Back in the bunk rooms, Robert asked Eddie, "So you really coming with me tomorrow?"

Nodding his head and with a serious look on his face, he said, "Yeah, Robert, I'll go with you tomorrow."

Well, that tomorrow came quickly.

His heart was pounding. He had those experiences as a kid where an older gentleman in the congregation might come up and shake his hand, and it felt like could see right through him. Eddie had no particular desire for that to occur here in San Diego. Still, Eddie knew deep down that this was just another of Satan's attempts to keep him from going where he needed to go.

Robert greeted Eddie, and the two of them headed out of the dorms on a bright Sunday morning to the San Diego Church of GOD. As Eddie walked into the church, he could not help but feel at home. Everything seemed so familiar—the pews, the hymnals, the smiling faces, the sweet playing of the piano, the feeling of love in the air. Not for a moment were any of Satan's lies true, for he felt like he belonged. As a matter of fact, he had longed for home, and this setting provided just that feeling.

MUSIC COMES IN SPRINGTIME

"Good morning, young man. Nice to see you here. My name is Sister Clark. What is yours?" A friendly middle-aged lady approached.

"Hi, I'm Eddie," he replied.

"It's great to meet you, Eddie, and good to see you again too, Robert."

"Good to meet you as well," Eddie replied cheerfully. How the time had passed since he had been around godly men and women!

"Good morning, folks! Let's stand together and worship the Lord. Please turn to page number 243 in your hymnals to 'I Saw the Light.'"

Even the dear hymnals seemed familiar. Eddie didn't exactly know what he was coming to church for, but just being there again really impressed on his heart a need for personal change.

> *I was a fool to wander and stray*
> *For straight is the gate and narrow's the way*
> *Now I have traded the wrong for the right*
> *Praise the Lord, I saw the light*
> *I saw the light, I saw the light*
> *No more in darkness, no more in night*
> *Now I'm so happy, no sorrow in sight*
> *Praise the Lord, I saw the light*

As Eddie stood there, hymnal in hand, standing next to Robert, and singing these lyrics, he knew he had wandered from the light. He had grown up in the church and knew all the songs in the hymn book. But what would it mean for him to "trade the wrong for the right?"

They sat down and listened to the pastor preach. On that morning, he had decided to preach about forsaking our old ways and turning to Jesus in our everyday lives.

"In 2 Corinthians 5:17, it says, 'Therefore if any man be in Christ, he is a new creature: old things are passed away; behold, all things are become new.' My question for us this morning is, Do we truly believe this? Are we willing to crucify the old man and his lusts and passions and allow Christ to transform us into new creatures?

"It's not enough to simply come to church, say there is a GOD in heaven, and then live our lives in sin Monday to Saturday. GOD tells us to repent, to lay aside every weight and the sins that so easily beset us, and to run the race with endurance. Will we become new creatures, or do we secretly desire to live the double life?"

That last sentence hit home for Eddie. He believed in GOD but deep down knew he didn't live like he believed it. For the first time, he realized that GOD was watching him and seeing his every sin and evil thought. That terrified him. Then he thought back to the words he had just sung, "Now I have traded the wrong for the right." Would he allow GOD to take his broken sin-filled body and life and turn it into something new—into a child of GOD? He longed to be free and to be made new.

Yes, there was an altar call at the end of the service. But Eddie did not go forward. He desperately wanted to, but he also wanted to have more time to really think things through. There was a Sunday evening service happening at seven o'clock, and he was determined to attend with Robert. He had resolved to go to the altar if he was serious by then.

That afternoon, he spent time thinking, praying, and reading passages from his old Bible. He read in 1 John 1:9, "If we confess our sins, he is faithful and just to forgive us our sins, and to cleanse us from all unrighteousness." Then he remembered what Robert, his dear friend, had told him not long ago: believe. At that moment in his heart, on August 19, 1945, he didn't just acknowledge it, but he believed that Jesus is the Christ, the Son of GOD.

He went forward to the altar that evening and gave his heart to Jesus. "GOD, make me a new creature. I am so broken, Lord. I have chased after the things of this world and tried so hard to fit in and fill the empty hole in my heart. Nothing has worked. And I just want to come home." Tears filled his eyes. "I want to come home to You, like the prodigal son, and become a child of GOD."

While at the altar, as the piano played softly, a wave of peace flowed over him, peace like a river. He confessed his sins before GOD and knew that truly he was forgiven.

MUSIC COMES IN SPRINGTIME

Robert knew what the smile on his face meant. As Eddie approached, he threw his arms around him and gleefully said, "I'm proud of you, Eddie! GOD has a real plan for your life. Welcome to the family!"

"I love you, brother," Eddie beamed as he embraced his friend. "Thanks for praying for me and helping me to believe."

And you know what? The closing song for the service that evening was "A Child of God"! How fitting!

Praise the Lord! my heart with His love is beaming,
I am a child of God;
Heaven's golden light over me is streaming,
I am a child of God.
I am a child of God,
I am a child of God;
I have washed my robes in the cleansing fountain,
I am a child of God.

Later that night, still full of joy and peace after having resolved to fully follow Jesus, Eddie sat down and wrote a letter to me, Carolla, a girl he missed very much. But I'll let him tell the story.

August 19, 1945

Hello again, my darling,

> *It is 10:40 and I just got back from church, a few moments ago. Really am happy tonight though darling, for tonight that empty spot in my heart was filled to overflowing. You know it's really good to know that God forgives a person of his sins, not once, not twice, but many times. I'm happy to be able to say tonight, that God has once again forgiven me of my sins. I went to church tonight with the intentions of yielding my life to Him and I thank Him for giving me the strength and courage to do so. My*

prayers and your prayers have been answered. And thanks so very much for remembering me Darling, and please continue to remember me for I do so want to live a good Christian life. I know through His help that I can do it too. I'm thankful from the bottom of my heart tonight for the privilege of serving Him again...

Sis. Clark wanted me to stay for the social after church tonight but I told her that I had two very important letters to write and she understood. Couldn't hardly wait to tell you for I feel so good about it. If everything goes right I can expect to tell you on the phone before you get this letter. I hope that I can. As soon as I finish with this letter I'm going to write and tell Mom about it. No kidding darling it really is wonderful and I only wish that you could be here with me. However far from there I kinda think you are sharing it with me,

I guess I should be able to write on and on about it but I really can't express myself properly. May I say again that I am truly thankful...

Well, Darling, it's after 11:30 and I still have a letter to write to Mom, so maybe I'd better close for now. Pray for me Darling, and I'll do the same for you. So until next time, it's goodnight, sweet dreams, my Darling. I'm thinking of you.

Always,
Eddie
Edwin H. Fritzler RM 2/c

CHAPTER 13

Love and War Together, Part III

Eddie's time in San Diego would soon come to a close. In France, the D-Day landing on Normandy of the Allied forces, which was the beginning of the end of the war in Europe, had occurred just over one year and two months prior in June 1944. Less than two weeks before Eddie got saved, the United States, from the aircraft *Enola Gay*, dropped the world's first atomic bombs over Hiroshima and Nagasaki, Japan. Between 129,000 and 226,000 people died as a result of the deadly destroyers. The once heavily populated cities turned instantly into colorless otherworldly barren wastelands.

Robert, Ronny, and Eddie continued to spend time together during their last month in California. Eddie especially appreciated Robert's encouragement and help as he navigated life aboard the ship as a new Christian. He had many questions, and the two spent hours talking about various aspects of the Christian life—from grace to the sovereignty and love of GOD.

This new season of life Eddie embraced wholeheartedly. Ronny especially noticed how Eddie seemed more rooted and grounded in what he believed. It seemed to him that Eddie had somehow turned into another Robert! But then again, Ronny secretly desired to be like Eddie and Robert. He wanted to experience the same joy and peace they felt. Life for him seemed pretty dull and monotonous, especially before the war.

LOVE AND WAR TOGETHER, PART III

Of course, there was always more exploring to do, new paths to forge, and new adventures to be had. There was a world out there of discovery and novelty—places to be and people to meet. Yet he had his doubts as to how life would turn out after the war. The last thing he wanted to do certainly had to be returning to rainy Seattle. If for nothing else, he wanted to stay in warm and breezy San Diego and try to find meaning in that city. But that was one of the things that bothered him, subtly.

Robert and Eddie both had families to return to following the war—people who cared dearly about their lives. The same could not be said for Ronny. Sure, his adopted parents "cared" about him. But he had lived a life of riot and havoc in his early days; they were weary of him. Returning to Seattle meant returning to a world void of meaning and to a world of broken trust and relationships.

What would it be like…to go home to a warm, quiet, and comfortable home, where I feel loved? My own little hobbit hole, he thought to himself.

Yet Eddie and Robert both knew Ronny first needed Jesus. Ronny couldn't change all the circumstances in his life even if they seemed outright unfair. But he could allow the Creator of the universe to change his own life and make things new and right.

His attitude toward Robert changed. No longer would he sneer behind his back after what seemed like a sermon. Instead, he just listened to what he had to say and rarely spoke. But all the while, he took in what Robert and Eddie told or "preached" to him.

September of 1945 came, and the three amigos finally had to bid one another farewell.

"Well, gang, it's been great to get to know you! I'm gonna miss you, guys—a lot! But I'm ready to return home to my mama and dad and Carolla back in Oregon." Eddie spoke.

"Hey, we've been through a lot together. Remember how many stressful times we had down in the radio room? It was hot, sweaty, dirty, dark, and adrenaline pumping—what a time! Our team on the old *Hunter Liggett* had moments of triumph and moments of silence. But the work was all worth it in the end. We just played a small part of it," Robert reminisced.

MUSIC COMES IN SPRINGTIME

"I admit, Southern Cal is not going to be the same without you, guys," Ronny revealed.

"Are you staying here in San Diego?" Eddie asked.

"I'm not leaving the area. Don't worry. I'll write my parents in Seattle and explain it all. There's just a few things I want to take care of here, you know. Besides, I'll be seeing you guys in a little while anyways. Our job isn't done yet. The captain said we have a special assignment soon with no mention of details."

"Well, then, it's only goodbye for a little while then. We've parted ways before. Don't forget to read that little Bible I gave you, Ronny."

"I won't forget, Mother!" he teased.

"Goodbye, guys," Eddie said.

They had a group hug, and then the time had come to go their respective ways. Robert went back to Texas, Eddie to Oregon, and Ronny stayed in the city of sunshine.

The whole flight home to Portland, all Eddie could think about was Carolla. He loved flying and looking down on the vast world below him. Beneath the clouds, he could see the fertile farmland and vineyards of California, all in vibrant color in early September. Occasionally, he beheld trucks and cars wandering the earth like sloths. But the closer he came to Portland, the greener the world became. And the green reminded him of home sweet home.

Portland itself seemed both changed and unchanged. The war was pretty much over now, and people would soon celebrate the return of the brave soldiers. A feeling of patriotism and excitement filled the air, a feeling the citizens of America had long awaited with anticipation. How many mothers, fathers, sisters, brothers, wives, and sweethearts had waited for this day! The hour of darkness, many believed, had finally come to a close. It was a rare city to not see an American flag nearly everywhere. It was a time when our national anthem sang loud, clear, and proud for all the world to hear. Little children and the old and wise took to heart the idea of our nation being a brotherhood from sea to shining sea. Many tears were shed. Some mourned for the lost soldiers, dead on the battlefield. Some cried for joy because their prayers had been answered.

LOVE AND WAR TOGETHER, PART III

But Portland remained Portland. On that corner was Rich's grocery store, and dear old Mrs. Nelson lived nearby in the white house, with the white picket fence and red roses. Eddie became ecstatic over the feeling of familiarity back home. And the feeling of familiarity increased the closer he came to the house he knew and loved.

"Eddie! Darling, you're home," his mother cried as she ran through the kitchen to greet her son.

"Mother! I can't tell you how good it is to see you! Nor can I fully express how good it is to be home," he cried as he embraced his mother.

"We received your letter recently. Oh, Eddie, is it true that you have decided to follow Jesus with your whole heart?"

"Yes, Mother. I can honestly say that I have decided to follow Jesus, no turning back."

And who should walk in the front door at that moment but Al and Roy.

"Eddie!" they both shouted.

"Al! Roy! You have both grown taller since I saw you last. And you look more like men! Come here," he said as he hugged his brothers.

"It's good to see my family coming back together again!" their mother shed a tear.

"Aw, Ma! You promised," Al said.

"I know." She cried while blowing her nose. "I just can't help myself."

"What are you making in the kitchen? It smells delicious!" mentioned Eddie.

"We're having your favorite stew and cornbread—with a strawberry rhubarb pie to complete it."

"I'm starving. Anything of yours sounds amazing."

"Eddie! The way you said that makes me think you don't even care what I make. Forget the fact that I wanted to make you something special," she voiced.

"No, Mother, I didn't mean it like that. It is my favorite. I just said that I would eat anything you make." He grinned. "Trust me, I sincerely miss your food."

MUSIC COMES IN SPRINGTIME

"Oh, thank you!" she replied more gently with her hand on her heart. "As you can see, it's been a very emotional day for me."

The family had a wonderful time around the dinner table that evening, and Eddie enjoyed reuniting with his dad. His older brothers had not yet returned from the war, and he himself still had to return to San Diego. As Ronny had reminded them, they had a special assignment from the captain to perform. But at least it wasn't supposed to last long. And the end was in sight.

"Please pass the cornbread, Mother," said Al.

"I can't believe it has already been a year since we last saw you, Eddie! Tell us about what has happened in the last year and how life has been on the training ship in San Diego," his dad remarked.

Eddie had so much he wanted to mention, but he broke it down into a few groups. He talked about how the training program had progressed onboard his old ship and how life was like in California. But he also mentioned his two favorite buddies, Robert and Ronny, and told of their stories. And lastly, he told them about the most important thing that had happened during the whole war, and that was his conversion.

"Praise the Lord, son! I can't tell you what a joy it was to receive the letter. It will be a treasure we will never throw away." His dad beamed.

"Before making the decision, I really wanted to have the kind of faith like Robert. He's such a genuine guy. It doesn't matter what anyone thinks of him, says to him, or says about him—he just doesn't care. He only cares about pleasing God."

"Eddie, you may not know this," said his mother, "but I spent many hours praying that God would send you a Christian friend onboard the ship. I greatly desired for you to have someone to help build your faith and not destroy it. Through what you are telling me, I now realize God has answered my prayers."

"Amen," his father concurred.

"Oh, mother! I forgot to mention this, but I called Carolla at the airport, and she said she's coming to our house as soon as she gets off work."

"Yes, she called me. We can expect her probably any minute now."

"You know, son"—his dad leaned over to Eddie and had that look on his face—"if you truly had the desire to marry Carolla, I want you to know you have my blessing."

Eddie wasn't surprised.

"I've watched her," he continued, "over the last few years and have observed what appears to me a quality, godly, and pretty young lady. And you don't even need to ask whether she spent hours on her knees in prayer for you or your brothers. Her heart's desire is set on serving others, and she would make a great helpmeet."

"Oh, Dad, look! Her car is just pulling into the driveway," Eddie exclaimed.

His heart raced. It had already been a year since he had seen her last and had dreamed so much of this moment.

"Carolla!" he exclaimed with a grin the size of Texas. "Oh, Carolla! How I missed you!"

"Eddie," I said just as happy with half a tear in my eye. "Eddie, I have missed you so much as well." We hugged each other. "I don't want to keep you. I know you want to have some family time. But my dad offered to let us use his car whenever we want."

"Carolla, can we go out tomorrow then? I want to tell you all about the last year, including my conversion!"

"I've really been looking forward to hearing it!"

"Well, then, I will too!"

No couple could have looked any cuter than the two of us cruising around Portland on our way to all our old favorite locations. Of course, Eddie wanted to cruise along the old Columbia River Highway, and it brought him chills to be back in that part of the country he knew and loved so much.

It was early September, and the sun still shone while the leaves began to slowly turn golden. He took me up Crown Point back again to the Vista House, and we stood there gazing out on the sunset. It was there he told me all the details of his conversion. The whole story brought me to tears. I knew inwardly how much praying I had done for Eddie, and the day that letter came will be one I will never forget.

MUSIC COMES IN SPRINGTIME

As the air turned crisp and cool and I wrapped myself tighter in my coat, I asked, "So, Eddie, you mentioned how you have a special assignment that still must be completed. When will you be leaving again? Do you know how long it will take?"

"I can't tell you exactly how long, Carolla, but I assure you, the time will pass quickly. Before long, we won't have to be parting like this again." He spoke softly.

A bird flew overhead and chirped in a most pleasant way as the sun fell beneath the hilltops.

"My darling, I love you," he gently said and paused. "I need you. All along during the war, I realized you were praying for me. For the duty of our country, we may have had to part ways for a season. But I don't want to ever be parted from you again." Breathing heavily, he spoke.

I slowly ran my fingers through his lovely curly hair. "I love you, too, my dear. I always have loved you!" I looked intently and beheld the face of my beloved. "I can't believe this is happening."

He gave me a side hug, and we stood in the same romantic idyllic spot we had stood at just a year prior.

What more could I ask for? I was enthralled with the scenery around me, wrapped in the arms of my best friend.

*****

We so thoroughly enjoyed our time up the gorge, and then real life came into play. It started raining that evening, and some guy, probably drunk, ran into us at the intersection of Killingworth and Union in Portland! Eddie and I were not hurt, but he immediately took the blame for the destruction of my father's car. His face turned red with embarrassment wondering what my dad would say or think. We were stranded and had to wait for a while before a friend of ours picked us up. (We probably looked weird standing in the rain like that, but at that point, I really didn't care.) Dad harbored no ill feelings and was nice to Eddie about it—reminding him that it was not his fault and that he was really a responsible driver. Well, we missed the freedom of having a car!

Anyway, we found other ways to get around—like taking the bus. I took a few days off from work. Actually, I had not missed a single day for any reason during my time at the shipyard. But the war was nearly over, and I knew where my priorities needed to lie.

On a foggy morning, which happened to be the very next day, we headed to Mount Tabor Park. After only a short while, the sun rose, and the fog cleared. As soon as we set foot in the beautiful park, a flood of memories rushed through my head. Unbeknownst to Eddie, this was the place where I had my epiphany. This was the place where, for the first time, I felt true peace and resolve concerning the war. This was the place where I had pondered and fully understood my mother's wisdom: Music comes in springtime.

Eddie ran past me as I jolted from my reverie. He had remembered to bring his camera on this trip and had seen this colorful butterfly atop a red rose. Of course, he had to find just the right angle to take the picture! And then something else caught his eye. I drifted back into my reverie.

After a few more photos, he came back and held my hand, and we walked pleasantly through the park. We found this beautiful grassy area beneath some fir trees, and he had me pose for some picture-perfect moments. I wore a light-pink dress, one of my favorites, and felt flattered to have my pictures taken! Afterward, I took some of Eddie; he wore his handsome Coast Guard uniform. It was really funny, honestly! I didn't realize he was such a poser. But then, he actually said the same thing about me as well!

The most special photographs, of course, were of the two of us together. I wouldn't trade those special moments in time for anything in the world. For some reason, the park seemed especially empty that day, and it felt like we were the only two people in the world. After a short jaunt, we came and sat down on a lovely little bench, the same one, I recognized, where I had my epiphany. The scene felt so familiar! The sunshine, the towering trees, and the gorgeous symmetrical white and red roses all about. As I gazed at all these, Eddie grasped my hand.

"Carolla, my darling. Will you marry me?"

My heart stopped beating. "Yes," I said instantly, "I will gladly marry you."

"I will always love you, my darling," he said emphatically.

"And you, I will always love, my dear."

"Whew!" Eddie sighed. "Well, what do you know! We're getting married!" he shouted and started flailing his arms wildly.

"Oh my word! We are!" I started laughing and shouting too! We sprang from the bench and started dancing in place a little. What an adventure life had been! Who would have known that I would have become engaged on that little park bench? It might have been September, but following a heavy war, I could finally say music had come in springtime!

One day later, the first people we announced our engagement to included my aunt Estella and my uncle Hubert, who lived over at Giles Lake. My uncle probed us as to how we were going to "break the ice" with the family as my parents had invited the Fritzlers and the Krause family over to our house for dinner the next evening.

"You know what you should do? I have an idea! Make out a written announcement of your engagement, you see. Then, while your dad, Carolla, is praying for the meal, Eddie, you slip the announcement onto his plate. See how long it takes him to figure it out!"

"Doesn't Herman probably already know though, dear?" Aunt Estella asked.

"No, I'm not sure he does," Eddie chimed in. "I actually forgot to ask for his permission to marry Carolla!"

"You're kidding! Well then, my boy, you may be in for some surprise tomorrow night, let me tell you!" Uncle Hubert said half joking, half serious.

Eddie gulped. I just smiled. "Dad fully approves. I am 100 percent sure on that." I spoke reassuringly.

Well, one evening later, my parents, Jacob and Mary Fritzler, Fred and Margaret Krause, and Eddie and I all shared a meal together at our home. It's surprising to me that no one really made any comments about us being a couple, of course, until after the announcement.

Mom worked really hard and prepared a delicious meal for the evening. As usual, she covered the table with a white tablecloth and put fresh flowers on the nearby buffet. In 1945, people dressed up for all sorts of occasions, big and small. Tonight was no exception. We all came dressed properly and neatly. The dinner served included roast chicken and all the trimmings, plus peach pie and ice cream for dessert. Eddie had been to our home on multiple occasions and loved my mama's cooking! (I secretly hoped my food would measure up!)

Eddie had the folded-up announcement and kept it under his leg at the table. After a few minutes of conversation, while waiting for the potatoes to be brought to the table, Dad led everyone in a word of prayer. One moment after closing my eyes, I reopened them and found Eddie very cautiously slipping the piece of paper onto Dad's plate. We both exchanged glances and smiled mischievously.

"Amen!" said we all.

After a moment, Dad was getting ready to serve his plate with a helping of salad. Then he noticed the white piece of paper obstructing the plate!

"This is odd. Who put this here?" he asked.

Everyone turned toward him as he opened it and read aloud: "Carolla and I are engaged!" Dad hung his open mouth in midair.

My parents were speechless for a moment, but not in the least disappointed. Dad smiled and spoke first. "Congratulations! I knew this day would come. Actually, I've sensed it for a long time."

"My baby! You're engaged!" Mother felt the impact a little deeper. "All three of my children off and married." She sighed. "It hardly seems possible! But, Eddie and Carolla, I am very pleased and happy for you."

"Yes, welcome to the family, Eddie."

Eddie's parents both were overjoyed with our engagement. It was Eddie's father who had given him the "okay" to make the move anyway.

Now we had a lot to talk about at the dinner table! Marriage plans, house plans, work plans, and the list went on and on. It was official, and the news, public!

Two days later, we had the same group of people in our home, plus Eddie's old friend, Alfred Dietz, to celebrate Eddie's twenty-second birthday. Funny that we again had fried chicken and all the fixings on this occasion, but with a banana cream pie for dessert.

MUSIC COMES IN SPRINGTIME

Additionally, Mom Fritzler baked a delicious cake with white frosting to celebrate his birthday. Toothpick United States flags replaced ordinary candles.

The cake was set in the middle of the table, and after the scrumptious meal, we all sang "Happy Birthday to You" to Eddie. Wearing his Coast Guard uniform, he grinned from ear to ear and held my hand as his mom cut the cake and handed him a slice. I smiled, but with a faint inward sigh. It was a beautiful Sunday evening, but I knew that before long, Eddie would hop on a plane and go right back to San Diego although the war had nearly come to an end. I missed him even before he waved goodbye to me on that plane. But I knew worrying about the situation would not help in the slightest way. I had to keep my chin up and remain thankful and positive. *He won't be gone long*, I knew.

Eddie remained positive. For one thing, he told me, at least he was going back to some nice hot weather! It had started raining here in Oregon the last few days, and feeling the warm sunshine on my back would have felt nice, I admit.

He rejoined his good buddies, Robert and Ronny, and the three of them picked up where they had left off. Shortly after arriving, they understood their assignment. Although the *Hunter Liggett* had been used as a training ship in San Diego, after the war ended, it had been chosen to help transport troops home from the South Pacific.

The repatriation of the more than eight million American servicemen became known as "Operation Magic Carpet." Hospital ships, aircraft carriers, battleships—these all had a new role to play in the transporting of the brave American soldiers home.

The Army had been aware of the need to establish a protocol for transporting soldiers home two years prior, in 1943. Army Chief of Staff General George Marshall delegated the task to committees, and later the operation was placed under the control of the War Shipping Administration (WSA).

Operation Magic Carpet was no small feat. It required delicate planning and coordination between the Army, Navy, and WSA, and it lasted almost a year, from October 1945 to September 1946.

LOVE AND WAR TOGETHER, PART III

USS Hunter Liggett joined the valiant operation on December 10, 1945. Robert, Ronny, and Eddie rejoined the rest of the ship's crew as their captain explained the details. Part of the interior of the ship had to be redesigned slightly to accommodate the vast numbers who would soon become homeward bound. Some ships, such as aircraft carriers, actually had three-to-five-tiered bunk beds arranged in their hangars.

It meant a lot to Eddie to see the faces of the American soldiers as *Hunter Liggett* journeyed to Ulithi, Guam, Pearl Harbor, and the Palaus. In San Diego, the three radio operators had helped to load the ship with adequate food and supplies for several weeks of journeying. Space for storage was at its premium, but no one really cared. The war had ended! Period. Everyone on board *Hunter Liggett* considered it not even a right but a privilege to return to the South Pacific to retrieve their buddies who had given everything within them for freedom.

They had set out from San Diego in December, and Eddie, Robert, and Ronny enjoyed conversing in between preparing for the servicemen's needs. The whole ship came alive in preparation. However, Eddie quickly realized that something was missing. Serving their physical needs alone would not be enough. These men, who would soon board the ship, needed more. After the chaos, they needed care and support. After the emotional trauma, they needed healing and love. After the horror, they needed rebuilding and encouragement. Many wounds went deeper than what could be seen with the eye alone.

These thoughts had Eddie just before landing on their first island. Minutes later, he looked out across the water and beheld the large gathering who had been waiting so long for that ship to arrive. How they waited patiently but eagerly! Before long, soldiers began to pour onto the ship's deck in droves. Leaning on a metal wall on the top deck, Eddie watched as emotions varied. Some men walked slowly onto the platform, keeping their composure, but daring not to look back at the island behind them. Others came in silent tears, with painful glances backward. Many came to islands such as these, but fewer left them. "To this place, I will never return." Spoke many a man.

The feeling in the air was both joyous and somber. They were grateful to find themselves aboard an American ship but yet also feeling the pain of leaving fallen fellow soldiers behind.

Eddie, Robert, and Ronny all helped make the soldiers comfortable in any way they could—whether that be bringing food to the weak or offering encouragement. Most remained silent as to the horrors they had been through. Yet a few offered to share their stories.

One night, as Eddie carefully took a bowl of soup to a man who had suffered from dehydration, he found himself engulfed in a story. The man, whose name was John, looked longingly at Eddie as he graciously served him a meal. Sweating profusely, the marks of war covered the man's face and body.

"Here you go! A nice warm bowl of soup. Eat it carefully and very slowly."

"Thanks," the man whispered hoarsely. "It's much appreciated."

"You are more than welcome. What is your name?"

"I'm John. How about you?"

"I'm Eddie. It's nice to meet you."

"Yeah. Same. Just being in a safe place, surrounded by safe walls, and having a warm meal is more than enough to be grateful for." *Cough!* the man went a few times.

"Though we all have been through the fire, GOD blesses a grateful spirit like yours."

"It hasn't always been easy. I had no real peace in the foxholes." The man choked up. "Night times were the worst! We knew the island by day, but the enemy by night. All hell let loose as they slithered around in the dark with deadly bayonets. You never knew who would you never see again by morning!" The tears began flowing.

"I'm sorry, John! I'm so sorry."

"My best friend, Danny, and I were in the same platoon. We went through it together! Some nights, when searching for a foxhole or a crevice in the rock to rest, even if you wanted to, you couldn't identify people. It was just too dark. But Danny and I had a faint whistle we came up with to alert either of us of each other's presence.

I had been terribly weary and struggled to crawl on the ground to find a place of refuge for the night. To make matters worse, it began raining—in torrents. Before long, my face became caked in mud, and the visibility around me greatly faded. Desperate, I groped about and eventually came to what I knew to be a foxhole. But the question haunted me, 'Who is already in there?'

"One could not simply blindly believe that the man inside was friendly. But then, I heard it. Above the rainfall, I heard Danny's whistle. I was safe to enter! I couldn't figure out how he had recognized me, but I was thankful for that. My heart leaped as I slowly lowered myself into the tight and dark space. But as I began to whisper, Danny quickly covered my mouth with his hand. I understood, and he let go of his hand and instead put his arm around me. The two of us sat there: exhausted, sweaty, and dirty, in silence. Silence. Silence. Not a thing flashed before our eyes.

"My heart had been sprinting earlier, but now, it only ran and then slowed some. Still alert, I breathed. Danny breathed. And then instantly, the plot of land above us became an active war zone. *Thud! Thud! Thud!* Rapidly. I knew the sound of an AK-47 quite well. Through the narrow opening, I watched the sky flash with a boom. Danny and I could make out that the conflict commenced very close to where we were located. Who was involved and how many, we could not tell. I thought I could make out a faint cry for help. The cry was so faint, in fact, that I strained my ears as best I could. But then, all I could hear was the boom and the whistle and the crash of many weapons of war all around me. And suddenly, I heard words in English directly above me, 'Fall back! Immediately.'

"Chaos continued for a while and then gradually faded away. Seemingly moments later, Danny and I wondered with dread anticipation whether we needed to leave the hole or not. We waited. We could not tell how long, but we waited patiently and as calmly as we could. The faintest bit of light told us it was the early hours of the morning. Without realizing it, we had been waiting for a few hours. Uncomfortable in the tight and dirty space, we carefully peeked out of the hole to ensure safety. Danny and I looked each other in the eyes, and we both gave that 'approving' nod.

"Danny climbed out ever so stealthily, and I followed right behind him. We were on the ground. But then that same voice—that same quiet cry for help—came again. Both of us figured out the direction of the voice and crept toward the location. We crawled past several bushes and small war-sick trees before reaching a deathly wounded man. He, indeed, needed help. Who knew whether a medic was in the area or not. Regardless, his cry for help was so faint he could easily be passed by unnoticed.

"We were there and had a duty to our fellow American soldier. I had some crude first-aid supplies in my bag and immediately began administering them. But he needed much more medical help than I could give him. Danny tore the man's shirt off and wrapped it tightly around his chest to restrict the sickening blood flow, for it was obvious he had been shattered by pieces of mortar. The man needed water desperately, and I slowly gave him some from my canteen.

"We knew his condition had become critical, and he needed to be brought back to a field hospital. I grabbed his legs, Danny took his arms, and we began to walk cautiously but quickly back toward where he could receive help. But before we had gone twenty yards, we heard the sound of bullets whizzing past our heads. The enemy had been waiting for us near our foxhole. *Thud! Thud! Thud!* We hit the ground and then tragically realized the man we were trying to help had been hit by enemy fire again. There was nothing we could do.

"Danny and I crawled, then ran as fast as we could. We turned a corner in the road and immediately came face-to-face with gun barrels and the enemy themselves. Danny instantly put himself between them and me, and in the blink of an eye, I watched him be shot down, hitting the ground dead like lightning. I saw his blood. My friend was dead, and I had seen their murderous faces!

"A small ravine lay to the left, and without thinking, I jumped—hitting the solid ground hard. Groaning, I heard their fire, but I crouched, in shock, mostly unharmed. I had fallen behind a large rock, which had protected me, as if by Divine protection, from death. By Danny's sacrifice and GOD's grace alone, I narrowly escaped from that situation alive. Danny gave his life for me!" The man broke down.

LOVE AND WAR TOGETHER, PART III

"Greater love has no man than this, than that a man lay down his life for his friends," Eddie comforted him and sat in awe over the story.

"Thank you," said Eddie, "for sharing that story with me, John. I know that it was painful for you to share that story. But it needs to be told—to remember and honor Danny and to reflect on how precious it is to even be alive."

"You're right." John gazed off to the side. "You are right. The story needs to be told."

Eddie found himself among many men who had suffered greatly during the years of intense battle. He strove to meet not only their physical but also their spiritual, mental, and emotional needs as well. On many nights, as he returned to his tight quarters, he remembered the stories the men had shared with him. Many prayers needed to be offered for those men.

One night, as it became quite dark, while Eddie and a few others organized and arranged some supplies on the deck which had come from one of the islands, he had this thought. *The stories of many of these men will never be told. They will go back into society and remain nameless heroes. Not many of them will be decorated by the president himself. The rest will go down in history as common men.* The thought saddened Eddie. But even in this quiet realization, he knew that he could make a difference in the lives of these men.

Yes, many of their stories would never be told. Many chivalrous details would be lost to time. Yet even in the short amount of time that Eddie had with them on *Hunter Liggett*, he could be the one to show them honor. To uplift them. To encourage them. To offer to pray for them and stand by their side.

"What is today's date?" a soldier asked Robert one day.

"Why, it's December 24, Christmas Eve!"

"Christmas Eve!" Eddie could hardly believe what his friend had just stated. Yes, he knew in advance he would be gone and away from his family this Christmas. But life aboard the ship had been so busy he had forgotten to count down the days. And before he knew it, that special day had come.

MUSIC COMES IN SPRINGTIME

"Ronny! Robert! Come here. I want to talk to you, guys, for a minute," Eddie said just moments later as they passed through the dining hall.

"What is it now?" Ronny asked.

"I have an idea. Guys, it's Christmas Eve! Do you know if anything special has been planned for this evening or tomorrow?"

"Not to my knowledge," replied Robert.

"Well, we need to do something. It needn't be fancy, but why don't we organize a Christmas carol sing-along for everyone on the top deck? We could set it for, say, seven-thirty."

"Do you think the captain would approve?" Ronny questioned. "I sure hope so because it sounds like a lot of fun!"

"Eddie, great idea!" exclaimed Robert.

"I'm going right now to find the captain to ask for permission." Eddie ran off.

And wouldn't you know it? The captain, indeed, approved, and at seven-thirty, or 1930 in military time, Eddie, Robert, and Ronny stood on the windy, almost dark, deck with flashlights. Some men already gathered around them, and others slowly joined the group.

"Robert," Ronny whispered. "I don't know if I'll know all these carols."

"You'll be fine, Ronny. Just mouth what we say. We definitely need your help tonight."

"Can I have your attention, please!" Eddie shouted as more than one hundred people gathered around and had begun talking loudly.

"Tonight is Christmas Eve. This is a very special time of the year where we have the privilege of remembering our dear Savior's birth. Let's take some time this evening to sing some old familiar carols! Shall we?"

The response was enthusiastic. Robert and Eddie waved their arms and led the group first in "Hark! The Herald Angels Sing." How they sang it beautifully and with resolve!

Hark! The herald angels sing
"Glory to the new-born king
Peace on earth and mercy mild

LOVE AND WAR TOGETHER, PART III

> *God and sinners reconciled"*
> *Joyful all ye nations rise*
> *Join the triumph of the skies*
> *With angelic host proclaim*
> *"Christ is born in Bethlehem"*
> *Hark! The herald angels sing*
> *"Glory to the new-born king"*

More and more men began to appear and sing with them. You could see it on their faces: The songs were touching their hearts. It seemed as if the whole ship had come alive with music! The feeling in the air had become joyous—one filled with remembrance and celebration. You could see the strain lifted off the faces of these men as they sang "Joy to the World!"

And the last song that evening was "Silent Night." The stars had come out over the Pacific Ocean, and the mesmerizing water below could still be heard. Many shed tears as the first few words were sung:

> *Silent night, holy night*
> *All is calm, all is bright*
> *Round yon virgin, mother and Child*
> *Holy Infant so tender and mild*
> *Sleep in heavenly peace*
> *Sleep in heavenly peace*

Heavenly peace. That summed up the exact feeling they aboard the *Hunter Liggett* had that evening. And it was just what they needed.

After hours of precious singing, Eddie returned back to his crowded quarters. But he didn't mind. The singing had lifted his spirits high to the point where he had a difficult time falling asleep. He thought about the birth of Jesus and how His mission on earth had been to save those who were lost. Christ had called us to follow in His footsteps. And then he realized, that in some small way, he was obeying GOD by being a part of Operation Magic Carpet. For it had been used to "save" the American soldiers from off of these islands and bring them home. Eddie understood the parallel, and he thanked GOD for this opportunity.

Lastly, before he fell asleep that evening, or Christmas morning, for it was after midnight, his thoughts drifted across the Pacific back to Oregon. He thought of his dad and mom and especially of his girl, Carolla. In the dim light, he took out a small picture that he had stuffed in his pillow.

"Merry Christmas, my darling!" he whispered and sighed. "I love you." And he held the photo close to his heart.

*****

For Eddie, one of the most powerful things he saw during Operation Magic Carpet included Pearl Harbor in Hawaii. As their ship docked in Oahu, Robert, Ronny, and Eddie had a few minutes to spare to see the wreckage. They carefully treaded the area. Eerily, some ships could still be seen sunk beneath the water.

"This is where it all began for us," Robert said with eyes fixed on the devastation, "just a little over four years ago." It was a sight to behold and a sight to ponder as well.

Operation Magic Carpet came to a close for the men aboard this ship. The mission had been accomplished, and the brave American soldiers had returned home. In January of 1946, Eddie said goodbye to the many men he had met on this incredible journey, including John. Then he, at last, said a final goodbye to Robert and Ronny.

"Keep reading that Bible Robert gave you, Ronny." Eddie pointed directly at him.

"I already have been, rest assured," Ronny said with his usual hint of sass but with a smile as well. And maybe a tear as well.

Robert interjected. "GOD be with you 'til we meet again, guys! Group hug!"

As to the illustrious ship, *USS Hunter Liggett*, she was formally decommissioned on March 18, 1946, just days after being returned to the Army in Olympia, Washington. She was awarded four battle stars.

But enough about the ship—and enough about the war—for it is over! The war has been raging now for years. Let us return home.

Now the military still had plans for Eddie. He was to be transferred to West Point, Washington, but had a less than three-week leave in between assignments. Of course, he couldn't wait to come home to his soon-to-be bride.

*****

"Darling! Oh, I missed you over the last few months! Happy new year 1946! To our Savior be the glory. This war is over." Eddie spoke gleefully.

"Oh, Eddie!" I ran toward him happily. "I'm thrilled you are home! But what happened to your beautiful curly hair?"

"They cut a strip down the middle of it when we crossed the international date line in the Pacific."

"Oh! Really? [I tried not to show my sadness, but I was greatly disappointed. I loved his curly hair! It never looked the same after they cut it.] Anyways, a slight change of hairstyle won't change the man I really love."

Married men with children were the first to come home. Art Smith, Emil Dietz, and Ray and Mike Fritzler all came back before Bud Timmons and Eddie.

But they all came back. Inwardly, I knew there was so much to be grateful for. Many a mother—many a sweetheart—had no son or lover to welcome home. My dear friends had endured so much. But GOD had providentially seen them through back to our earthly home in America.

Bob came home with a traumatizing story. As you may recall, he went into the Navy, and his ship traversed the Atlantic Ocean. On one occasion, they were hit by a German submarine U-boat, and water began gushing into the lower section of the ship. The only chance they had of saving themselves involved immediately shutting the watertight doors, so the rest of the ship would be not flooded. Their own comrades, performing their duties, were on the other side of the doors. The water levels inside rose fast. But there was nothing they could do. The doors shut tight, and Bob and the rest had to listen to the agonizing cry of their friends to let them in. They beat on the doors. "Help! Open the door! Save us. We're drowning," they screamed. Bob and the other men burst into tears, and some fell to their knees and began praying. Although nothing humanly possible could have been done to save those men, Bob struggled with feelings of regret. He still suffered from hearing the cries of the men he worked and lived with every day. But it was their sacrifice that allowed the many others aboard the ship that day to be saved.

That was a lesson I tried hard to begin to understand. Because we learn in scripture that "greater love has no man than this, than that a man lay down his life for his friends."

Oh, so much had happened. And Eddie talked to me of all the healing these men needed. But we, back home, had so much to be grateful for. That thought brought me to tears.

Though I had so many emotions in early 1946, the greatest was the reality of love. I loved Eddie dearly, and he loved me the same. Eddie had less than three weeks of leave between Operation Magic Carpet and becoming stationed in West Port. So we made the most of every moment of those few weeks and planned our wedding day for February 1, 1946.

We did not have a lot of time to plan or money to spend but a lot of love for each other. There have been fancier weddings out there, but I didn't mind. I felt like a princess about to marry her prince charming.

The day of our wedding came, and I cherish every detail. Brother Kempin performed the ceremony, and we had Mike and Esther, Bob and Pluma, and Roy and Naomi Kempin as the bridesmaids and groomsmen.

Many candles lit the stage, and the flowers were placed beautifully about. How I had waited for this day! Eddie and I had known each other for several years now, and I had always wondered and wished—but here we were. Before I knew it, I saw my man wearing his Coast Guard uniform, and he saw me dressed in my beautiful white flowing dress. The glorious music played.

"Eddie," Brother Kempin asked, "do you take Carolla to be your lawfully wedded wife? To have and to hold from this day forward, 'til death do you part?"

"I do," he said.

"And, Carolla, do you take Eddie as your lawfully wedded husband? To have and to hold from this day forward, 'til death do you part?"

"I do," I said. *'Til death do us part.*

"I now pronounce you man and wife. Eddie, you may kiss your bride."

If ever there was a moment where time seemed to stop, it was that time.

"Ladies and gentlemen, may I present to you for the first time, Mr. and Mrs. Edwin Fritzler!"

We were married! Husband and wife! Woohoo!

Following the ceremony, we cut the ornately decorated white cake, which included figurines of a man in the Coast Guard and his bride underneath an American flag. It was perfect and very fitting for us. I fed him a reasonable bite, but of course, he stuffed a ton down my throat! My mouth was completely full, and I was dying laughing as well. (I must have been a sight!)

We were young, but the two of us had a love as strong as a mountain. Because of the circumstances, we were not able to have a honeymoon. But my prince charming had come for me! And that was all I wanted.

Days later, Eddie reported for duty at West Port, Washington. He was on for forty-eight hours and then off forty-eight hours and would hitchhike rides back and forth as we lived in Portland. I remember early mornings taking him across the Columbia River into Vancouver and then dropping him off to hitch a ride. (I always disliked leaving him there, but it allowed us to save money.) Ironically, he was so regular that, many times, the same people offered him a ride! He always thanked them and really had an amazing talent for striking up conversations. (Remember, this was 1946.) But sometimes, he would refuse rides from people that didn't look good to him. On only one occasion did he ever have to catch a bus for part

MUSIC COMES IN SPRINGTIME

of the way because he needed a ride that would take him back to the base on time.

Thankfully, this season of life lasted only about a month, and he was soon discharged from the military.

At this time, we rented a sweet little home at about Thirty-Ninth and Killingsworth in Portland. It actually came furnished, and each of the two bedrooms included a twin bed. However, there was no refrigerator, and we had to put the milk bottle in the sink and let the water run over it to keep it cool! The water itself was heated with a gas burner underneath the water tank. A small front porch made an excellent addition to the home, and we enjoyed many evenings sitting outdoors in chairs Eddie had made. These were the days where, even in Portland, and when the weather permitted, many people spent their evenings out on the front porch.

The simple pleasures—rocking in a swing, chatting, plucking a guitar, reading the newspaper, knitting, and saying hello to neighbors across the way—were enjoyed by all. Eddie and I grew closer together through our times out on the front porch—gazing out at the sunset, which brought back wonderful memories.

Oftentimes, on these simple yet sweet evenings, we talked about our hopes and dreams for our future together. We wanted to have lots of kids! I didn't grow up with any sisters, and so I greatly desired to have daughters of my own. I dreamed of dressing them in my homemade dresses, teaching them how to cook, and showing them how to love GOD and be ladylike. Eddie and I wanted both girls and boys. He dreamed of owning a farm someday and wanted so badly to have a plot of land he could care for and call his own. And of course, he needed a son to help out around the farm. Portland had been a nice city to live in, but we both wanted to have our place and space out in the open country. We wanted to have animals and live the good old country life.

But for now, we just sat there on the porch, talked, and dreamed. Like most Americans, we didn't have a lot of money, but we were very grateful for what we had. A 1936 Oldsmobile met our daily needs even if it pulled to the left when you stepped on the brakes. (You had to be very careful about that and plan for space accordingly!)

LOVE AND WAR TOGETHER, PART III

Oh, but we loved our life, and we loved each other. I continued working at the shipyards, and thankfully, the pace slowed down following the war. Eddie worked for Brother Timmons carrying hod (backbreaking brickwork) but later found employment at Swift and Company running the bacon slicer.

Not too long after starting work there, he woke up in the middle of the night with a shriek after a nightmare that his hand was still in the slicer! It took him a minute to realize he had both hands! A day later, his hand got caught in the machine. Eddie wasn't seriously hurt, but he saw the writing on the wall and started looking for another job. (Wow, I learned to start taking dreams a little too seriously after that!)

And the Lord provided. My dad had a wonderful job working for Portland Provision Meat Company, and he helped Eddie to find work pumping hams and bacon. It could truly be said my man brought home the bacon in both ways! Eddie enjoyed the work and wanted to stay in the meat business long term.

Through it all, we walked hand in hand. Life had already been a great adventure, but our life together had only just begun.

CHAPTER 14

The Years That Followed

So much happened over the next few years in life, and every time I blinked, it seemed that change was on the horizon. But, dear reader, I do not wish to tell you of all the details of the many adventures Eddie and I were afforded over the next several decades. The number of stories would fill another book, and that is for another time and place. However, I do wish to share with you some of the rich happenings that occurred along the way.

On our very first anniversary, in 1947, Eddie and I moved into our first-bought home on Holman Street. It cost us $3,500, but I had war bonds saved up which helped cover a significant part. At this home, Eddie and I learned the art of remodeling and how sometimes (actually always) that requires patience! Most of the time, we just kept trying until something worked, but I am very thankful for my dad's guidance as well.

The basement came with a dirt floor, and Eddie and I decided to dig the basement out and put in a furnace as well as a place to wash clothes. We planned on pouring concrete to create a wall, and Eddie had built the forms. Well, needless to say, that "wall" never worked out. The "ready-mix" truck came and began pouring wet heavy cement; the forms gave way, and it looked like the bow of a ship! We were so disappointed! Bob, who was helping us, chimed in, "Let's pour it on the floor." And so Eddie reworked the forms right there, and we soon had part of the floor finished! What lessons learned!

In May of 1948, our oldest daughter, Sally Emmogene, was born at Emmanuel Hospital in Portland to proud and happy parents! We had been receiving record rainfall during that May after a heavy winter, and while in the hospital, the nearby city of Vanport flooded. The city had been constructed as a war housing project in 1942 for those in industries such as the Kaiser Shipyards and was located between the Columbia Slough and the Columbia River, near Portland.

Before the flood, Vanport had sprung up as the second-largest city in Oregon and had become a thriving community. But it was completely eradicated when an earthen railroad dam gave way. Fifteen people died because of the powerful flood, and Portland was ablaze with sirens and rumors for several days.

But our dear sweet baby stole our hearts. Sally had pretty reddish-brown hair which curled after it grew. As I quit work outside the home forever, I enjoyed spending time sewing all of her dresses and sweaters.

She grew to love and appreciate music, to a great extent, and could sing from a very young age. When she was little, we moved the piano my parents had bought for me into our home. Sally could play tunes she had heard at church or watched on TV with both hands on the piano when she was only five or six years old. (I remember her loving the *Lone Ranger* and *Roy Rogers* theme songs!) Eddie and I were thrilled to have a child with more musical talent than either of us possessed.

When Sally was a few months old, we attended the Church of God camp meeting in Clackamas, Oregon. How many vivid and wonderful memories I have of camp meetings! This had been a family tradition for many years now as you may recall. My mother began attending in Enterprise the summer before I was born. But now, I had my own family to take to the weeklong event. Eddie and my dad came every night to the rousing services after work, and we cooked supper for them. Eddie, as a faithful dad, took Sally's diapers home each night to wash them and bring them back fresh the next day!

MUSIC COMES IN SPRINGTIME

Our family had wonderful friends we had met over the years through camp meetings, and it became one of the most special traditions in my life. The passionate evening services held in old barns or big tents, the singing of thousands of worshipful voices, the meals partaken with dear brothers and sisters, I looked forward to these every year. Memories made there remain priceless.

Back home, one of my favorite activities included the Women's Missionary Society meetings which took place at our church. Several of us mothers met on Thursdays to quilt, and we always enjoyed the visits. Often, while our hands and fingers were busy at work, we tried to solve all the world's problems! Why, many issues could be discussed over the years—the Cold War, nuclear weaponry, the hippie movement, Vietnam. There was always something to talk about!

In January 1951, I gave birth to my second daughter, LaVisa Nan. What a sweet and cute blondie! Our little one possessed a very good temperament and never cried. With an ever-growing family, Eddie decided to add two more rooms to the house; the space was much appreciated.

We had many wonderful neighbors in Portland, and the girls enjoyed playing with their friends. One of our neighbors in the 1950s, the Chandlers, had a huge antenna on their house to get better TV reception. One night, Eddie and I stayed up late trying to steam wallpaper off of our living room wall (the girls were asleep). And who came storming into our living room but Mr. Chandler himself. He informed us that our steamer had disrupted his TV reception and asked if we would shut it off until his program had finished. Trying to be good neighbors, we complied.

TV became popular in the 1950s, but we couldn't afford to waste our time in front of a screen. There was always some project to work on. We built our own garage and chicken house. I dreamed of having my own playhouse as a little girl, and Eddie decided to build one for our girls. This little house had its own porch, a nice window with shutters, an electric light, and painted walls and ceiling. Over the years, our kids used it as a house, grocery store, church, or whatever their little minds could dream up.

Eddie and I remained very close with our parents. Sadly, in June 1952, Eddie's dad passed away. He had been such a wonderful man, and we felt the loss deeply. Eddie's mother, who had been through a lot after his passing, died in 1964.

We went through a lot of cars in our married life! As no new cars were manufactured from around 1942–1945 during the war, it was difficult to find one. I'll never forget pulling out of the driveway after having just purchased a brick red Willys for $400, and the seller's son shouting, "Dad, did you tell them what it does when it rains?" I about had a heart attack! *What does happen when it rains!* The alarming thought ran through my head. Well, it didn't take long to find out! The car had a seam down the middle of the hood, and it leaked like crazy. Eddie actually put his overcoat under the hood so the distributor wouldn't get wet!

A few years later, we bought a beautiful red-and-white 1957 Ford—a custom model but had no radio. I loved the heater (which was an option in those days). We even splurged and paid extra for a passenger-side visor! (How we take so much in our cars for granted these days!)

Our true heart's desire was to live in the country—out in GOD's open field. Even while we lived in the city, Eddie built a stanchion and bought a cow. But because, of course, we had no pasture in town, she spent her days simply standing in the barn and eating hay. The fresh milk was nice, but she ended up coming down with mastitis, so we had to get rid of her. However, we still kept up that farming spirit! Bob and Pluma had already moved to a farm in Aurora, Oregon, and they raised pigs, berries, and hay. Eddie, the girls, and I spent many Sunday afternoons driving around the Willamette Valley looking for a place of our own.

While pregnant again, we finally found our dream farm, which had twenty-eight acres of usable land. Tualatin-Sherwood Road, a major thoroughfare, divided the property. On the south side stood a home, garage, and a stand of oak trees. To the north stood a barn, another outbuilding, cleared land for crops and pasture, a stand of pine trees, woods with oak trees and rose bushes, and two creeks.

But at this point, the exterior appeared in much better shape than the interior of the home. The farmhouse was sunken in the back and had no foundation or plumbing. Shiplap and wallpaper covered the lower floor while the upstairs remained unfinished.

In June of 1955, Eddie and I welcomed our baby boy, Edwin Herman, into the world. Our little boy would grow up to love farming just as much as his dad one day. How proud we both were to now have two daughters and one son. Eddie had always said he needed a boy to help out on his farm someday. Ironically, he brought the farm papers for me to sign while I was still in the hospital!

We now had a farm of our own. But there was a lot of work to be done, and I mean a lot! The backyard of the house, as well as the upstairs, was full of old cans and junk. We had an area in the lawn the size of a big straw pile that needed to be burned. Cat manure caked every corner of the home, and we had to chisel it out. Bees had made their home in the west wall, and though we got rid of them, you could still smell honey whenever the sun shone!

Bob and Ursel Livingston, friends of ours, and Eddie jacked up the house and leveled it after he poured some footings. He then dug a septic tank and poured it all in one day with a small cement mixer. Man, was my hubby sweaty! I made sure he had plenty of water and refreshments to keep him going. As he worked alone on this project, he had to finish it quickly so the tank wouldn't leak. The house came with no bathroom, only a lovely little path to an outhouse, and so I requested that project take precedence next!

Eddie put one in a section of our screened back porch, and the bathtub found a home in one of the downstairs bedroom closets. It wasn't five-star living by any means, but we didn't really care. We were soon to raise our family of five out in the country, and that was all we wanted.

So many more projects had to take place before we could move in, which ended up being that November. We took out the chimney in the kitchen and opened the door to the living room with an arch. The living room itself had only shiplap, deadening felt, and old wallpaper which had cracked at every seam when we leveled the house. By taking off the stairway door, we made a room at the top of the stairs for the girls.

One of my favorite improvements included replacing the windows. How I enjoyed looking out at the expansive field and at the old barn! It was our million-dollar view. We could see Mount Hood from the kitchen window and Mount Saint Helens from another (until she erupted in 1980).

Many friends came and helped us with our projects, and we were very grateful for their willingness and the giving of their time. Sally and LaVisa helped out whenever possible too. Between the two of them, they moved a lot of garbage!

That first winter in the farmhouse was bitterly cold. It came with little, if any, insulation. The air blew straight into the house from underneath as there was no foundation. We wrapped the pump in an old rug as there was no pump house, and the water froze each night. What a winter! But we survived! When there's a will, there's a way. We learned to let the water run and keep the fire going. Sometimes, I ironed leaning right up against the stove and still felt cold.

But I loved the color of our home! We painted it a dark red, with bright white trim, and later added a white fence in front. Two old wagon wheels flanked the steps to the front porch. This was my kind of country living right here! Everyone in the area knew where we lived when we said, "We live in the red-and-white house with the white fence on Tualatin-Sherwood Road." I was so proud of Eddie and our family for working so hard to make this dream a reality.

We paid $12,250 for the farm but also spent extra to buy an old case tractor and some farm machinery. Eddie also purchased some apparatus so we could put loose hay in the barn, which was sinking in the back and leaning south. The barn came with a long row of milking stanchions and a wooden floor and trough built in to scrape the manure, with a hay mound upstairs. (It looked like it couldn't take the weight from all those years of pulling up loose hay into the hay mound.) And that brings up a funny story.

We borrowed money so we could have another cow, and once, after she went missing a long search for her, we found her meandering in the loose hay up in the hay mound! I couldn't believe the heavy cow hadn't fallen through the floor in one of the many holes! But thankfully, we brought her down safe and sound.

MUSIC COMES IN SPRINGTIME

That barn was so much fun for the kids. They loved jumping around in the hay, playing hide-and-seek, and building forts.

Now every farmer has his moments, and my husband is no exception. One time, the cow kicked Eddie, and so furiously, he kicked back. But I think she got the best of him because he forgot he was wearing rubber boots instead of his steel-toed work boots! He had a very sore toe for a long time. (I probably shouldn't have, but I enjoyed mentioning "you reap what you sow!")

Oh, but Eddie and I loved each other, and we loved Sally, LaVisa, and little Ed. As a youngster, Ed loved to sit on the parked tractor and pretend he was farming; he lit up when around the farm equipment!

My dad, after living in America for fifty years, went back to Germany with Mom to visit family. They had a wonderful time there. He noticed the boys wearing lederhosen, which are leather, short pants, and sent back a pair for Ed. The lederhosen was loved to death, and Ed wore them every chance he got! I remember seeing my little guy running around outside like a mad dog in those pants!

All the kids spent a great amount of time outdoors, playing and helping to work on the farm. Our family really didn't have a lot of money, but we made it with such things as we had. The blessings of the Lord were upon our family! And we grew closer together out on the farm.

I had our fourth and final child, Candace Belle (Candy), at Emmanuel Hospital in February 1959. That girl came out so fast I didn't have time for a spinal! What a beautiful little baby and a good sleeper too. Sally and LaVisa loved helping to hold and take care of her. But they didn't care for diaper duty so much! I would put her to sleep in her buggy right next to the stove in the living room, and she would sleep for hours. Sally and LaVisa just stood right next to the buggy, waiting for her to wake up so they could hold her!

By age two, Candy had thick, long hair, and the girls loved combing and braiding it. With our growing family, Eddie partitioned the upstairs and made the area into three bedrooms—one for each of the older kids. Sally and LaVisa usually ended up sleeping together though! It warmed my heart.

Back to our old, old barn. Because of its terrible condition, Eddie decided to tear it down and make a new one. He intended on keeping weaner pigs in the new barn. To that end, he poured a slab of concrete that was slightly sloped to the north so the waste from the pig pens could be easily scraped through the opening provided under the edge of the siding and to the ground below. Building a barn by himself was no small feat, and he never considered himself an expert. He bought used timber, put up a section of it, then braced it on all angles to continue on until he made it around the building. The new barn had a sheet metal roof with Plexiglas skylights and contained room for milking, a covered feeder for horses and cows, horse stalls, and hay storage.

Wow, we didn't realize how fast weaner pigs grow up! Their food is expensive, but they can be ready for market in one year—weighing in at two hundred pounds! (Cows take at least two years to grow large enough for market). Eddie built a portable pigpen and used the tractor to move it to a new location once the pigs had eaten all the grass in one place.

The contraption worked fine for a while until one day it didn't. Eddie accidentally moved the pen onto uneven ground, and all those "cute little pigs" ran out! I thought it wouldn't be too difficult to catch them. Well, was I ever wrong! Our entire afternoon that day was spent chasing pigs! I became a filthy mess in the process. We had to cancel a dinner engagement with Bob and Pluma, and the whole thing was just crazy. Eddie reminded me he had pigs for a time when he was a kid, and his dad had a hard time loading them in his truck to take them home. Why do any sane people keep pigs? I guess it's the allure of bacon!

That was not the only time our animals escaped. We also had a boar that didn't care for being kept in a pen. He was mean and vicious, and I got very nervous when I had to chase him. Once, I had chased him back to his pen, and then he turned around and started chasing me. One moment I was the boss, and the next I was literally running for my life! I ran until I couldn't run anymore. But when I stopped, he ran right past me! All that wasted effort: He wasn't even trying to chase me.

MUSIC COMES IN SPRINGTIME

Eddie and I built extensive fences for the cows, horses, and hogs. But still, the pigs escaped through a hole under the fence. Once, when Candy was three, I left her inside to go chase the pigs back to the barn. Those pesky things knew exactly where they had come from and ran right back through the hole in the fence and into the field! For some reason, that made me really angry!

Before the bore, Eddie had to take the sow to be bred. He and little Ed worked and worked to get it into the trailer, and it took forever. During the process, little Ed blurted out, "Dad, I don't think she wants any babies."

We may not have been the most successful of farmers, but we got to do and share all these moments together—which was our ultimate goal. I spent many hours mowing the lawn, preparing meals, planting with Eddie on the tractor, taking care of the kids, and then repeat! But that was our busy life on the farm, in the charming, romantic, red farmhouse.

With little farm machinery of our own, we had to have our hay custom baled. Occasionally, it became wet, and that meant really heavy bales! How I remember those hot and dusty days of picking up the hay in the field with hay hooks! It was dirty, itchy, and sweaty work! No one in our family really had a great passion for helping to put it into the barn, but it was something that needed to get done, and we all did it together.

One of my favorite activities included gardening. I loved our fresh beans, corn, tomatoes, squash, and every vegetable imaginable. We planted corn down by the creek for several years; they produced big bountiful ears. But one year, some China pheasants pulled up about 90 percent of it and ate the seeds; that was the last year we planted in the lower field.

I thoroughly enjoyed making jam and pies from our nectar berry plants. We all loved the berries, and I froze many packages for the winter. I always canned at least fifty quarts of beans and froze many packages of corn. We had a delicious pear tree, and I canned many jars of pears as well as bought peaches. I made pickles in an old crock. We grew our own pork and beef and out-of-this-world bacon. We drank milk from our own cow and occasionally made our own butter. So scratch what I said earlier. In many ways, we were successful farmers!

Eddie decided to dig a basement for a furnace and room to store wood; this time, our basement was a success! It took eight cords of wood to heat the house with the new stove. Eddie and Ed could go out into the woods and cut three-and-a-half cords in one day.

The two of us moved our bedroom upstairs, and our old room downstairs turned into what we all called "the other room." It became our music room, with a comfy couch, and at one time, it housed two pianos and an organ. The kids always loved making music in the little room, which was toasty as it sat over the furnace.

Behind the house, we had an old dug well—bricked up on all sides. Once, the water smelled so foul I couldn't bring myself to drink it. After an investigation and some cleaning, Eddie discovered several moles and other dead creatures. Ugh! A deeper and cleaner well lay on the property but on the wrong side of the road. Eddie and I worked very hard digging a ditch to lay the pipe so we could use that well. However, this well went only about fifteen to twenty feet deep, and there was never enough water. Baths were very shallow, and the water had to be shared. The dirtiest kid went last, and that was usually Ed. We couldn't keep the grass green in the summertime. When the well ran dry, it was hard to get the pump to prime.

During the summertime, our girls and boy stayed plenty busy. Not only did they play hard, especially out in the woods, but they also worked hard—on the farm and for other people. Sally and LaVisa normally picked raspberries at our friend's farm down the road. The owner's wife even made LaVisa a little bonnet to protect her from the sun! Our girls picked berries every season: strawberries, raspberries, blackcaps, and boysenberries. When Candy was a little older, she picked blueberries. Little Ed picked as well and also spent many days out in the hot sun, baling hay for two of Tualatin's longtime farmers.

Our son had an amazing knack for machinery. I believe his first words were truck sounds! He could figure out how to set the disk and other parts as a very young boy. Eddie listened to him and appreciated his input. Driving the tractor and truck in the field was one of his favorite things long before he could drive on the road.

MUSIC COMES IN SPRINGTIME

There are a lot of things in life I wish would never change. As a mom, I occasionally wished my children could always stay the same and never grow older. I suppose most moms have felt that at some point. But regardless of my feelings, my little babies grew and grew. Still, some of the day-to-day practices in life never changed, and I am grateful for that. Whenever he dressed up, Eddie always wore a bow tie and wound his pocket watch and put on his wedding ring every Sunday. (As he worked with machinery, he was afraid of losing a finger if he wore it to work.) My man was the most handsome usher in our church!

As a family, we always ate dinner together at four-fifty, right when Eddie came home from work. I knew it was my job to cook for my family every night. All my meals were made from scratch, and I made homemade dessert with every meal. My hope was that my whole family knew how much I loved and cared for them.

Eddie always worked very hard at his job even though it was difficult work at times, and he had a long commute into Portland. Often, he reminded our kids that it was his job to make money for the boss. Every job he started, he finished. Regardless of the circumstances, he was always honest and always lived a life of integrity.

We rarely took vacations, but it was a special family tradition to drive to Wallowa County, nearly every year, to visit relatives. As you know, my family is from the area, and I lived there for a few years as a little girl. The place holds so many rich and precious memories. All of nature seems to scream out GOD's magnificent glory in that place.

We visited Grandpa and Grandma Hodge, as well as several aunts and uncles on these trips. My mother's sister Via and her husband, Mike, let us stay on their ranch for our weeklong getaways. Often during our stay, we would head out for picnics and rides into the beautiful countryside. We ate sloppy taters over a campfire at nights, and the kids loved playing in their irrigation ditch. Their favorite thing to do included heading up into the high mountains, hiking, and enjoying the many lakes. Our family favorite, throughout the years, has been Wallowa Lake.

How Eddie loved the Wallowa mountains! As he grew up in Kansas, which is as flat as a pancake, he couldn't get enough of

THE YEARS THAT FOLLOWED

Eastern Oregon. Besides our family trip to the area, for many years, Eddie went to the high lakes for a week. He started backpacking and got a pack of donkey and later horses. This rocky and steep trek he enjoyed with my brother Bob, Uncle Mike, and many other relatives. I always loved the fish they caught! His favorite spot in the area was a place called Minam Meadows, with beautiful alpine grass and surrounded by the most serene peaks. This was his special "cove," and he loved to go there and have time to think and pray.

My husband asked for so little in this world and truly lived a selfless life. With an immense amount of responsibility, I was so happy for him to have times of respite and refreshment in the Wallowa mountains.

Behind our home, Eddie built a shop building; it had a storage loft accessed by a built-in ladder. This allowed for more covered storage behind the building. Just outside, we had our own gas tank, which the Clackamas County Grange Supply regularly filled. The gas tank was handy for our farm machinery and also teenagers with cars! Around the same time, he put in a carport, plus a nice room in the back of the house to be used for sewing, as well as for fruit.

How the memories roll on! In October 1962, Oregon experienced a terrible windstorm, dubbed the "Columbus Day Storm." Forty-six people were killed on the west coast as a result. The top wind speeds recorded were at 115 miles per hour. Damaged homes, farms, and buildings dotted the landscape.

I had dropped the girls off for piano lessons, and on my way home, the wind began quickly picking up. Once we arrived home, the wind became even stronger, and a huge branch fell from our enormous oak tree. Then I watched a tragedy, for lo and behold, a 150-foot fir tree fell right through the middle of the barn that Eddie had just built! The wind speeds were so loud and voracious that I did not hear it fall. I felt sick.

While on their way home, Eddie, Sally, and LaVisa remember fir bows blanketing the landscape on every road, along with downed power lines. They took several back roads to make it home.

Though the wind blew viciously and cruelly that day, the next morning, it was calm and unusually warm. The family went outdoors to assess the damage and found our barn literally cut in half, with one beam holding it together. Six sows and six litters (one hundred) of pigs had been housed in the barn. Yet thankfully only one little pig had been killed by the tree and another injured. We spent the morning chasing those little things all over the field, trying to herd them home.

A variety of side effects resulted from the Columbus Day Storm. We lost power for a week. Eddie had to draw water from our well with a bucket and rope! The phones were out for two weeks. Our local insurance company went broke, and we and many others didn't get paid our total insurance coverage. But that's life. One good thing happened, and that was the wind blowing so hard that the old truck parked behind the house had become shiny!

How discouraging, though, for poor Eddie! He had to rebuild the barn. Another substantial storm occurred as he was attempting to rebuild. To say the least, it was a long process.

One time, Sally accidentally flushed my partial plate down the toilet! Eddie was madder at me for putting it in a place where it could be flushed than he was at her! He opened the septic tank and had "Ye Olde Honey Pot" come and pump the tank. I asked if I could help, and he said no. Instead, I decided to spend the afternoon baking pies, but I overheard him say, "That's why men die young—because they have to live with women."

They got clear to the bottom—and no teeth. Eddie went looking for them with the "honey pot" guys. Finally, at the back of the truck tank, they found the teeth, and Eddie brought them home. I will tell you one thing for sure; was it ever hard to get those things clean enough to put back in my mouth!

The kids didn't mean to cause trouble most of the time. Instead, they always had plenty to do using their creative energies on practically every inch of those twenty-eight acres. They played "pony express" up and down the lane and built forts in the field and in the woods. Eddie helped them make trails for our horses in the woods, and the kids gave them names like "Slug Head Trail" and "Goblin's Gulch." Sometimes the kids would be gone for hours, just playing and using their imaginations. All their friends and cousins loved playing in the woods together, especially on Sunday afternoons.

Sometimes their innocent play scared me half to death! Sally and her friend Mary were playing down by the creek and became quite thirsty. Instead of coming back to the house, they decided to drink from the creek. Later, when I found out about it, I was beside myself because of what had happened to my own uncles. People could die from drinking water from a creek! They ended up not becoming sick, but the whole thing gave me quite the scare.

Speaking of our creek, I remember picking blackberries with Eddie and the kids down by the creek one time. We were having a grand old time but didn't realize that our cow had gotten out. She was standing right behind us, eating out of our crate! It gave us quite the start, but at least it was something to laugh at as well.

My little son! He loved to hunt and roam about in the woods with his friends. I guess there's just about nowhere else a boy would rather pass the time. Once, he climbed a tree and went too far out on a limb. He not only fell but landed right into a cow pie! What a mess! Poor Eddie got poison oak probably because of what the cow had eaten.

Our story would be incomplete if we left out all the animals. Through the years, we had many beloved pets. They gave our children a sense of responsibility. We had a goat named Loppy, who loved to be rocked in a metal rocking chair by LaVisa and also ate the tassel off her stocking hat! Sadly, the goat ended up becoming aggressive, and Eddie sold him for $1 and gave the money to the kids. We also had a white domestic duck named Swanee. After making a huge mess in our yard, I had the kids take her and her eggs and box down to the swamp. She needed a new area to live in. Well, guess who followed Sally and LaVisa right back to the barn!

We owned several cows, both dairy and beef. Sally had the job of milking the dairy cows, and we paid her twenty-five cents per milking. As previously mentioned, we had several pigs and, at one point, bantam chickens. Although we loved the eggs, the chickens could simply destroy a barn lot. Eddie was grateful when the skunks got them.

MUSIC COMES IN SPRINGTIME

After settling into the farm, our next big dream included owning horses. We spent several Sunday afternoons driving to various farms and horse traders. Once, a horse we were considering bit five-year-old LaVisa right in the stomach! That obviously didn't work out. But the Lord gave our family the sweetest horse we will never forget.

Someone at Eddie's work had a Welsh pony who was about 11.5 hands tall. Our horse Lucky was an older horse and had a problem with laming, especially when the seasons changed. Eddie bought her for $25, and for a while, he rubbed her legs down with horse liniment. Eventually, she became stronger and rarely lamed. She really was the best horse any kid could hope to have. The kids loved to ride Lucky down the trails in our woods. City kids thought they were real horsemen when they rode her because Eddie didn't have to lead her.

Sally had Lucky in 4-H and rode her in our local Sherwood Robin Hood Festival parade; she was her best friend. One year when it snowed, Eddie rode Lucky and held the top of the rope, which was tied to the sled, and gave the kids the best rides ever. At times, we had three kids all on top of her, and our gentle horse didn't mind at all; she was a jewel. When she lost her teeth, Eddie ended up buying special food for her. He just didn't have the heart to put her down.

Throughout the years, we also owned several other horses. One day, we found a beautiful sorrel mare grazing among our cattle. Eddie checked the neighboring farms to find out who owned her. One of these said we could have her if we wanted her. She was a registered Thoroughbred with a bloodline back to the infamous "Man o' War" horse. (The "Man o' War" horse is generally considered to be the best American racehorse of the twentieth century and died in 1947.) This horse, named Oatmeal Cookie, had been a racehorse (Battle Trout) but had been expelled from the track because of her behavior at the gate. She hadn't worked out as a broodmare and was just too much horse for the kids and Eddie. We finally had to sell her.

As Lucky became too old for 4-H, we looked for another horse. We bought Sugarfoot, who was a sorrel American saddlebred barrel racer. He was a very nice horse who would stop suddenly when your foot left the stirrup. Sally rode him at 4-H and in the parade. Eddie gave her an ultimatum when she went to college: either she could sell him, or he would. He ended up selling her for $50.

Later, Eddie bought two more: Cherokee Princess and Nebo. As Nebo had health problems, he was traded for another horse that Eddie named Fanny. Fanny was a healthy horse who turned out to be with foal. She gave birth to Little Tater, named after a comic strip baby. Cherokee Princess ended up being little Ed's horse. He was reluctant about breaking her in, but with time and patience, she turned out to be a good loyal horse. Ed had her in 4-H, took her to the fair, and also up to the Wallowa mountains.

Three other horses came into our lives over the years: Slim, Ira, and Paint. Eddie also wanted a few donkeys to be used as pack animals when they went up into the Wallowa mountains. So we bought Cactus, a long-legged black donkey, and Estralita, a gray one; they lived for what seemed like ages. They were good and useful donkeys; however, I do remember one story. Once, while Eddie rode Cactus, little Ed, for some reason, threw a rock at him. The donkey went mad and gave Eddie quite a ride which inevitably landed him on the ground.

And what would a farm be without dogs and cats? Our first dog, Mamie, named after President Eisenhower's wife, actually made the newspaper. She was a collie and had babies with a Lab. So they called her puppies "Collaborators." There was mean old Bosco, who had been picked up from the pound by Eddie and only liked him and scared the rest of us. We also had Chipper, Sidney, Wendy, Sammy, George, and Barney too! Not to mention a whole host of cats, which were Candy's favorite. She loved naming them all.

Besides chores, work, school, church, and just living daily life, one of the biggest priorities Eddie and I had for our children was music. We both felt music a worthwhile investment. Not only could it be used to bring praise and honor and glory to our GOD and King, but it could also be used to lift and encourage our fellow man. It is said of Bach that he wrote *"Soli Deo Gloria"* in his musical compositions, which means glory to GOD alone. We are musical beings and, as such, should value and treasure this wonderful gift from GOD. I have always loved classical music and thoroughly enjoy listening to my children play and perform. Eddie sacrificed so that our children could take music lessons. He once said, "I don't play. I just pay." But it was truly worth every penny.

Sally started taking piano lessons in Portland, and then we found another teacher for her in Sherwood when we moved to the farm. In due time, all of our children took piano lessons. They practiced in our little music room, which always felt warm and toasty as the room sat over the furnace. They became excellent pianists, playing songs I loved from composers like Beethoven, Chopin, Debussy, Brahms, and Liszt. The piano became Sally's main instrument, and she excelled at it greatly.

Strings were offered at Tualatin Grade School, and Sally, in the sixth grade, wanted to join. None of us had been familiar with strings or the violin, so Eddie went to a pawnshop in downtown Portland and bought a violin for $25. He had the violin repaired, and Sally enjoyed playing the beautiful instrument. Yet they only offered strings for one year at the school, so her violin days were short-lived. But we kept the violin. Eddie always wanted someone in the family to learn to play the violin as it was one of his favorite instruments.

LaVisa loved to make music on just about whatever she could find. She became a prolific flute player. Little Ed went on to play the trombone, and Candy, the Oboe. Mr. Collins was the music teacher at our kids' school—a nice older bachelor who loved the kids and poured his life into them. He encouraged them to go to solos and ensemble contests. All our children received many honors and went to "Music in May" (an exclusive music festival held at Pacific University). We were always very proud of their accomplishments; they now are all fine musicians. Eddie made sure they always had the best instruments available and sacrificed much so they could have lessons.

Our family's lives have been intertwined with the Church of God since the 1920s when my parents got saved. Following their conversion, my parents taught my brothers and me the value of attending church. But they didn't just advocate for a once-per-week attendance and then go about life as if they could do whatever they pleased. My parents made the church the center of their activity.

THE YEARS THAT FOLLOWED

They were fully vested in the work of the Lord at their congregation. They loved the people of GOD who attended and made them their best friends. Eddie and I continued in our parent's footsteps. We attended Holladay Park Church of GOD, near downtown Portland, as a family twice on Sundays as well as on Wednesday evenings. As Eddie was on the board, he had additional meetings to attend.

We felt blessed to have such a supportive church family who continually encouraged our children. The pastors, over the years, remained faithful to GOD and taught us faithfully. This was a wonderful environment in which to raise a family. Our kids were active in youth activities and attended lots of summer camps at Camp White Branch. The church provided musical training as well. Holladay Park had an amazing band directed by Uncle Emil and later Ivan Puller, as well as an adult choir and children's choir. Over the years and decades of attending, the children sang and played their instruments for worship, and as adults, the girls all directed church choirs.

How the years rolled by so quickly! Our beautiful daughters and fine young son all grew up. Given the investment we made in music lessons, our girls attended Warner Pacific College and ended up teaching elementary music. Ed went to Portland Community College to study mechanics. They have all been active in music in their churches and have been a blessing to so many people.

All four of our children married believers, much to the joy of Eddie and me. Sally married John Kuykendall on June 12, 1970. LaVisa married Steven Arnold on August 26, 1972. Ed married Nancy Jacobson on September 8, 1979. Candy married Mike Bratcher on January 10, 1981. They all got married at Holladay Park. Helen Wilson played the pipe organ for all their weddings just as she had done for ours.

Candy graduated from college in 1980 and went on to do her student teaching with LaVisa. Her wedding was originally set for November 15, 1980. In September of that year, Eddie and I decided to visit John, Sally, and our three grandchildren in Walla Walla, Washington. We stayed for a few days, and Eddie enjoyed having the chance to play with the grandkids—Mindy, John (BJ), and Joey. We next headed to Wallowa County to visit more family. Before coming home, we stopped in Clarkston, Washington, to see Sally's in-laws, Dutch and Jo Kuykendall, and Eddie celebrated his fifty-seventh birthday there on September 26.

We came home on a Saturday. On Sunday, LaVisa and Steve had us over for a birthday dinner. On Monday morning, September 29, 1980, Eddie went to work, and I spent the day making Candy's "going-away" dress. In the afternoon, a call came from Portland Provision Meat Company. Eddie had passed out. I called Ed, and we rushed to the hospital, and LaVisa and Candy met us there. But he was gone—three days past his fifty-seventh birthday. I took his hand and kissed him one final goodbye.

Although the wedding invitations had already been printed, Candy, being sensitive to our devastating loss, postponed her wedding until January 10, 1981. We added a card to the invitations explaining the reason for the change of date. Although I was in a fog that night, I walked Candy down the aisle in place of her dad. I literally felt the prayers of the congregation holding me up as I walked with her down the long fifty-foot aisle.

Eddie was a very unselfish person and a wonderful husband for thirty-four years, not nearly long enough. He worked hard for all of us and always thought of his family first. On all our projects, we worked together; we made a team. I could not have asked for a better husband and friend.

The Christmas Eve following Eddie's death, the kids did the music for the service at church. It was something we needed to do as a diversion to honor Eddie. Following that special service on Christmas Eve, we decided to form a "family band"—since all of the children and grandchildren play instruments. This is now my favorite tradition at Christmastime.

I believe all my family enjoys coming together and playing cherished carols, and I surely enjoy listening to them play. Each year, in addition to our band, we sing the "Hallelujah Chorus" from Handel's *Messiah*. Over the years, the band has improved as more and more of the grandchildren and great-grandchildren have learned to play instruments. We now have the very violin Eddie bought at the pawn-

THE YEARS THAT FOLLOWED

shop back and playing again! I only wish that Eddie could see the fruits of all the lessons he paid for. He would be so proud.

Before Eddie died, the zoning on the farm had been changed from agricultural to heavy industry. We knew we couldn't continue to live on the farm forever. Several offers came to buy the farm. Eddie talked with one of our friends, and he said the property was valuable, and we should keep it. We ended up listing it with Mr. Yoder in Woodburn for a while and got an offer, but it didn't work out. Next, we used a realtor from Tualatin who tried to sell it for us. He secured a fee option from Southern Pacific Railroad and only gave half of it to us. Time ran out, and we did not renew our contract with them.

Duane Moore, from Southern Pacific Railroad, wanted to deal directly with us as our realtor. We trusted him; he said that we should have gotten the entire fee option instead of just half that the Tualatin realtor had given us. We were given two more fee options from the railroad through Duane Moore. They wanted to bring their tracks on the north end of the place across the wetlands and use it for Southern Pacific.

After Eddie died, Duane Moore continued to go to meetings at Tualatin City Hall and fought valiantly for me. They had no interest in changing their zoning and facing environmentalists who wanted to save the frogs. The environmentalists really wanted to condemn more of the land. They dug holes hoping to find Indian artifacts so they could take more of the property. The city ended up taking 4.81 acres as wetlands even though some of it was highland and had fir trees growing on it (which is interesting because fir trees do not grow in wetlands).

The city wanted to build a sewer line on the north side of the wetlands and said they wouldn't give us a "minor petition" if we did not give our consent. At first, they offered us $1,000 for the sewer line. We felt it was important to retain our entrance onto Tualatin-Sherwood Road to make our property more marketable. So we didn't readily sign their request. We ended up getting nothing, but they did grant out a "minor petition," allowing us to separate our twenty-four acres into three parcels. The economy was so bad in the 1980s that nothing was selling.

MUSIC COMES IN SPRINGTIME

Mr. Moore got nothing for all his work trying to help us. He went to countless meetings and had binders full of requests and meeting notes. I was just fifty-five when Eddie died and had not worked for years. The three fee options that Mr. Moore got kept me going until some of the land could be sold. Eddie's meat cutter pension lasted for five years and was $225 per month.

I will always feel that GOD sent Mr. Moore to help me as I don't know what I would have done. He did so much for me and even negotiated compensation for the UPS turnaround that went through our property. He would not take any money for that transaction. Duane Moore was then transferred to Texas. Years later, after I had sold some of the land, I tried to find him. I wanted to send him a letter and some money for all that he had done. A friend tried to find a Duane Moore in Texas on the Internet, and he found one. When I called to talk with him, I knew it wasn't our Mr. Moore. I often have wondered if he was a real angel.

To GOD be the glory, I was able to sell some of my property. Ed was a huge blessing at this time as he continued to farm the land and cut wood. He also went to the meetings at the Tualatin City Hall with the "frog lovers."

In 1986, Steve, LaVisa, and I bought ten acres in Tualatin and divided the property into two parcels. They lived with me while building their home, and then mine was completed in 1990. I felt blessed to have so many people help with this whole process.

To avoid having to pay capital gains tax, we needed to sell the house on the farm and reinvest in another within a year. GOD provided. A man up the road wanted to buy it and move his business. The deal closed just a few weeks before the deadline. We traded the farmhouse for our new property. The man who bought it never ended up moving his business there but later sold the property. I believe GOD sent him at just the right time. He was a Christian man; surely, GOD was at work.

One more thing I would like to mention. Our farmhouse was on a road with few neighbors. Before Eddie died, people constantly stopped by our place to get gas or help from Eddie. After he died, it was like the Lord made the farm invisible. No one stopped for gas or came to the house while I lived there alone. Only one time, on a Thanksgiving morning, did one trucker need to use our phone to call his company. Truly, GOD provided for me and protected me.

There is so much more I could write, dear reader. But our time is fast coming to a close. As my dad passed away in 1975, my mom lived with me for a few years until her death in 1995; those were precious times. The years continued, and with them brought more and more grandchildren and great-grandchildren. I took the family to Disneyland, the San Diego Zoo, and Universal Studios in 1995, and then Disneyland again in 2001. We had such a special time together as a family. We drove the first time and then flew the second. And I'm glad because that would have been a lot of bathroom stops for a big group of twenty-eight people!

The world around me continued to change rapidly—especially as we entered the 2000s. My state of Oregon, which was a hinterland when I was a girl, fast became a booming and bustling area. And the technology these days is astounding! My great-grandkids often have to help me navigate it all!

I watched with the world the events of 9/11 and the war on terror. But this is not the first time in my life that I have seen trouble and sorrow. No, I have seen much in my lifetime. And the whole conclusion of the matter, as it says in Ecclesiastes 12:13–14, is this: "Let us hear the conclusion of the whole matter: fear God and keep his commandments: for this is the whole duty of man. For God shall bring every work into judgment, with every secret thing, whether it be good, or whether it be evil." I know Who is in control of it all.

Life has not ceased to bring joy and activity. After Eddie passed, I started doing treasury work at the church with Ray, Eddie's oldest brother. I really got to know and appreciate him better. I signed the checks for the church and tried to support the activities and mission of the church as much as possible.

As always, I continued to be busy in the kitchen—baking countless pies, cookies we call "Wyoming Whoppers," rolls, butter horns, and bread. In addition, I love to quilt and have made one for every new couple in the family, in addition to socks and Christmas stockings for all the grandkids and great-grandchildren.

MUSIC COMES IN SPRINGTIME

My GOD and my family continue to be my life. We are now in the 2020s. Every moment I have the chance to spend with them, I count as precious. Steve and LaVisa host a cousins' camp for all the great-grandchildren once a year, and I love to see everyone at these gatherings. Nearly every Christmas, we gather and continue our special tradition of a family band. How I love that music!

My family has thrown me birthday parties for landmark years, such as eighty, ninety, and ninety-five. I am now even older than that. At these gatherings, we always sing Church of GOD hymns, which are my very favorite. I have spent my entire life in the Church of GOD, and the hymns I sing are timeless truths that will never, ever grow old. And I get to sing them with all my family! I have four wonderful children who are all married, thirteen grandchildren, and thirty-three great-grandchildren.

I can never thank GOD enough for His faithfulness and guidance throughout our lives. One thing I know: The salvation we profess works. I take no credit for the children, grandchildren, or great-grandchildren who have committed their lives to Christ and the church. It is only their personal decision that has made their commitment possible. I am very grateful to the Lord for my family.

With tears in my eyes, I realize this book has come to a close. Thank you, my dear reader, for joining me on this journey. Life has been a fantastic adventure. There have been struggles and hardships, tears, sweat, and blood. But there have also been hopes, joys, triumphs, blessings, and victories throughout. I see both the mountain peaks and the valleys but only need to dwell on the mountain peaks. Truly, I can say, music has come in springtime.

EPILOGUE

The process of writing this book has greatly impacted me, my own view of family history, and how I view life as a whole. I hope that you, my dear reader, are able to adopt that same mindset and approach. May we all look at life from a holistic perspective at times—to step back and appreciate what is good and what is beautiful in this world.

I am truly grateful for my family and the legacy they have given to me. My great-grandma Carolla, grandma Sally, and so many others have all given me this heritage—this family treasure. Now I want you to do the same with your family. I know there is a lot of hurt and abuse in this world, and sometimes, it remains hard to think of the positive. But my prayer is that you might cherish and enjoy your own family history. Not everything from the past or from our relatives will be romanticized, but strive to look for the good. Search out and learn the stories behind your own family history. Where did your family come from? In what culture did they live in? What are their stories of victories, challenges, triumphs, or even defeats? How about romances or even wars? Learn as much as you can and remain deeply grateful for whatever "gold nuggets" you mine. I can tell you from experience—it is truly rewarding. What's amazing is that in so doing, you deeply connect yourself with the past. This allows you to feel rooted and grounded and understand your own time and place in history. You have nothing to lose but everything to gain!

Tell your story. Everyone has a story to tell. Maybe even consider putting it in writing. I look forward to, one day, hearing or reading *your* story!

BIBLIOGRAPHY

This list certainly is not exhaustive. In writing this book, I have had to draw on a number of people and resources over the years, and for all these, I am truly grateful. My biggest resource included the four family history books written by my great-great-grandmother and great-grandma. I should also mention the countless hours of stories from various family members and friends. The following resources helped me gain a greater historical perspective and improved accuracy in the details of this book. If you are interested in further research, I hope these are helpful for you:

"Atomic bombings of Hiroshima and Nagasaki." Wikipedia. en.wikipedia.org/wiki/Atomic_bombings_of_Hiroshima_and_Nagasaki. Accessed 17 May 2022.

"Fun Taffy Facts: Its Origins and Why You Pull Taffy." *Warrell Creations*, 24 January 2018. www.warrellcorp.com/blog/fun-taffy-facts-origins-pull-taffy/. Accessed 30 January 2022.

"Germans from Russia in Kansas." *Kansas Historical Society*, December 2017. www.kshs.org/kansapedia/germans-from-russia-in-kansas/12231. Accessed 3 December 2021.

"History at the Vista House." *Vista House.* vistahouse.com/history/. Accessed 9 April 2022.

"Island City." *Union County Economic Development Corporation.* ucedc.org/union-county-community-pages/union-county-overview/island-city/. Accessed 23 March 2021.

Kramer, Arthur. "Migration of Germans to Russia." *University of Washington*, American Historical Society of Germans from Russia. 17

BIBLIOGRAPHY

March 1999. depts.washington.edu/heritage/Organizations/Russia/Seattle%20AHSGR%20pamphlet.htm. Accessed 3 December 2021.

"Man o' War." Wikipedia, en.wikipedia.org/wiki/Man_o%27_War. Accessed 5 October 2022.

"Old Joe Clark." *Songs for Teaching*. www.songsforteaching.com/folk/oldjoeclarkb.php. Accessed 21 March 2022.

"Ten Beloved German Christmas Traditions." *Germanfoods*. germanfoods.org/german-food-facts/german-christmas-traditions/. Accessed 12 December 2020.

"USS Hunter Liggett." Wikipedia, en.wikipedia.org/wiki/USS_Hunter_Liggett. Accessed 2 Apr. 2022.

"Vanport, Oregon." Wikipedia, en.wikipedia.org/wiki/Vanport, Oregon. Accessed 2 July 2022.

ABOUT THE AUTHOR

First and foremost a Christian, Jared Kuykendall is also known as the "family historian" and writes from a philosophical framework around romanticism. An Oregon native, he now lives in the beautiful forested hills of Centralia, Washington, with his family. Jared works for Mount Capra Products, a small food and nutrition company, and holds a bachelor's degree in applied management from Centralia College. When not writing, he enjoys playing the piano, reading, singing, biking, and spending time with family and friends. A skydiver, runner, and avid nature enthusiast, Jared loves life and looks to promote the value of remaining grateful for all things—the adrenaline rush, the simple things, all things family, and Jesus.

Printed in the USA
CPSIA information can be obtained
at www.ICGtesting.com
JSHW021231091023
49638JS00004B/9

9 798889 430865